The Croom Family and Goodwood Plantation

The Croom Family and Goodwood Plantation

Land, Litigation, and Southern Lives

William Warren Rogers and Erica R. Clark

William Warren Rogers
Erica R. Clark

to Shirly + Oliver —
We want you to
see Goodwood in
person soon! .
Love, Erica

The University of Georgia Press   *Athens and London*

© 1999 by the University of Georgia Press

Athens, Georgia 30602

All rights reserved

Designed by Kathi Morgan

Set in Monotype Walbaum by G & S Typesetters

Printed and bound by Maple-Vail

The paper in this book meets the guidelines for
permanence and durability of the Committee on
Production Guidelines for Book Longevity of the
Council on Library Resources.

Printed in the United States of America

03   02   01   00   99   C   5   4   3   2   1

Library of Congress Cataloging in Publication Data

Rogers, William Warren.

   The Croom family and Goodwood plantation : land, litigation, and
southern lives / William Warren Rogers and Erica R. Clark.

     p. cm.

   Includes bibliographical references and index.

   ISBN 0-8203-2069-2 (alk. paper)

    1. Plantation life—Florida—Tallahassee Region—History—19th
century.   2. Frontier and pioneer life—Florida—Tallahassee Region—
History—19th century.   3. Goodwood Plantation (Fla.) 4. Croom
family.   5. Croom family—Trials, litigation, etc. 6. Tallahassee
Region (Fla.)—Biography.   7. Tallahassee Region (Fla.)—Social life
and customs.   8. Tallahassee Region (Fla.)—Race relations.
I. Clark, Erica R.   II. Title.

F319.T14R65   1999

975.9'88—dc21   98-40767

               CIP

British Library Cataloging in Publication Data available

To Velma Lassiter Croom
and
Dr. Ada Belle Winthrop-King (1900–1997)

Contents

Illustrations

Preface

In the first decades of the nineteenth century, waves of settlers from the upper South, Georgia, and Tennessee (swelled by ripples of migrants from the North) moved into the booming Southwest, the term for the present-day lower South states plus Arkansas. The immigrants came to the area's newly opened lands in such numbers that four new states were admitted to the Union: Louisiana (1812), Mississippi (1817), Alabama (1819), and Arkansas (1836). The settlers had a variety of reasons for uprooting their lives. Some came with ill-defined or undefined motives, and others, if they were children or slaves, had no choice in the matter. The institution of slavery was legal in all the newly formed states.

Economic advancement was the most compelling reason for moving. The vast Southwest was capable of producing cotton in abundance and furnishing domestic and world markets with a staple perfectly suited to the burgeoning industrial revolution. The cotton gin guaranteed that there was money to be made. In contrast, much of the upper South's soil had become depleted after generations of unscientific cultivation, and the fertile land to the south was a powerful magnet.

The region appealed to planters and perhaps even more to their sons, anxious to establish independence and achieve success on their own. Wives were consulted, and the decision was often mutual. While

proposed moves were undoubtedly abandoned sometimes because of opposition from wives, it was the planter who usually made the original
and final decision. The challenge of the frontier and the adventures of
starting new lives in an unknown country were significant motives for
the exodus.

In numerous instances the plantation system that had evolved slowly
in the upper South—large landholdings farmed primarily by slave labor—was transplanted to the lower South and found immediate imple-
mentation. Yet the majority of the pioneers were people who owned
only a few or no slaves. They seized the opportunity to advance their
fortunes and became yeoman farmers who homesteaded on smaller
tracts. As the lower South developed towns and urban centers, some of
the middle class became artisans, craftsmen, clerks, and store owners. A
professional class also emerged in the towns. Whatever their economic
status or gender, the white pioneers of the Southwest believed that regardless of what lay behind, success lay ahead.

Rather than bending west with the contours of the country, some of
the migrants proceeded in a more direct line south to Florida. Events
similar to those in the Southwest were taking place there. The promises
of Florida as a future agricultural kingdom were touted by word of
mouth, personal correspondence, and newspaper descriptions with no
less hyperbole than descriptions of Alabama's Black Belt, Louisiana's
river bottoms, or, later, the Delta of Mississippi and Arkansas. Yet the
history of antebellum Florida's plantation region is less well known and
written about, perhaps because it occurred in a relatively small area and
because many basic records became available later than in other southern states. Even so, works of sound scholarship have been produced;
Julia Floyd Smith's *Slavery and Plantation Growth in Antebellum Florida, 1821–1860* (1973), Clifton Paisley's *The Red Hills of Florida, 1528–
1865* (1989), and other monographs and articles are important studies
and valuable guides.

After its acquisition from Spain by the Adams-Onís Treaty of 1819,
Florida was organized as a territory of the United States in 1821. The
race for land followed quickly, and there was a population explosion in
its northern section. For example, between 1825 and 1840 Tallahassee

and Leon County grew by 1,049 percent. Native Americans were displaced from their land by treaty and warfare (the First Seminole War, an extension of the War of 1812, began in 1818, and the Second Seminole War lasted from 1835 to 1842). South Florida, however, experienced almost no growth because that region had major interior transportation problems and, even worse, land far less adaptable to cotton and traditional row crops.

This book deals primarily with one large family of planters, the Crooms, and their lives and deaths in frontier Florida and the South. It is also the story of other planter families and of slaves, slave drivers, overseers, yeoman farmers, judges, lawyers, preachers, businessmen, and professional people. Women are no less important than the men portrayed, and Frances Croom, Eveline Croom, Ann Hawks, Ann Croom, Ann Bellamy, and Henrietta Smith, to name a few, were remarkable people. The decision to leave familiar surroundings and move to the unfamiliar, often lonely (sometimes hostile) southern frontier, as well as the adjustments after arrival, involved a different set of attitudes and reactions for planters' wives than those experienced by their husbands. What is explored here in some depth has been broadly and expertly researched by Jane Turner Censer (*North Carolina Planters and Their Children, 1800–1860* [1984]) and Joan E. Cashin (*A Family Venture: Men and Women on the Southern Frontier* [1991]). This book directs attention to emerging generations, as children became adults and played their part in the narrative. Complicated relationships and continuity within families, especially for planters such as the Crooms, were crucial to the Old South's order.

The present volume addresses religious commitment (mainly to the Episcopal Church), farming and plantation management, slavery, business, social life, money, and education. The work includes the convoluted circumstances of a lawsuit that lasted twenty years. At the personal level it changed the lives of the principals. Beyond that, the litigation resulted in a landmark decision in cases involving presumption as to the order of survivorship in a common disaster. The case highlights the book's major concerns: people and the attendant forces of ambition, rivalry, success, failure, and tragedy.

This is not a genealogical work on the Crooms, although a chart containing a limited "family tree" is included. Even so, the Crooms and their remarkable network of kinsmen, the Whitfields, and their in-laws, the Bellamys, as well as the Smiths, the Winthrops, the Hopkinses, and other families and individuals, are discussed in detail and in passing. Nor is it strictly the history of Goodwood plantation, but the impressive mansion that was constructed there and the Goodwood lands are central to the account. The final plantation house, built in the 1840s, followed a pattern common in the Old South in that it was preceded by other less impressive and less permanent structures. The aesthetically appealing home has been restored by a private organization, the Margaret E. Wilson Foundation. Historians, architects, preservation architects, and artifact conservators consider it one of Florida's most important antebellum residences.

Events in New York, North Carolina, Georgia, Alabama, and Mississippi are related and are important to the narrative, but the Florida frontier is the focus. Conditions and developments there are considered in the larger setting of the South and the nation. Most of the research is based on family letters, courthouse records, and recently uncovered manuscript court cases. As planters, the major characters here were part of the South's aristocratic class. While conscious of their position and proud of that status, they were hardworking, competitive, largely nonpolitical people who were interested in the process of government but whose lives centered around family, religion, and land. They faced the universal conflicts that are timeless and common to all men and women. How they did so in the context of their own place and era was unique to them and is the subject of this book.

Acknowledgments

Like all authors, we owe a debt to many persons and institutions. During the time spent in writing this book a number of people and the places where they work provided the help that enabled us to complete this book.

We wish to thank James Arrington, James Berry, Dr. Edwin Bridges, Dr. Canter Brown, Dr. David Coles, Alice R. Cotten, Susan Whitfield Cowles, William Cowles, Nancy Dobson, Wynne Dough, Richard G. Fulmer, Dr. Leon Golden, William A. Grant, John Green, Mattie Grice, Dr. Sally Hadden, Sarah Bruce Harris, Ernest R. Hilliard, Elizabeth Johnson, Mary Helen Jones, Dr. Marcy L. Koontz, Dr. J. Patrick Lee, Laura Hopkins Long, U. Bowdoin Marsh, Dr. Margaret Moore, Joan Morris, Joanna Norman, Betty Odum, Clifton Paisley, Joy Paisley, Dr. Paul Pruitt Jr., Betty Reeves, Anita Richardson, Dr. Larry Rivers, Dr. Warren Rogers, Fran Santagata, Dr. Bawa S. Singh, Dr. Sidney R. Smith, Elizabeth Stegall, Robert Suter, Dr. Joseph Tomberlin, Dr. Raymond Vickers, Anne Webster, Karen Wells, Martha Brown Whitner, and Daniel Winchester.

Special thanks are extended to Caroline Claiborne of Goodwood Museum and Gardens, Inc., who read the entire manuscript twice and gave valuable editorial suggestions; Dr. Joseph G. Cushman Jr. gave the manuscript a thorough review; Renee Gledhill-Early provided much-needed aid in helping locate materials in North Carolina; with his expertise Peter Kraft provided the essential maps; Dr. John H. Moore, an authority on antebellum agriculture, saved us from error on several crucial points; Dr. Dorothy McInerney, biographer of Elizabeth Croom Bellamy, read the manuscript and made helpful suggestions; Larry Paarlberg, executive director of Goodwood Museum and Gardens, Inc., gave freely of his time, wisdom, and enthusiasm; Herschel Shepard, restoration architect, was a major source of advice; Dr. Jerrell Shofner, a leading expert on Florida history, read the manuscript and offered important insights; Randolph Whitfield, closely related to the Crooms and Whitfields, gave wise counsel and loaned primary materials to the project; Martha Zeirden located important sources for the wreck of the *Home* and the Charleston phase of the book.

We are grateful to the staffs of the state archives at Montgomery, Alabama; Tallahassee, Florida; Atlanta, Georgia; Jackson, Mississippi; and Raleigh, North Carolina. The personnel at several courthouses provided valuable material, and we express our appreciation to the people in Alabama at the Greene County Courthouse, Eutaw; Montgomery County Courthouse, Montgomery; and Sumter County Courthouse, Livingston; in Arkansas at the Chicot County Courthouse, Lake Village; in Florida at the Jackson County Courthouse, Marianna; Jefferson County Courthouse, Monticello; Franklin County Courthouse, Apalachicola; Gadsden County Courthouse, Quincy; and Leon County Courthouse, Tallahassee; in Georgia at the Muscogee County Courthouse, Columbus; and in Mississippi at the Bolivar County courthouses in Cleveland and Rosedale; Leflore County Courthouse in Greenwood; and Sunflower County Courthouse in Indianola; in North Carolina at the Craven County Courthouse, New Bern. Malcolm Call and Jennifer Comeau at the University of Georgia Press and copy editor Grace Buonocore provided professional help and personal support.

A number of people at libraries and museums provided their time and resources, and we are the beneficiaries of considerate attention from the staff at the Mobile Public Library; Florida State Supreme Court Library, Tallahassee; Historic Tallahassee Preservation Board; Special Collections Room at Florida State University Library, Tallahassee; P. K. Yonge Collection at the University of Florida Library, Gainesville; Special Collections, University of Georgia Library, Athens; Lenoir Community College, Kinston, North Carolina; New Bern/ Craven County Public Library, New Bern, North Carolina; Southern Historical Collection and also the North Carolina Room at the University of North Carolina, Chapel Hill; Charleston Museum, Charleston; South Carolina Historical Museum, Charleston; and the South Caroliniana Collection at the University of South Carolina Library, Columbia. We deeply appreciate the patience, understanding, and advice of our respective, but, thankfully, not always respectful, spouses, Miriam Rogers and Ronald Clark. Errors of fact and omission are our fault, and we accept responsibility.

William W. Rogers, Tallahassee
Erica R. Clark, Tallahassee

The Croom Family and Goodwood Plantation

1

"Fertile Country ... Never Failing Streams and Fine Springs"

After long coveting Florida, the United States finally acquired the thumb-shaped peninsula from Spain by the Adams-Onís Treaty of 1819. The actual transfer was delayed until 1821, and Florida was not organized as a territory until 1822. The new territory became the object of land-hungry southerners as soon as sales were made public. The most eagerly sought tracts at the land offices were in what came to be called middle Florida: the five future counties, going from east to west, of Madison, Jefferson, Leon, Gadsden, and Jackson. Joining the migration from the upper South were various members of the wealthy Croom family of eastern North Carolina. Over time the Crooms persuaded various kin and neighbors to join them, creating a ripple effect that was repeated many times on the southern frontier.

William Croom, head of the family, led the way. From his desire to accept the challenge and, no less, to earn the rewards of the Florida frontier would come Goodwood plantation. In noting the various motivations for migrating by planters, a recent scholar has shown the powerful force exerted by the prospects of acquiring more land and slaves. Croom and others were further attracted by propaganda about

Florida's potential. William Pope Duval, the territory's first civil governor, said of Florida that its "fruitful soil, and delightful climate and . . . picturesque beauty may bear a comparison with Italy or Greece." He predicted, "[A] few years will demonstrate the value of Florida to the United States and thousands of Southern planters will realize in this country that wealth for which hitherto they have toiled without success."[1]

When Croom was born, on January 4, 1772, probably at his father's plantation on Lower Falling Creek in Dobbs County (later Lenoir County), North Carolina was still a colony of Great Britain. The next twelve months saw the Boston Tea Party and similar protests by the colonials. Before the year was out, Parliament passed the "Intolerable Acts," and the American Revolution was only three years away. William's father, Major Croom Sr., was the son of Daniel Croom. Accepted by genealogists and family members as the progenitor of the North Carolina Crooms, Daniel was born in county Limerick, Ireland, about 1683. He migrated to Virginia by the early 1700s and established himself as a solid citizen. Daniel lived mainly in Henrico County, where he leased land and later received a land grant of 400 acres from King George II. Before he died in 1734, Croom had three or four children by his first wife, Elizabeth, and three by his second wife, Susannah.

Daniel and Elizabeth's second son, Major, sold his inheritance in Virginia, and in 1743–44, at the age of twenty-one, he established a plantation in eastern North Carolina on the south side of Falling Creek and the north side of the Neuse River. Major Croom's brother Abel and his half brother, Jesse, also migrated to North Carolina. Major married Olief (Olive?) Avery, and the couple had seven sons and a daughter. After Olief died, Major married a woman whose first name was Susannah. It was not long before Croom's deeds gave credibility to his martial first name. In 1771 Major and his oldest son, Joshua, were hired by Governor William Tryon to haul matériel when he marched against the Regulators on North Carolina's western frontier in 1771. Both Major and Joshua were enrolled in the revolutionary militia. Major was a member of the New Bern District's committee of safety and in 1779 held the post of commissioner of magazines.[2]

Major's sense of honor and patriotism was inherited by future generations of Crooms, as was his love of land and the machinations involved in real estate transactions. His military services later earned him a land grant of five or six thousand acres from the state. Beyond that, he purchased land in Lenoir County on more than forty occasions and became a wealthy planter.

William Croom, with the example of his father and brother—Joshua served in the colonial House of Commons and later in the legislature—before him, also entered public service. At twenty-one he succeeded Joshua in the state Senate and was reelected five times. As a senator, Croom pushed legislation supporting agriculture. He was an officer in the state militia and during the War of 1812, as a major general, commanded three brigades of militia from Lenoir and Jones Counties. In July 1814, Croom assembled his men to defend the nearby port of New Bern from an invasion that never came. Yet the threat was real. Units from the British fleet had sacked Portsmouth and Ocracoke Islands off the North Carolina coast. Older citizens remembered that during the American Revolution the British had occupied New Bern briefly and burned some plantation homes.[3]

Once the War of 1812 ended, William Croom retired to Newington, an estate three miles east of Kinston, seat of government for Lenoir County. Kinston, established in 1762 but not incorporated until 1826, was only thirty-one miles west of New Bern. Croom was a town commissioner and served on Kinston's governing board when it was incorporated. Newington was the former property of General Richard Caswell, first governor of the state. About this time Croom began reducing his public activities, but he increased his real estate ventures. He purchased several plantations—Tower Hill, Rountree, Friendship Hall—and other properties nearby.

Hearing stories about Florida's rich lands (one territorial official described the area around the future Goodwood plantation as a "fertile country growing sugar cane and sea-island cotton, and watered by never failing streams and fine springs"), Croom cast his land net to the south.[4] He was driven more by a restless spirit than by the need for more land, but the wealthy planter was not averse to increasing the legacy that his

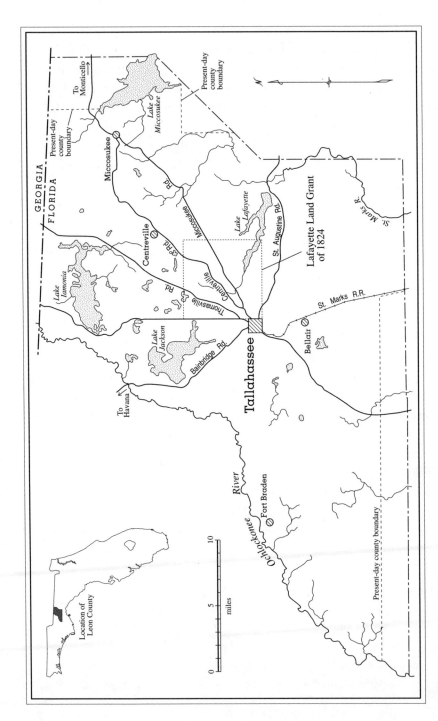

GEORGIA
FLORIDA

To Monticello

Present-day county boundary

Present-day county boundary

Miccosukee

Lake Miccosukee

Miccosukee Rd.

Lake Iamonia

Centreville

Lake Lafayette

St. Augustine Rd.

St. Marks R.

Lafayette Land Grant of 1824

Centreville Rd.

Thomasville Rd.

Lake Jackson

St. Marks R.R.

Bellair

Bainbridge Rd.

To Havana

Tallahassee

Ochlockonee River

Fort Braden

Present-day county boundary

N

Location of Leon County

0   5   10
miles

Map of Leon County, 1855

family would inherit. By the mid-1820s he had visited north Florida and purchased tracts in Gadsden County, but his speculations were cut short. On May 9, 1829, the exact day that the fifty-seven-year-old Croom had set aside for another journey to Florida, he died at Newington. He had been sick for eleven days with a violent fever that no amount or variety of medicine could control. His doctor described the illness as a "bilious fever." Croom was typical of most planters in that he divided his large estate equitably among his wife and children, including his daughters. He was buried in the family cemetery on Rountree plantation near Tower Hill.[5]

William Croom, like other affluent southerners in the antebellum South, had more than one wife and fathered two sets of children. No less common was his propensity and that of succeeding generations to use surnames, regardless of the offspring's gender, as given names, both first and middle. The result was a tortured maze of relationships that has created nightmares for historians, not to mention genealogists. Retaining family names made confusion coequal with continuity but was considered worth the price.

Croom was married twice, first to Mary Bryan, daughter of Winifred and Colonel Nathan Bryan, a native of Craven County. Bryan served North Carolina as a member of the House of Commons in the 1780s and 1790s and as a member of the Fourth and Fifth Congresses (1795–98— he died in 1797). William and Mary had four children: Hardy Bryan (to avoid confusion he will always be referred to as Hardy), Susan Matilda, Bryan, and Richard.

Mary Bryan Croom died on October 7, 1807. Some eighteen months later (April 20, 1809) William married again, this time, Elizabeth "Betsy" Whitfield. Betsy was the daughter of General Bryan Whitfield and Nancy Bryan Whitfield, the general's first wife. The Whitfields lived at Spring Hill in Lenoir County. Elizabeth, who brought land and slaves as her dowry, bore William five children: Ann Bryan, William Whitfield, John Quincy (died in infancy), Elizabeth "Betsy" Jane, and George Alexander. Elizabeth died in Kinston on June 27, 1831, and was buried beside her husband. Religious faith was an enduring characteristic of the family, the people they married, and succeeding generations of Crooms. Almost without exception they were Episcopalians who assumed leadership roles in various churches on the frontiers of Florida and Alabama.

Although William Croom established planting interests in Gadsden County, buying land there in 1826 and 1828, he never became a citizen of the Territory of Florida. One son by his first marriage, Bryan, did, while Richard, also a child of the first marriage, may have, but only briefly because he moved to Alabama about 1835. Even so, Richard bought large tracts of land in Florida and was practically a dual citizen, as he and members of his family variously visited and lived there. Hardy, Mary Bryan Croom's other son, periodically considered becoming a citizen. His blood relatives and various acquaintances would contend that he actually established legal residence, but others would insist that he did not. If Hardy was not a Florida citizen, he exercised various privileges of one, including voting. He also signed numerous legal documents listing himself as a Floridian. The question of Hardy's citizenship was important because, later, his status in the territory became crucial to the ownership of Goodwood plantation. On March 8, 1816, Susan Matilda, about whom little is known, married Edmund Whitfield of White Hall in Wayne County, North Carolina. His parents were Needham (1758–1812) and Elizabeth Hatch Whitfield (1760–1812). Within five years Susan Matilda was dead.[6] As for the children from William Croom's second marriage, both Betsy and Ann became Florida citizens, as did William and George Alexander.

Hardy and, to a slightly lesser extent, his brother Bryan were responsible for establishing Goodwood plantation. The name Goodwood probably did not come into usage until the late 1840s, but by the 1850s, it began appearing frequently in various letters and has been in common use since. Although other siblings and kin were intimately involved and their activities are discussed, this narrative's initial and major focus is on Hardy and Bryan Croom. Hardy was born in Lenoir County on October 8, 1797. During much of his forty years of life, he was beset by chronic ill health, mainly lung problems—possibly tuberculosis but probably malaria. Hardy was highly susceptible to chills, colds, and coughs. Even so, he was active—he liked to ride horseback, was a strong

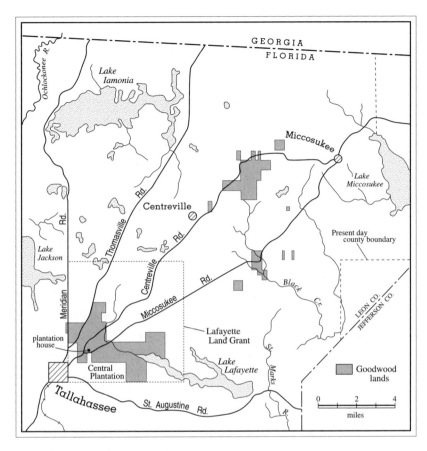

Map of Goodwood Plantation, 1855

swimmer, and had few equals as a traveler in an age when going places was a physical ordeal. He managed to combine intellectual and scientific interests with those of practical business, planting, and, on a limited basis, politics.

Born toward the end of the Enlightenment, Hardy bore the stamp of that epoch's influence on America—and its special effect on an elite group of southerners. Aristocrat, intellectual, writer, lawyer, amateur botanist and scientist, reluctant politician, linguist, planter, and slaveholder, he followed a pattern not unlike that of Thomas Jefferson. Hardy may have attended the Spring-Hill Seminary of Learning, chartered in Lenoir County in 1802. He was among the ten members of the class of 1817 at the University of North Carolina at Chapel Hill. Chartered in 1789, the school attracted the sons of planters and graduated men who became leaders in North Carolina and other southern states. The school was the college of choice for most of the Crooms and their kin and close acquaintants. Because he was an excellent student (and from a leading family), Hardy was awarded an A.M. degree in 1820. Even though earned master's degrees were not instituted at the university until 1885, the honorary recognition was always a badge of achievement.

Hardy had an oval face with a broad forehead and sharp chin. High cheekbones and almond-shaped blue eyes framed an aquiline nose, and he had a wide but well-formed mouth and light brown, slightly wavy hair. These features, combined with his slim, almost delicate build—he was slightly less than 5′10″ in height and never weighed more than 135 pounds—gave Hardy the appearance of an English Lake Poet. Soon after taking his degree, Croom studied law with a young New Bern citizen, Francis Lister Hawks, who graduated from the University of North Carolina in 1815 and later gained fame as an Episcopal bishop, historian, and educator. The two men read law with William Gaston, a barrister and a teacher of law in New Bern. A Federalist and later a Whig, Gaston was a member of the state legislature, serving as Speaker of the House of Representatives. One of Craven County's most illustrious natives, Gaston also represented his district in Congress and was a member of the North Carolina Supreme Court. Gaston's biographer noted that he trained a number of lawyers, to whom he "devoted himself unsparingly and patiently, giving each his earnest attentions and courteous consideration."[7] He clearly influenced the two young men, who practiced together for a brief time. In addition to his practice of law, Hardy served occasionally as a justice of the peace in Lenoir County.

Hawks remembered later that Hardy had no intention of making law his profession. According to the future bishop, Hardy had a "natural amiability of disposition" and "was a good scholar, particularly attached to classical learning." He also liked botany, geology, mineralogy, and American history, and he planned a book on "some of the colonial events" of North Carolina. In short, Hawks noted, "he loved letters with a pure and beautiful love."[8] Hardy's idealism was seen in a Fourth of July oration he delivered at Kinston in 1825: "Throughout the civilized world, my friends, we behold one great and general strife, the strife of *principles;* the Liberal and the Despotic, the *Ormuzd* and *Ahriman,* the good and evil of the political world. Such being the case, we may well invoke all the energies of the good old cause, the cause of human rights."[9]

Another example of Hardy's scholarship, one with ironic coincidence, was his translation of the first two cantos of Voltaire's epic poem *La Henriade.* Concerning Henry IV of France and religious freedom, the work was inscribed by Croom and presented (along with many gifts from other people) to the marquis de Lafayette during his triumphal visit to the United States in 1824–25. Hardy may have given it to Lafayette personally when he visited either Raleigh or Fayetteville in March 1825. Hardy had no idea that a decade later he would begin Goodwood plantation by buying land in Florida that had been given to Lafayette by the United States.[10]

Croom kept in close touch with family, friends, and professional acquaintances. Although only ten when his mother died, he loved her deeply and cherished her memory throughout his own life. As a thoughtful man, Hardy might be expected to have reflected on the morality of slavery, and no doubt he did. But he made no public statements. In numerous private letters he never mentioned the philosophical or economic justification for the peculiar institution. Yet Croom was a man of impeccable honor. His correspondence clearly establishes him as a kind master, admiring, trusting, and assigning responsible duties to some of his bondsmen.

During his one term in the North Carolina state senate (1828–29), Hardy voted for a measure that permitted emancipated slaves over the age of fifty to remain in the state. He also introduced a resolution to have the judiciary committee investigate the practice of withdrawing benefit of clergy from a slave convicted of attempting to poison a white person. Still, he accepted slavery and did not question it as integral to southern life and culture. He bought, sold, and hired out his slaves—as did the other Crooms, male and female.

Important as a base for the Crooms, the previously mentioned New Bern was an attractive and prosperous port city located at the confluence of the Neuse and Trent Rivers, about forty miles west of Pamlico Sound. People moved into the area as early as 1702, but the main settlement was made in 1710 by Swiss and German colonists under the leadership of Baron Christoph Von Graffenried. New Bern was the colonial and then state capital from 1746 to 1792, when Raleigh was laid out as the seat of government. It remained an important city throughout the antebellum period.[11]

In New Bern, on June 19, 1821, Hardy married Frances Smith, daughter of Nathan Smith, a wealthy resident, who owned plantations and town property. Her mother was Henrietta Harrineau Lee of Plymouth, North Carolina. Although not beautiful, Frances was attractive. She had an oval face, high forehead, and long nose (a physical feature inherited from her father's side of the family). Her mouth was small with faintly pursed lips, and she had a slightly pointed chin. Combined with her brown eyes, chestnut-brown hair, delicate neck, and sloping shoulders, these features gave her the appearance of unusual fragility. Frances had health problems no less serious and in fact more traumatic than those of Hardy. She suffered from what were described as "nervous attacks" but were actually epileptic seizures. As for Nathan Smith, he bought and sold land and when necessary went to court over boundary disputes. He was also successful as a planter and was already a prominent citizen when he died at thirty-five on February 26, 1823. He left

Frances, nicknamed Fanny, and his other children inheritances that included town lots in New Bern. Hardy and Frances were given Lot 15, worth an estimated $6,600. Smith's other daughters were included in his will, but the bulk of the estate's lands and slaves went to his wife, Henrietta, and his son, Nathaniel.[12]

Hardy and Fanny had five children. Two of them died young: Eugene Lafayette when he was eighteen months old, and Frances Elizabeth one month short of her first birthday. Of those who survived, Henrietta Mary, the oldest, was born on April 28, 1822, William Henry on December 29, 1827, and Justina Rosa three years later.

As noted, Hardy represented Lenoir County in the North Carolina state senate in 1828. His tenure was largely an act of public service and undertaken in the tradition already established by his immediate family and close kin. Although health problems militated against his performance as a legislator, Croom voted on most bills. In addition to his positions on slavery, the reluctant senator worked on financial measures, local elections, and banking regulations and introduced a bill establishing a poorhouse in Lenoir County.[13] Following his father's death in 1829, Croom resigned his seat.

Unlike Thomas Jefferson, Hardy had no particular taste for holding office. Yet he closely followed political developments in the United States and Great Britain. As the Whig party evolved in the 1830s, he adhered to its principles. Hardy was succeeded in the statehouse in Raleigh by William D. Moseley, also of Lenoir County. Moseley knew the Croom family and was a graduate of the University of North Carolina, class of 1818. Moseley moved to Jefferson County, Florida, in the late 1830s. There he established himself as a planter, served in the territorial Legislative Council, and, as a Democrat, was elected in 1845 as the new state's first governor. In Florida, Moseley became reacquainted with several of the Crooms.

Leaving Frances in New Bern, Hardy spent much of his time in Lenoir County helping manage his father's property, especially Friendship Hall plantation. There in 1828 he supervised construction of a new smokehouse. In the ginning and packing of the cotton crop, he shifted over to the new and more profitable mode of making square bales instead of round ones. Hardy was one of the executors of his father's estate (along with a brother-in-law from each of William's wives). He inherited a number of slaves who had been placed under his supervision, as well as livestock and Falling Creek and Friendship Hall plantations.[14]

Even before he purchased Florida property outright, Hardy was interested in the territory. In the early spring of 1830 he thought the estate's Florida land would have to be sold. His conclusions were based on conditions in New Bern, about which he wrote Bryan, "The times are such as we never had before. Almost half the merchants of this place are broke." Yet when Hardy visited Florida in the fall of 1830, he was so impressed that he changed his mind. Croom wrote Frances that one field hand in Florida could produce as much as two in North Carolina.[15] Without doubt economic conditions in coastal North Carolina helped spur his Florida ambitions.

In October 1831, a few months after his stepmother died, Hardy sold his plantation in Lenoir County. The purchaser, his brother Richard, paid him $10,000 and, on moving to Friendship Hall, agreed to harvest and dispose of the crop. Hardy hired one Malachia Fields to take his slaves to Florida—the overland journey took twenty-nine days and was accomplished without mishap. Fields was experienced in such matters and had rendered the same service for Nathan Bryan Whitfield, a kinsman of William Croom and an executor of his estate. Whitfield later moved to Marengo County in Alabama's fertile Black Belt and established a large plantation that he named Gaineswood. The home he built there rivaled Jefferson's Monticello and remains one of Alabama's most stately mansions.[16]

Hardy and Frances moved to New Bern, settling into her parents' comfortable home. The two-story structure had a double piazza in front and was one of the town's finest residences. It was located on Lot 12, on the north side of South Front Street near the town's wharf. Title to the home remained with Henrietta Smith—in 1834 Hardy paid her $150 for two years' rent. The precarious health of both Crooms was a factor in the move, as Frances especially did not want to reside in Lenoir County. Henrietta did not live with them—in 1833 she wrote Hardy, who was in Florida, "We spent a pleasant evening at your house last night."[17]

Hardy lived in New Bern but, by choice, was something of an outsider. He neither sought elective office nor took an active part in Craven County politics. Acquaintances said that he did not vote or exercise the usual privileges of citizenship. Hardy used New Bern as a way station, a point of departure for forays north to New York and south to Florida. Maintaining a peripatetic schedule, Croom sometimes let a month pass before picking up his mail at the New Bern post office. Yet he was well known in the town because of his personality and achievements and as Fanny's husband, a man of mark who had married into a leading local family. The couple's children were baptized in New Bern's Christ Church (Episcopal), but for all their prominence, Hardy and Frances wore their affluence lightly. As Zachary Slade, a carriage maker, remembered later, "[They] always treated me with kindness & respect beyond any reasonable expectations of mine, both families being of the highest circles of society in New Bern." [18]

If Croom viewed the town as a temporary domicile, he envisioned Florida as his future. Working with Bryan, he planned to expand farming operations by purchasing and renting more Gadsden County land and concentrating on cotton and sugarcane. As he wrote Bryan, they could combine their resources, adding, "I doubt not that *with prudence* we shall be in a [position] to do well." [19] For the brothers "to do well" required hard work: looking after their slaves, hiring efficient overseers, purchasing supplies and farm equipment, caring for livestock, supervising land clearing, planting, plowing, hoeing, weeding, building and maintaining fences, and harvesting and marketing their crops.

In 1831, Hardy's slaves were hired out in either Leon or Gadsden Counties, probably both. The brothers owned a number of slaves jointly, and on occasion, the elder Croom sold one of them. In 1831, John Kennedy, a Lenoir County neighbor, paid him $500 for Joe, a forty-year-old bondsman. In the spring of 1832, Hardy took some of his slaves, as well as some belonging to his mother-in-law, from Florida to New Orleans and sold them. While there, the ever inquisitive planter-scientist considered buying cotton lands in Mississippi along the Yazoo River or hiring out some of his and Bryan's slaves (he never did). [20]

While engaged in selling his slaves in Louisiana, Hardy was the guest of a man named Wilkinson, who owned a plantation forty miles south of New Orleans. Hardy's nine slaves were also quartered there. Wilkinson's hospitality was excellent, although Hardy declined the planter's offer to sell him land. Oranges grew there, but mosquitoes were bad, and the country was "not so *comfortable* as Florida." Taking his blacks to New Orleans, Hardy sold five women and three men for $4,000. He also sold a ten-year-old boy for $350. "You will see," he wrote Bryan, "that negroes are high here."[21]

Leaving New Orleans on the new steamboat *Henry Clay,* Hardy went up the Mississippi River before traveling east to Norfolk, Virginia. From there he journeyed to Philadelphia, where he met his family (who had been in New York) and returned to New Bern. Whatever scenic and botanical pleasures the journey provided were paid for at the cost of Hardy's physical well-being. As he ascended the Mississippi, the weather became colder, and his health worsened. "The consequence is my health has suffered a serious injury. The state of my lungs I fear is worse than it has ever been before. . . . There is some doubt whether the ensuing winter will not be too much for me unless I could get within the tropics." His recovery was gradual, in fact, "very slow": "The issue cannot at present be foreseen, although I do not anticipate any sudden fatality."[22]

Eventually, Hardy divided his time between his land in Lenoir County, New Bern, his land in Florida, and New York City. Charleston, South Carolina, was added later, and he visited many other places. Carefully avoiding the Florida heat, he spent part of each summer in New York City with excursions to Newport and Saratoga, where he and Frances had family and friends. He also renewed himself intellectually in New York, visiting museums and libraries, attending lectures, and engaging in conversations with men of science. But for all his travels, between 1830 and 1837 Hardy was in Florida for longer periods than anywhere else.

Hardy and his family, and, even more, his in-laws, were always arranging some seasonal rendezvous. There is no evidence that his wife or daughters ever came to Gadsden or Leon Counties. William Henry accompanied his father to Florida several times, first in 1830, when he was only three. On one trip to the territory, Hardy wrote of his son: "His buoyancy of spirits is very great. At every House he has a romp with the children, every person he meets he salutes with some familiar address, & is a general favorite wherever he goes." Once, William went to school in Gadsden County, probably Quincy Academy, which had been established in 1832.[23] Hardy frequently wrote of his children's desire to visit Florida.

After 1823, Frances and the children were often in the company of her siblings and widowed mother, as well as her mother's sister, Mary F. Camack. After her husband, Robert Camack, and her daughter Rosana died, Mary inherited large tracts of land in Ohio from them. Yet she continued to live in New Bern. Her role there was more than social: she helped attend Frances, whose health problems were subject to unpredictable crises. The family relationship was ongoing, both in North Carolina and in out-of-state visits to friends and relatives. Frances was one of five children, including the aforementioned Nathaniel. Her brother was not well and spent time in St. Augustine, Florida, and elsewhere attempting to restore his health. Nathaniel died without children, as did Henrietta, his sister, who married John B. Carroll, a New York broker and commission merchant. Another sister, Elizabeth Armistead, would become the only surviving child. As early as 1821, Richard M. Armistead, Elizabeth's husband, was unable to attend to business, and she was given control of her inheritance. A man with family ties in Edenton, North Carolina, Richard died after what was described as "a short illness" on March 19, 1824, in Philadelphia, Pennsylvania. Susan Evelyn, born the year of her father's death, was the Armisteads' only child. It seems probable that after Nathan died, Henrietta lived in New Bern with her widowed daughter Elizabeth. Hardy helped look after his mother-in-law's interests, and on one occasion she gave young William Henry a present of three slaves.[24] Hardy was far too much the gentleman to have an open confrontation with his wife's mother, but their relations would become obviously strained. His brother Bryan would also learn how formidable, despite her age, Henrietta Smith could be.

Henrietta Lee was born in 1780 in Plymouth, county seat of what became Washington County (1799). She grew up in the town, located on the western end of North Carolina's Albemarle Sound, and later met and married Nathan. Henrietta had children and wealth but was a widow by the age of forty-three. From then until her death, she managed her affairs with a natural flair for business. Henrietta's appearance matched her character. She had dark hair and eyes, a slightly beaked nose, a generous mouth, and a strong chin. Large and heavyset, she was impressive and dignified, everything about her suggesting strength and determination. Henrietta's love for her children, whose interests she protected, was returned in full measure. Although she never lived at the Goodwood mansion, the widow Smith came to Leon County and played a pivotal role in the plantation's history.

By 1832, even Henrietta wanted to visit Florida, but not Elizabeth Armistead, whose opposition was the strongest among family members. As Hardy wrote Bryan from North Carolina, "My health continues to improve & New Bern to decline. You cannot conceive how the place has altered. Mrs. Smith and all the family would move out if it were not for Mrs. Armistead."[25]

Hardy shipped some furniture and china, as well as a number of his books, to Rocky Comfort, Bryan's Gadsden County plantation. Most of the books were scientific monographs, and there were enough of them to make Hardy's personal library one of the largest in the territory. Hardy assumed correctly that Bryan would permit him and his family to live at Rocky Comfort for a while, "in order," as he put it, "that my wife might feel so little as possible the want of society."[26] That fall (1832), Hardy was "seized with ague and fever" but by October was preparing to join Bryan in Florida: "I am very desirous to be with you and am resolved to remain 12 or 18 months at least."[27] Hardy's stay was not nearly so long, and, as often happened, the plans fell through for bringing his family.

While attending closely to his planting operations, Hardy kept up his scientific studies and research. In his travels he compiled careful notes and charts of his botanical observations, collected specimens, and always sought the company of botanists and naturalists. Hardy was a member of the Literary and Philosophical Society of South Carolina, as well as a corresponding member of the Academy of Natural Sciences of Philadelphia and the New York Lyceum of Natural History. For a man of his interests and physical condition, Florida was an exotic paradise, and North Carolina, while interesting and the sometime subject of his research, suffered by way of contrast. Writing to Bryan in Gadsden County in 1831, Hardy complained of conditions in his home state: "Today and yesterday are the coolest days I have ever felt in the month of July. I keep fires to make me comfortable. My health suffers considerably by the wet weather and I heartily wish myself in some better climate."[28] It was no surprise that a number of his articles and catalogs on plants were on the flora of Florida.

In 1833 Hardy's "Memoranda of a Journey from Newbern to Raleigh by an Amateur Botanist" appeared in the *Harbinger*, a Chapel Hill newspaper, and in 1833–35 three of his articles were published in the *American Journal of Science and Arts*.[29] In 1837, his catalog of plants native to New Bern appeared, and, typical of his scholarship, its thirty-nine pages were followed by ten more devoted to eighty-four footnotes. Croom encouraged citizens of New Bern such as George Wilson to pursue botanical studies, sharing his own work with him and putting him in touch with professional scientists.[30]

Croom discovered a rare coniferous tree in Gadsden County and named it *torreya taxifolia* in honor of his famed botanist friend Dr. John Torrey of New York City. Torrey, a medical doctor and professor of chemistry at Columbia and Princeton, was America's pioneer taxonomic botanist. That is, he was engaged in naming new species, subspecies, and genera and arranging them into families and orders. Torrey became the mentor and friend of leading botanical investigators, and he and Croom developed a close relationship. In 1836, Torrey read a paper (subsequently published) to the New York Lyceum of Natural History and credited Hardy as one of those who aided him in its preparation.

Croom first sighted the Torreya tree near Aspalaga in Gadsden County. It was an important finding (the first evidence of the species in the United States). Later the tree was found in limited areas of California, China, and Japan. Related to the yew tree, the Torreya is six to sixteen inches in diameter, grows twenty to forty feet high with numerous spreading branches, and bears a small fruit. Its wood is dense and close grained, flows a blood-red turpentine, and gives off a strong, unpleasant odor when burned or bruised. Greatly prized as an ornamental tree in Europe, the Torreya had an economic use for Floridians: resistant to insect attacks, it made excellent rails for the territory's early railroads. When Croom discovered another rare plant, Dr. Torrey named it *croomia pauciflora* as a tribute to him.[31] Hardy also wrote for a popular audience and was such a frequent contributor to the *New Bern Spectator* (previously known as the *Spectator and Literary Journal* and also as the *Spectator and Political Register*) that some people thought he edited the newspaper.

Hardy and Bryan soon bought land in Jackson County, Florida (west of Gadsden County), but their holdings were not extensive.[32] Created August 12, 1822, the county was named for Old Hickory, who, among his other accomplishments, served briefly as the territorial governor of Florida. If the Tennesseean's tenure was short lived, his influence was lasting. A number of the territorial leaders were protégés of Jackson. Hardy bought and rented some land in Gadsden County, and the brothers engaged jointly in planting activities. Florida's potential seemed vastly different from the realities of New Bern, where Hardy declared in 1830, "*Bankruptcy* is the order of the day."[33]

Writing from Rocky Comfort in December 1831, Hardy informed his wife, "I have concluded to occupy and cultivate in cotton the place my father bought near Bryan's with part of the hands, and employ [others] with a part of Bryan's on the river, in making sugar."[34] From 1830 on, Hardy maintained a close interest in Florida affairs.

Bryan Croom, born October 8, 1801, was less intellectually active than Hardy but much more physically fit. Medium in build, he had a high forehead, slightly angular face, full eyebrows, and an open expression. He had a broad nose and, unlike the clean-shaven Hardy, affected a mustache and beard that, neither well groomed nor scraggly, gave him a slightly unkempt appearance. Hardy more closely resembled his brother Richard than Bryan. Even when he was ill, Bryan drove himself, prompting Hardy to remark on one occasion, "His imprudence is such that he has not yet recovered his health." Another time, Hardy urged his younger brother, "Be careful of your health, take quinine, and use every effort to re-establish your [well-being]." Unfailingly level-headed, Bryan was also known for his sense of humor. There was no question about where he would attend college, and Bryan was one of twenty-nine students who graduated from the University of North Carolina in 1821. As a part of the graduation exercises, he debated fellow student Robert Cowan on the question "Have the Moderns Equaled the Ancients in Eloquence?" Bryan married Eveline Singleton Hawks on July 27, 1826. Eveline was from a respected, well-to-do New Bern family and was the first cousin of Francis Lister Hawks.[35] Born in 1800, Eveline never escaped a lifelong problem of having people misspell her name. It was frequently rendered, even on her tombstone, with an *a* as Evelina, but much more often with *e* as the last letter. Throughout this book the spelling is Eveline.

The Crooms usually had fairly large families, but Bryan and Eveline never had any children. Unlike other sons of planters, Croom did not migrate to become less emotionally and economically dependent on his father. When Bryan came to Florida in 1826, he was no doubt in the company of his father. He bought land in Gadsden County, where he and his wife settled down on Rocky Comfort plantation. Eveline's brother, Benjamin B. Hawks, and her widowed mother, Ann Singleton Hawks (a prominent and capable woman who owned a number of slaves and land lots in New Bern), lived with them. In 1834 and 1845, Ann sold her North Carolina property and continued what became a permanent residence with Bryan and Eveline. She and Eveline maintained a deeply affectionate lifetime relationship that was intimate even for a mother and daughter. A young man in his twenties, Benjamin was a lawyer who was not overly serious about his profession. As a gentleman planter he followed the lead of the Crooms and had a close intellectual relationship with Hardy.[36]

Bryan's land included Sections 13, 17, 18, 23, and 24 (or at least large parts of them) in the rich Little River Survey in the Forbes Purchase and contained 2,000 acres. The Forbes Purchase was a privately owned expanse of 1.5 million acres that sprawled across parts of Franklin, Liberty, Wakulla, Gadsden, and Leon Counties. In the period 1763–83, when Great Britain owned Florida, the major trading firm there was

Panton, Leslie and Company. Possessing Florida a second time (1783–1819), Spain permitted John Forbes and Company, successors to Panton, Leslie and Company, to handle most of the colony's trade. Over time the Spanish government became heavily indebted to the Forbes Company and canceled its obligation by granting the corporation land that became known as the Forbes Purchase. When the United States organized the Territory of Florida, it claimed the vast acreage, and an extended lawsuit resulted. The courts finally ended the litigation by ruling against the United States in 1835, but even before that the Forbes Company was surveying and selling its property. Much of the Forbes Company's empire had limited agricultural potential, but the Little River area in Gadsden County, which was surveyed by Daniel F. McNeil in 1824, contained excellent cotton land.[37]

Rocky Comfort Creek ran through the region and gave its name to the small community where Bryan and Eveline had their plantation. The Croom family patriarch, William (who did not remain), and his son Bryan (who did) were among the pioneer settlers of Gadsden County. They established plantations in the Little River Survey, and in 1827 Bryan and Robert Forbes, an early migrant, bonded one David Ochiltree as the Rocky Comfort postmaster. The act was strong evidence that by then Bryan had settled permanently in Gadsden County.[38]

According to his father's will of 1829, Bryan inherited two of his North Carolina slaves and all of his bondsmen in Florida. Croom also gave Bryan "all [his] right of lands in Florida" and provided up to $3,000 from his estate sales to help his son purchase more acreage in the territory. Instead of relying solely on cotton, Bryan practiced agricultural diversification and made money from manufacturing sugar. The cane crop also supplied his household and slaves with syrup. By 1830, Bryan's sixty-three slaves made him one of Gadsden County's largest planters.[39]

Bryan and his mother-in-law made an arrangement for him to employ her slaves: she permitted Bryan to have one-half of the slaves' hire in return for her and her son Benjamin's board. Bryan agreed to pay a "reasonable hire" for the other half due her, and the settlement took the form of selling her a slave named Matilda and her children for $3,000.

Both Ann Hawks and Bryan accepted the amount as the equivalent of hiring her slaves, and no other action was taken until 1837, when the arrangement was revised.[40]

Together with Hardy, Bryan owned 479.5 acres in the short-lived county of Fayette. They sold the property in 1833 for $5,000. Bryan also owned the land on both sides of the Apalachicola River that was used for ferry landings, but he sold the acreage in 1833.[41] The landings connected Fayette County (formed in 1832 but reincorporated into Jackson County in 1834) on the west bank and Aspalaga, a hamlet on the east bank in Gadsden County. The community never advanced far beyond the planning stage. In the fall and winter of 1837–38, the French naturalist Comte Francis de Castelnau visited middle Florida and on a journey down the Apalachicola River described "the village of Aspalaga, if one may give this name to two wooden cabins situated on an elevation."[42]

Gadsden County was established June 24, 1823, and named for James Gadsden, who served in Florida with Andrew Jackson in the First Seminole War in 1818. Daniel F. McNeil, the county surveyor, laid off Quincy as the county seat, and the first land sales were made July 7, 1825. John Quincy Adams, secretary of state at the time, would later, as president, sign the deed for the town site. The Massachusetts native was no doubt flattered to have the village named for him. Quincy developed into one of antebellum Florida's principal towns, rivaling Tallahassee as the hub of a wealthy agricultural area. Rocky Comfort was eight miles south of Quincy and was connected to the town by a post road. A log courthouse, built in 1825, was destroyed by fire in 1849. Because crucial records were lost when the courthouse burned, it is impossible to pinpoint when William Croom or his sons bought land in the county, but later purchases and sales are recorded. Together with family letters, newspapers, and trial records, they make possible an accounting of the Crooms' property.[43]

In 1831, Hardy wrote Bryan urging him to retain possession of Croom lands in Gadsden County, especially "that part which was cleared by [his] father's hands."[44] As the 1830s began, Hardy and, much less often, Bryan were making regular trips between Gadsden County and New Bern. The brothers were close and worked together well. For example, on one occasion Hardy sold a lot in New Bern for Bryan (one probably inherited by Eveline) for $225. He immediately bought Bryan "a pair of handsome bay horses" for $250 and ordered a "fashionable carriage of the best materials . . . to be painted olive, with two sets of harness," for $625. Hardy drove the team of horses and delivered them to Bryan at Rocky Comfort (the actual driving was probably done by Edward, Hardy's indispensable coachman). The carriage was shipped from New York to Magnolia or St. Marks, Tallahassee's gulf ports situated about twenty miles south of the capital, and picked up there. Hardy explained the transactions later.[45] If their partnership seemed casual to the point of indifference, it was based on total trust, an innate anticipation of the other's thoughts, and was more binding than any legal contract.

In January 1832, Hardy purchased ninety acres of public land in Section 25. The property joined Rocky Comfort plantation on the northwest and was incorporated into the brothers' farming operations. By late spring of that year, Bryan reported to Hardy that their crops in Gadsden County promised success. The corn was in good condition, and their stand of short-staple Mexican cotton, despite damage from cutworms, was satisfactory. The Mexican variety, crossed later with other types, could be grown all over the upland South and helped make cotton the region's major crop.

The long-staple Sea Island cotton crop, which opened later and brought more money per pound, promised a bountiful yield. Bryan discussed the white supervisor whom they had employed: "Oliver is certainly a most excellent overseer, & I think we can prosper at farming with him at the head. The negroes are satisfied with him & he gets along with very little trouble to himself or me." With their farming operations expanding yearly, it was little wonder that in the summer of 1832, the more settled Bryan wrote Hardy, "I would impress you seriously with thinking of moving to Florida."[46] Oliver's efficiency must have declined, because a year later Hardy, mistrusting his employee's ability to weigh cotton, informed Bryan that the overseer was "too often drunk." Hardy warned, "If he should indulge in this way too much, you ought to admonish him, and if he should whip too cruelly, you should moderate him."[47]

As experienced men of the soil, Hardy and Bryan well knew that whether one was a planter or a farmer, the capriciousness of nature determined success or failure. Despite the bright outlook earlier in 1832, things had changed by October. Hardy responded stoically to Bryan's report: "Our crop of cotton, especially my Mexican has been a good deal injured by the rains. It seems there must always be some slip between the cup and the lip. But let that pass, we [*sic*] do the best you can. You do not inform me what preparations you have made in addition to your farms, for ginning out the crop, but I hope you have procured another roller gin, and fitted it up. In regard to our crop at the river, if you do not propose to gin and boil the cane, let it be cut, and carefully put up before frost." Ever the practical planter, Hardy added, "My views for the next year are these—If you can get land enough in your neighborhood for *all* our hands, we will employ them in cotton, and rent out the river place, and sell the corn and cane." [48]

The brothers were also entangled in a lawsuit in Florida over land and money involving the hiring of slaves. As a precaution if he could not get down in time for court, Hardy enclosed instructions for Bryan to give to his attorney in Tallahassee—including his statement that if the case was lost, then an appeal should be filed. Then, easily putting aside economic and legal woes, the older Hardy informed his brother, "I got for you the musical dictionary but it is written in French, and I fear [it] may not be very useful." [49]

As for Bryan's suggestion that Hardy move his family to Florida, Frances, whose health influenced her thoughts, was not so sure. While Hardy was at Rocky Comfort in January 1833, she wrote him, "Mama told me to tell you she was preparing with all haste to emigrate with us; I have not heard sister say what she intends to do. It seems though almost a pity to leave our State just as times are getting better. . . . Tell [Bryan and Eveline] I shall be glad if we can be near neighbors when we all get out there." [50] She was responding to Hardy's desire to bring all his slaves to Florida and his attempts to persuade the Bellamy brothers—Dr. Samuel C. Bellamy, his half sister Betsy's husband, and Dr. Edward C. Bellamy, husband of Ann, his other half sister—to move there. [51]

Frances's caution was no doubt influenced by the mitigating circumstances of living on the Florida frontier, including the possibility and later the fact of another conflict with the Native Americans (the First Seminole War occurred in 1817–18). She was also disturbed by the death of her brother, Nathaniel, in 1832. As noted, Nathaniel and his mother were the chief beneficiaries of Nathan Smith's will, with the son receiving land and slaves. Nathaniel was never well (the nature of his illness in unknown) and sought relief in Florida and elsewhere. He died under unusual circumstances in New Orleans. Later there would be charges that he was a wastrel who squandered his fortune. Whatever the situation, Nathaniel left a document without date or signature directing the disposition of his property. It was too incomplete and informal to serve as a will, and the family members, including Hardy and Frances, signed everything over to Henrietta Smith.[52] Harmony was preserved, but resentment remained and would flare again. Such events made the indelicate Frances cling closer to the familiar sanctuary that was New Bern.

All the while, Hardy and Bryan continued their planting operations. The scholarly debate over the economic aspects of slavery—whether it was inefficient and unprofitable or a system whose returns outnumbered its losses—is lively and ongoing among historians and other scholars. Planters such as Hardy and Bryan, unconcerned that they were making history, were occupied with making cotton and marketing it. Planting was always problematic, but to Hardy and Bryan the returns were worth the risks. Most of their business operations took the form of credit, and although they favored a few factors, they traded with a large number of merchants. The management of the Croom lands in Gadsden County and, later, Goodwood in Leon County included the effective utilization of their labor force. That they were equal to the task was seen early on.

In June 1833, Hardy gave Bryan instructions about employing the slaves after the crop was laid by and before picking time. The hands should begin "grubbing" in the oak land at one place. After grubbing twenty-five or thirty acres, they could begin to cut; Hardy added, however, "That land will require very little cutting, and I wish no more done than is necessary." Bryan was to employ a white man named McRainey to supervise the work. Showing skill in management relations, Hardy had purchased a gun for McRainey in Quincy and hoped he would enjoy using it. Some of the slaves at another place were to build a gin house and a cotton house, while the others were to clear new ground. Most important, he informed Bryan, "Begin to pick out cotton as soon as it is ready, and do not allow it to wait on new ground or any other work." One month later the vigilant Hardy repeated, "Begin to pick out as soon as the crop requires it, and make it an object to pick in the cotton as clean as practicable and not to let it suffer *heating in bulk.*"[53]

Time and trouble expended in traveling between North Carolina and Florida argued strongly for a permanent residence. The logistics of getting from New Bern to Charleston, South Carolina, might involve nothing more complicated than taking a steamer, although regular packet (commercial) service was not available, and making the connection could be difficult. It was also possible to travel by land from New Bern northwesterly to Kinston, then to Waynesboro, North Carolina, where a commercial stage was available (the town died out later when the county seat was moved to Goldsboro). From Waynesboro a road went through Camden, South Carolina, to Augusta, Georgia (there were also land routes to Wilmington, North Carolina, and Charleston).

If Charleston was the point of departure for Florida, the journey was likely to be by land. When the Crooms were initially active in Florida, the villages of St. Marks and nearby Magnolia had no established packet service. Barring unlimited time to wait, that route by sea was impractical. More likely, the traveler went from Charleston to Augusta and from there south and west through Georgia to Sparta, Milledgeville, Macon, and Columbus, where packet service was available down the Chattahoochee to its confluence with the Flint and Apalachicola Rivers just inside the Florida line. All that remained was a short trip east to Quincy and Tallahassee.

Yet there was an even more direct way, one taken by Comte Francis de Castelnau in 1837 and often duplicated with occasional route deviations by the Crooms. A traveler could leave Charleston at 6:00 A.M. on the 120-mile-long line that had begun in the late 1820s as the Charleston & Hamburg Railroad. Traveling over low, marshy country, the train ran along the winding Edisto River, passed through Midway, reached Aiken in midafternoon, and by 6 P.M. arrived at the small terminus village of Hamburg. From there an omnibus was available for the ride across the Savannah River to Augusta, an important inland town that shipped cotton and other produce to Savannah and beyond. This route was much faster and shorter than taking steamer service from Charleston to Savannah and then going up the Savannah River to Augusta.

Commercial connections between Augusta and north Florida were tied directly to mail delivery. Bi- or triweekly postal runs in two- or even four-horse carriages permitted the inclusion of a few passengers and meant profits for the owners of the stage lines. By the late 1830s the Florida Line—using a combination of steamers, mail coaches, and rail—connected New Orleans with Charleston via Augusta. Some travelers, including the Crooms, used privately owned conveyances, while others hired carriages or rode horses. Hardy, and perhaps Bryan as well, had a barouche (a four-wheel carriage with a collapsible hood; the driver sat on a box seat in front, and passengers faced each other across two double seats).

The forty-five miles along a narrow road from Augusta to Louisville took a day. Passengers moaned as their vehicle bumped tortuously along the roads—mostly old Indian trails widened to six or eight feet to permit the passage of wagons—studded with tree stumps sticking a foot out of the ground. Nor did the roads run in straight lines. Cutting down the ubiquitous pines was not difficult, but the builders made long and frequent detours around the hammocks that contained dense stands of tough hardwoods. As Florida loomed, fear was added to discomfort because the Second Seminole War was in progress, and isolated Indian attacks had been reported.

From the hamlet of Louisville the stage or carriage crossed the Ogeechee River, passed through Faisbridge (a community of people with the same surname), and stopped at the small town of Sandersville. From there the journey became more difficult, and reaching the village of Hawkinsville required fording the Oconee and Ocmulgee Rivers. Occasionally the trip was delayed because the driver lost his way.

It was impossible to time the arrival at a town so that it occurred at dusk. That meant stopping at houses along the way for food and sometimes for lodging. If no shelter was found, the travelers camped out. The simple fare in the lonely frontier homes was usually cornbread, sweet potatoes, pork, and cabbage. In Georgia and Florida the price ranged from fifty to seventy-five cents for a meal, but sometimes South Carolinians refused to accept payment and considered themselves insulted when it was offered.

From Hawkinsville the Flint River provided a good directional arrow, and travelers paralleled it south to Bainbridge, a settlement of about two hundred people in 1837. From there a road led to Marianna and west Florida through a country alive with animals and birds, especially squirrels and wild turkeys. If Tallahassee was the destination, a branch road extended from Bainbridge to Quincy. From there the weary sojourner traveled east on a twenty-six-mile ride that entailed crossing the Little River and the Ochlockonee River. The time required for the trip varied, but the four hundred miles between Charleston and Tallahassee always took several days.

The journey was never easy. Arriving in Florida by stage in 1831, Hardy remarked that the "*ladies* of the party became very much fatigued with the journey, & disgusted with the coarseness of the accommodations, & the exposure." A ball was announced for the next night in Tallahassee, and Croom expected that "in the gaieties in the capital they [would] forget or for-give the evils of the journey." Such was the route that brought Hardy and Bryan Croom and their kin to Florida and returned them most of the way to North Carolina. By late 1837, the Florida Line added branch routes to the itinerary described above. In the 1840s, old roads were improved, new ones built, and, better yet, Georgia constructed a number of railroads.[54]

Hardy wrote Bryan on June 28, 1833, complaining about the economic situation in New Bern, "Things are insufferably dull here and with nothing to do. I already desire to be on the road back to Florida, and were it not for the heat of the weather it would not be long before I would be so. I believe that things get constantly worse here; town property is worth almost nothing."[55] Hardy was also having trouble with his mother-in-law, and he informed Bryan that she had gone north until September. Working hard but also relaxing in marital ease at Rocky Comfort, Bryan must have sympathized with Hardy's complaint about Henrietta Smith: "I begin to find that all her promises to me are moonshine which is the worse because they were made from valuable consideration." Abandoning his usual restraint, Hardy added, "I leave here in October next never to return. Those who stay behind will not see me again unless they come to Florida. I have been trifled with long enough."[56]

A month later Hardy's mood had not improved, and he sent another letter to Bryan: "Since I wrote you last I took a trip to Lenoir, and went as far as Raleigh [accompanied by Isaac Croom, a kinsman and fellow Carolina graduate (1815)] to attend the 'Internal Improvement Convention' and see the ceremony of laying the corner stone of the Capitol. They make a sad business of public improvement in this State. The intelligent persons talk, but the mass of the people are a caput mortum, which I believe, nothing can move."[57]

Hardy kept his promise to come to Florida in 1833, undeterred by rumors of cholera in the port of Apalachicola and elsewhere. He mentioned others in New Bern (by then the Bellamys were convinced) and Kinston who were migrating as well. He wrote Bryan that he planned to bring young William Henry along and perhaps his daughter Henrietta Mary, who was "so anxious to go that [he did not know] how to refuse her."[58] Apparently, Bryan's letter informing him of an "attack of the caterpillars on [their] crops" was offset by the settling of the legal dispute in Florida. As Hardy put it, "I have not allowed it to weigh upon my spirits. . . . Indeed, I consider the *Hegira* of [James] Mills, and the demise of the other two [parties] as a fair set off to the caterpillars." The Crooms were involved in other civil court cases, but none of them were major.[59]

The visit to Florida restored Hardy's equanimity, because he returned to North Carolina. For one thing, he had benefited financially by hiring out forty of his slaves to the Tallahassee Railroad Company, engaged in constructing a line south to the gulf coast. The contract was for one year at $2,104 and would be renewed in 1834 for $1,990.[60]

Hardy's visits had become so regular and of such duration that he was among the forty men, including Bryan and Benjamin Hawks, who voted in May 1833 at Gadsden County's Cross-Roads precinct for a delegate to Congress. The three men would cast ballots there the next year for members of the Legislative Council.[61] By 1834 the Crooms, as well as many others, looked east toward burgeoning Leon County and became interested. Bryan and Hardy considered the area particularly appealing, and they found an excellent opportunity to purchase land there. A new phase of their Florida venture was about to begin.

2 *Planting and Planning*

Leon County was established December 29, 1824, and named for Juan Ponce de León, the first European to discover Florida. When the Spanish explorer landed somewhere between St. Augustine and the St. Johns River in 1513, he named the land Florida and claimed it for King Ferdinand V. In 1528, Pánfilo de Narváez and his expedition came ashore near Tampa Bay and moved north, exploring the Tallahassee region. An Indian word meaning "old fields" or "abandoned villages," Tallahassee was the site of an Apalachee village. About 1656 the Spanish established a Franciscan mission there and named it San Luis de Talimali. After San Luis was destroyed by James Moore, South Carolina's British governor, in 1704, the area was virtually abandoned. Following the Seven Years' War (the French and Indian War in America), Great Britain gained control of Florida. It remained in British hands from 1763 until 1783, when Spain reclaimed the peninsula as compensation for aiding the colonies in the American Revolution.

After the Adams-Onís Treaty of 1819, the United States established the Florida Territory in 1822 and installed a new governmental system. The British administrative policy (retained by the Spanish) of maintaining East Florida with its capital at St. Augustine and West Florida with its capital at Pensacola proved impractical. The old Apalachee village of Tallahassee, the mission site, and surrounding area had been sporadically repopulated by Creek and Seminole Indians, migrating south from Alabama and Georgia. Because of its halfway geographical location between St. Augustine and Pensacola and its attractive topography, the village was selected as the territory's permanent capital. Officially given its old name on December 11, 1824, the new town of Tallahassee was incorporated on December 9, 1825.

Surveyor Benjamin F. Tennille laid out the streets, squares, and lots, the last being offered at public sales. Located on rolling hills that were heavily forested, Tallahassee also became the seat of government for Leon County and, later, the state capital. Like Gadsden, Leon County had abundant rainfall and a long growing season. Predictions that Tallahassee would become the center of Florida's economic, political, and social life were soon fulfilled. The town and county grew from 996 people in 1825 to 11,422 in 1840, an elevenfold increase in fifteen years.[1]

Bryan's commitment to Florida was clear, and now Hardy was more enthusiastic, but Frances still had reservations. She was concerned about her health and did not wish to displease her mother. In February 1834, she cautioned Hardy, "Before you settle permanently, you give yourself sufficient time to judge." She reminded him, "You did not mention in what part of Florida you have settled, and recollect you were to write to Ma a description of your plans, for she would not feel advisable in doing anything of the kind without understanding the step she would take." Even so, "Ma desired me to mention that the winter has been very trying . . . [and] that she is determined on leaving North Carolina." Concerning her physical condition, Frances wrote, "I have scarcely left the house since you left, but expect to-morrow to accompany Ma to Adam's Creek [a stream that flows out of Carteret County into Craven County and enters the Neuse River], which will be some recreation for me and what I believe is very necessary for my health."[2] Fanny's father had owned a plantation on Adam's Creek that he left to his son, Nathaniel.

Because he was absent from New Bern often and for extended periods, Hardy provided for his wife's well-being. Besides depending on her mother and Aunt Camack, he employed Prudence Rice, a young white woman in her twenties, to be Frances's nurse. Prudence tended to Fanny's needs from 1833 to 1836, when she got married. Hardy also had a number of domestic slaves in New Bern, including Tabetha, the cook, who was in charge of the household, and a house servant named Crecy. William Morris, his agent in New Bern, also checked on Hardy's family during his frequent absences.[3]

The area that Hardy had not described to Frances or his mother-in-law (but would later, at great length) was Leon County. What attracted Hardy particularly was land in a valuable township known as the Lafayette Grant, parts of which became available for purchase and development. The marquis de Lafayette (1757–1834), the recipient of Hardy's translation of Voltaire's *La Henriade,* was a hero in the United States because of his aid to the patriot cause during the American Revolution. Later the Frenchman got caught up in his country's revolution and was arrested and imprisoned during the Reign of Terror. His life was spared, but his estates were confiscated.

The sympathetic American people approved when Congress gave the impoverished marquis back pay in 1794 and land in the Louisiana Purchase in 1803. Lafayette's fortunes did not improve permanently, and in 1824 during his triumphant tour of the United States, the time seemed appropriate to do something else for him. President James Monroe approved a congressional cash grant of $200,000 and a township (thirty-six square miles) of public land anywhere in the country. In Washington, Lafayette became friends with Richard Keith Call, a military and personal disciple of Andrew Jackson. Call had settled in Tallahassee, established plantations in Leon County (The Grove and Orchard Pond), and, at the time, was Florida's territorial representative in Congress. Call urged Lafayette to visit Florida. Although the Frenchman never did, he chose his land grant there and authorized Congressman John McKee of Alabama to select the township.

McKee reached Tallahassee on April 7, 1825, and examined the surrounding area before selecting Township 1 North, Range 1 East, in

Leon County for "Lafayette's Donation," as it was sometimes called. According to McKee, the grant, which had been surveyed by LeRoy May, was "in point of soil . . . superior to any other Township [he had] seen or heard of and its vicinity to [Tallahassee added] much to its value." He noted "the extraordinary number of Ponds that abound[ed] thro all the rich lands." "If people can enjoy health here it is certainly the most delightful region I have ever seen."[4] The area rose into red hills whose loamy soil produced bountiful crops. The terrain was covered by virgin pines and many hardwoods—blackgum, hickory, cherry, sweetgum, holly, maple, elm, walnut, cypress, sycamore, chestnut. Of the various oaks, none was so impressive as the omnipresent live oak. The long-lived tree with its massive symmetry and sculptured dignity became an enduring symbol of the Deep South. With its spreading limbs draped in Spanish moss, the live oak's daytime aura of quiet and tranquillity shifted at night to one of mystery and brooding.

Lafayette opposed the institution of slavery, and he attempted to establish a colony of free workers on part of his grant. At the same time, Leon County was attracting large numbers of settlers, drawn there by good land and their declining circumstances at home. A majority of the immigrants were yeoman farmers, but a large number were planters, from Maryland, Virginia, the Carolinas, and Georgia. Besides Croom, there were names such as Ward, Butler, Chaires, Randolph, Hayward, Eppes, Gamble, Bradford, Whitfield, Call, Hopkins, Williams, Cotten, Bannerman, McGinnis, and others—all people of substance who accumulated more wealth once they arrived.

Notable among the broadcloth planters was Prince Achille Murat, a dispossessed nephew of Napoleon, who immigrated to America and settled in Florida in the 1820s. He and his wife, Catherine Daingerfield Willis Gray, widowed great-grandniece of George Washington, owned Lipona and Econchatti plantations in Jefferson County. After Murat's death in 1847, his wife moved to Leon County. The descendants of these families often remained in the area and support one historian's generalization that "planters remained well-to-do across generations."[5]

The large landowners brought their families and slaves and established a plantation economy and culture similar to what they had known in the upper South. Leon became the center of Florida's cotton kingdom, and large plantations were established near Tallahassee, especially in the county's northern sections. The plantations ringed large and shallow natural lakes, including four major ones: Jackson (known as Okahee until its name was changed to honor Old Hickory), Iamonia, Miccosukee, and Lafayette (known previously as Prairie Lake).

In stark contrast to the planters and their expanding operations were three Frenchmen who were friends of the marquis and some sixty Norman peasants who arrived in 1831 and settled on a bluff overlooking Lake Lafayette. They attempted to establish vineyards and groves of olive and lime trees and planted mulberry trees for the nourishment of silkworms and an expected silk industry. The short-lived experiment saw the agricultural ventures fall victim to the weather and the settlers to sickness (they had no physician), as well as to the inhibiting differences of language, religion, and culture. The French settlers were anachronisms in rural Florida, and although a few remained in Leon County, others returned to France or migrated to New Orleans.[6]

Lafayette decided to sell his land—his first two agents were John Stuart Skinner, postmaster of Baltimore, and George Graham, United States commissioner of public lands—a tangled and drawn-out process that involved a number of lawsuits. The future Goodwood plantation lay in his township. On November 8, 1833, representatives of Lafayette agreed to sell the township to William B. Nuttall, H. W. Braden, and Dr. John A. Craig. The price was $46,520.[7] The men of the firm clearly were speculating in real estate, a widespread and already time-honored tradition on the American frontier. The trio's dreams of profits were only partially realized.

Nuttall was a Virginian who served as an overseer for his father, John Nuttall, owner of El Destino plantation, which lay east of Leon in Jefferson County. William B. Nuttall owned outright Chemonie, another Jefferson County plantation, and was a leading cotton planter, as well as a producer of sugar and a part-time lawyer. He was an officer in the Union Bank, an ill-fated institution chartered in Tallahassee in 1833, and intended to serve the interests of planters. Nuttall died in 1835.[8] Hector W. Braden was also a Virginian and an officer in the Union

Bank. Following the end of the Second Seminole War in 1842, Braden was among several Leon County planters who moved to Manatee County in south Florida to engage in the sugar industry. A native of Maryland, Dr. John A. Craig owned a plantation known as Andalusia (it bordered the northbound road from Tallahassee to Thomasville, Georgia, and extended to Lake Hall) and became a longtime resident of the county.[9]

By 1834, Hardy had made arrangements to buy land that lay in the Lafayette Grant and had begun farming there. On January 15, 1834, he purchased Section 27 (a section is 640 acres) from Nuttall, Braden, and Craig. The price was $4,785. Then, on January 18, Croom signed an agreement with Count Theodore Charles Laporte to purchase Section 26. A friend of Lafayette's, Laporte had made purchase agreements in France and settled on the grant. Failing in his efforts and bankrupt, the count sought relief from making land payments on Sections 26 and 23. Richard Keith Call also had paid $1,600 to the Frenchman toward the purchase of Section 26. Call acted as a sort of unofficial agent for Lafayette and at one point had made an unsuccessful bid to purchase half of the grant. Hardy agreed to pay Andrew Jackson's friend the amount of his investment and the remainder of the total price of $4,750 to the Frenchman. Count Laporte was returning to France and promised to work out the details with Lafayette. He would attempt to arrange the same terms—$4,750—for Section 23 or, failing that, secure Section 34 for Croom.

Hardy conceded the difficulty of cultivating places twenty-five miles apart and located in two counties, although he expected to let his half brother William Croom have his part of the Rocky Comfort operation. As it turned out, William, who had recently moved from Lenoir County to Gadsden County, had different plans, preferring the life of a merchant to that of a planter. Hardy favored Leon over Gadsden County and began concentrating his work there. In March 1834, he wrote Frances from "Lake Lafayette": "You will perhaps be both pleased and surprised to learn that I now make my trips between these places on horse back!" He added, "I think when you see our plantation here you will allow that it is the most splendid and desirable one that you have seen." [10] His title to Section 27 seemed valid, but that to Section 26 was unclear. Ultimately, Section 26 on the western shore of Lake Lafayette became a part of Goodwood. The plantation had been established.

Hardy tried to lift his wife's spirits, but being separated from him caused Frances to fall into depression. "My habits always require a constant change of excitement, and when I am left as I have been this winter, I am not surprised when I sink into nonentity," she wrote him. "We propose leaving in a few days for Plymouth [her mother's home north of New Bern], solely on my own account for refreshment. When we return, we think of going to Adam's Creek, which I hope will relieve that torpidity into which I have fallen, but when you return I hope all clouds will be dispelled." [11] Hardy soon returned to New Bern and was reunited with Frances.

Croom had white overseers in Gadsden and Leon Counties. The overseers at Goodwood, as well as Hardy (and later Bryan), were dependent on the judgment and skills of Fortune, a slave driver of rare talent. The driver's important task was to work under the overseer and direct the assignments of the slave force. What Fortune was to the plantation, the previously mentioned Edward, whom Hardy never referred to as a slave, was to his owner personally. Primarily a coachman, Edward was trusted to carry out individual assignments such as transporting horses and supplies between North Carolina and Florida. Hardy had no compunction about traveling with him by stage. Edward also drove Hardy, Bryan, and other family members back and forth between Florida and North Carolina—once he prevented a serious accident by stopping a runaway team.

With such aid, Hardy reported to Fanny concerning Lake Lafayette, "My crop has turned out finely. I want a few more negroes to enlarge it. I have bought lately three women and two children." Croom was undoubtedly referring to a purchase made from Jason Gregory, a Gadsden County man. Hardy paid Gregory $1,100 for Lydia (twenty-eight), Milly, Lydia's eleven-year-old daughter, Mariah (seven), Washington (five), and Charlotte (three)—yet it is difficult to see how Milly and Mariah were classified as "women." The document recording the sale listed Hardy as a resident of Gadsden County. [12]

When the marquis died on May 20, 1834, Hardy speculated to Bryan that Lafayette's death meant revoking the power of attorney of John Stuart Skinner and Robert W. Williams, two men with whom he had dealt. Hardy's newly acquired property was not clear of obligations owed by Call, and there were still some Frenchmen living on the land as well. In July, Hardy informed Bryan, regarding Section 26, "It is . . . my intention to keep possession of the place and to pay the debt for which Genl Call is bound as soon as I can do so. . . . You may say to Call that if my possession for the next year is not disturbed I will pay the value of the rent, say $500, towards the discharge of his liabilities and I will pay the whole as soon as I can safely do so and as soon as Williams will promise me a title on fair terms." [13]

Immediately, Hardy wrote Seth P. Lewis, a young resident of Tallahassee, hiring him to take charge of his lake property. Further, Hardy informed his brother, "[I have directed Lewis] to discharge those Frenchmen as soon as he can get clear of them and suggested that you [Bryan] would pay them 20 or 30 dollars for me, if you can raise it, or buy them some provisions if they need them." [14]

A relative remembered that Hardy even bought some town lots in Apalachicola (a thriving gulf port eighty miles away in Franklin County). The details are unverifiable because, once again, a courthouse fire destroyed the records. Yet the statement was confirmed by court documents and by Croom family members, who said that Hardy contracted for the lots but never completed the purchase.[15] Evidence of Hardy's activity in Leon County was revealed in a letter he wrote in August 1834, to Seth Lewis. The arrangement between the two men had been successful, for the absentee landlord-owner told Lewis, "I am glad to hear that the cotton is promising. Tell Fortune to do the best he can and I will reward him when I come out." The driver's importance was clear: "Tell Fortune to be careful of *fire* about the gin house and [to] begin to pick out cotton early. Some bagging will be sent by me to Magnolia by the first vessel from N. York in August, but if any should be wanted before this is received you [Lewis] can buy a little in Tallahassee." [16]

Although constantly busy with family affairs and managing his lands, Hardy continued his botanical observations and experiments and extended his writing to a broader audience. In 1834 he responded to a request from Edmund Ruffin, editor and owner of the *Farmers' Register,* to submit an essay on the soil and crops of middle Florida. The Virginian Ruffin (who later became a passionate secessionist and hater of all things northern) had acquired a wide reputation as one of the nation's leading advocates of scientific agriculture. Croom's reply summarized middle Florida's advantages and disadvantages. Beginning in 1828, three winters of severe freezes demonstrated the futility of producing oranges and other citruses. Croom grew sugarcane himself and described its proper planting and harvesting, but he declared its production expensive and risky. Hardy speculated in his best scholarly manner, "I believe that in no part of the United States is the sugar cane so good a crop as is cotton; *Quaeque ipse miserriama vidi, et quorum pars fai* [Which very sad things I myself have seen, and of which I was a part]." Observing that cotton was the planters' "principal pursuit," Croom discussed green-seed, Mexican, and Sea Island types. After estimating production per acre and describing saw gins and roller gins, Croom shifted to other crops. He saw little future for olive groves and approved of alternating oats and rye with corn and cotton. Ruffin's readers got an intelligent and useful report.[17]

Hardy became a frequent contributor of short pieces to the *Farmers' Register.* One was a gentle correction to an article by Thomas Spalding, a prominent planter who lived on Sapelo Island, Georgia, and was a well-known exponent of scientific agriculture. Croom noted that Sea Island cotton was not confined to the coasts of South Carolina and Georgia but had been grown in middle Florida since 1822. Other Croom items commented on new varieties of cotton, and one even proclaimed the virtues of okra. That vegetable, he wrote, had a beautiful flower, was a principal ingredient in creole gumbo, "when boiled, affords a delicious article of diet," and could be used as a substitute for coffee.[18]

In a land and era of limited medical knowledge and few doctors, health was a major problem for the entire population, and Hardy was always concerned about his slaves' well-being. "I want," Hardy wrote in 1834 to his overseer Lewis, "Dr. [John B.] Taylor to look at Ben and Will, and give them such medicines as they may require. Tell them if they do not take medicine and get well before I come out it may be worse for them."[19] Dr. John M. W. Davidson of Gadsden County also attended Croom's slaves, and later Hardy engaged the services of Dr. James Henry Randolph. For the years 1834–37, Randolph's bill for "attendance on negroes on plantation" was $69.30. Croom's personal physician in Leon County was Dr. John T. J. Wilson, who, like many southern physicians, was also a planter. No plantation, including Goodwood, failed to stock various medicines—castor oil, pills, ointments, and opium. Whiskey had its medicinal as well as social uses, and Hardy purchased it for nineteen cents a quart and seventy-five cents a gallon.[20]

One scholar has concluded that planters' sons who migrated from the eastern seaboard frequently abandoned the paternalistic attitudes of their parents toward slaves. Once on the frontier, they assumed a more racist view of slavery, refusing to recognize their slaves' humanity and family ties and forcing them to work under harsh conditions. The assumption that they owed their bondsmen little or nothing did not apply to Hardy or Bryan and was evident in their correspondence. Hardy's careful attention to his slaves was practical as well as humane, and it was noticed. Robert W. Williams, a neighboring planter and businessman, commented later, "In 1834, H. B. Croom's negroes passed by my house frequently. They were a likely gang."[21]

Plagued in 1834 by a lawsuit in Lenoir County involving his brother Richard and others, Hardy was delayed even though he "was exceedingly anxious to reach Florida" because he feared his business would suffer from his "long absence."[22] He did not get there until December, which explained why he remained into the spring of 1835. Hardy left for North Carolina on April 21, accompanied by Bryan, Dr. Edward C. Bellamy, and their families. The party made its way north through Georgia by an alternate route that included Macon, probably because Bryan was suffering from a bad cold, inflammation of the lungs, and high fever. If a doctor was needed, one would be available there. Because the group was traveling in Bryan's carriage and Hardy was anxious to get home, he took the commercial stage from Macon, arriving at New Bern sometime in May. The remainder of the summer was spent in New York and Saratoga with his family. Bryan and Eveline, probably accompanied by her mother, also spent part of the summer in New York City and visited other towns in the state—he found Congress Hall in Albany a place of "poor food—pretty good rooms."[23]

While in New York during the summer of 1835, Hardy wrote to Thomas Baltzell, his lawyer and friend in Tallahassee. The two men had been partners in buying eight town lots in Tallahassee and selling them for a profitable $2,100. Stern, incorruptible, dark featured—Baltzell had coarse black hair and black eyes—he had settled in Jackson County before moving to Tallahassee. Born in Kentucky, the able and stubborn Baltzell had risen from a penniless youth and was on his way to becoming a man of power and prestige: lawyer, jurist, and, finally, chief justice of the Florida Supreme Court. On occasion Baltzell entertained Croom in his home. Hardy had heard of an altercation between his friend and a judge and was distressed to learn of the lawyer's decision to retire from the bar of middle Florida and move to Apalachicola. "In addition to the loss of your society and that of your amiable lady at Tallahassee," Croom noted, "I feel some uneasiness concerning my law business." He asked Baltzell if he planned to vacate his house in the winter of 1836. If so, Croom explained, "I would like either to purchase or rent it, as I wish to carry my family to Florida next fall, and I shall be loathe to do it unless I can get a comfortable house." He added that he had placed his daughter and son in good boarding schools in New York. Baltzell reconsidered his decision to move, and Croom did not rent his house.[24]

The education of their children was a matter of major concern to Fanny and Hardy—besides the usual children's games, he taught them the names of his various shells and dried flowers. Henrietta Mary was taking individual instruction in French and music in 1833, and the next year the Crooms tried to find a private school in New Bern.[25] In 1835 Hardy took his two oldest children to New York, and after a few weeks he wrote Frances, "I have placed Henrietta Mary with Madame Chegaray, an excellent school. A few doors from her is a very good school for Boys, kept by two French gentlemen [the brothers Peugnet] and after a great effort of fortitude, I parted with little Will and placed him with them." Hardy was so pleased with the arrangement that he bought Fanny "a handsome riding dress, the prettiest [he] could find."[26]

Madame Eloise Chegaray's one-hundred-pupil school on the corner of Houston and Mulberry Streets enrolled boarding and day scholars. She was beloved by the students and maintained a good staff. Bright and hardworking, Henrietta Mary wrote her father, "I hope you will never regret having placed me here, as I am improving every day, and I do not think that all your trouble and expense will be without its benefits to me, and I hope that when I leave my education will be completed."[27]

Henrietta Mary's studies included lessons in writing, horseback riding, piano and guitar, and dance. Madame Chegaray praised the scholarship of her popular young charge, a voracious reader whose letters to her parents were spiced with wit and often contained poems she had written. In December 1835, Henrietta Mary had an ingrown toenail that became inflamed and required an operation. The experience demonstrated how primitive surgery was, even in New York City. She had to cancel most of her activities and four months later was still confined to bed. The young girl described her recuperation to her father: "While the caustiac [*sic*] was burning or rather eating my foot the pain was almost unendurable. I was in perfect agony and (shame to my fortitude) cried all that day and never did I feel so lonely — never thought I suffered so much with leeches and lancing before."[28] She sent out on Saturdays for presents to give to William Henry when he visited her every Sunday. "My brother . . . sits and talks to me about Florida and home," she wrote. "He is as considerate and attentive as a grown person and more than anyone here."[29] Although they missed the children, Hardy and Frances were confident they were being properly educated.

Back in New Bern in October 1835, Hardy wrote his botanist friend Dr. John Torrey in New York that he was starting on his "annual peregrinations to the South." He had sent Torrey botanical specimens from Florida and North Carolina, and there was much discussion of catalogs and the latest publications in their field. Croom wished he had the company of someone like Torrey, who would be his "'guide,' philosopher and friend at least in Botany."[30] The much-traveled Hardy Croom began making serious plans for the future in 1835. He reached Tallahassee in late October or early November and secured lodgings. No sooner had he arrived than he heard from Fanny reporting another serious attack. She was slow in recovering from it. Two months later she engaged in some self-analysis: "If I had been always so situated as to have been actively and profitably employed, my health would have been much better."[31]

Florida's climate agreed with Hardy, and for once he reported to Frances that his health was good. He added, "I have made a good crop better even than the last year. The negroes too have been more healthy, none of them have died during my absence and there has been but little sickness of a severe character among them—But among the whites there has been some fatal sickness." In a reflective mood, he wrote, "It is astonishing how high negroes are in this country. It is a good country for planting and merchandise but I cannot say that it is a desirable country to live in. Indeed I have pretty well concluded not to settle here. But to make all the money I can and lay out none of it in building."[32]

Hardy hoped that Fanny's mother and sister were well. He suggested that they should send their slaves to Florida and hire them out, but since the women were comfortable in North Carolina, they would be well served to keep their homes there. Such ruminations set Croom wondering about his family's future, and he wrote Frances, "Augusta is a fine place and there or at Charleston I would like to live if we could all agree on it. It would be a great pity to sacrifice all the good property they & we have in North Carolina. But if we should choose to go to some place of more society we might let the property lie for better times."[33]

About this time, Frances broached the idea of living in New York. Her sister Henrietta was about to marry John Carroll, a New York merchant and cotton broker in the firm of Carroll, Hawkins & Logan, located at 115 Front Street, corner of Wall. Hardy, she suggested, could ship his cotton directly to Carroll. The two men could go into business together, and her other sister, Elizabeth Armistead, could send her slaves to Florida for hire. Fanny speculated that having a good house in Florida would be pleasant but expensive. It would be better to have a slave plantation there without a main house. Before her namesake daughter got married, Henrietta Smith gave the couple the 1,100-acre Otter Creek place in Craven County, several lots in New Bern, and thirty-three slaves. The caveat was that should something happen to Henrietta, the estate would revert to her mother. The Carrolls spent their honeymoon in New Orleans. Unconvinced that Leon and Gadsden

Counties were safe from Indian attacks, they declined Hardy's invitation to visit Florida. Later, they settled into a three-story brick home on Horton Street in New York that cost $13,000, and the Croom brothers began using Carroll, Hawkins & Logan as one of their cotton agents. All the same, Hardy did not consider moving to New York. Bryan was even less inclined.[34]

While Hardy was in Tallahassee in the fall and winter of 1835–36, he solidified his title to Goodwood and, together with Bryan, expanded the plantation. Both the weather and the cotton crop were good, and the Lafayette Grant seemed more appealing than ever. Hardy described his land as a "desirable location for a family residence, being but three miles distant from the City of Tallahassee, the capital of the Territory, in the centre of good society, pleasantly situated on the border of Lake Lafayette, and combining many advantages for a permanent family seat."[35]

If Hardy continued to vacillate about the most desirable place to live, he and Bryan moved with resolve to buy land. On January 1, 1836, Bryan bought Sections 28 and 29 in the Lafayette Grant from the firm of Nuttall, Braden, and Craig. The price was $19,170, with $9,585 due on January 1, 1842, at 8 percent interest. The sale did not include a tract of eighty acres in Section 29 that was separately owned by a man named Fred Towle.[36] Bryan, who continued to live at Rocky Comfort, had the deed recorded to show that he was transferring half of the land to Hardy. The transfer indicated that the brothers shared the purchase price. In any case, Bryan and Hardy now jointly owned 1,200 acres in the Lafayette Grant. Added to that were the 640 acres of Section 27 that Hardy had purchased in 1834 (his title to Section 26 was still uncertain), making 1,840. In these early years Hardy was more involved in the future Goodwood than Bryan. He also continued proselytizing his North Carolina neighbors and others: they should migrate to Florida.[37]

During the fall and winter of 1835–36, Hardy continued to divide his time between Tallahassee and Rocky Comfort. His letters demonstrate that he cultivated crops in both Leon and Gadsden Counties. Croom wrote Frances in January that he had made a brief trip to Augusta (he gathered botanical specimens and probably looked the city over as a possible future residence) and planned to go to Mobile. He still thought Mrs. Armistead and others should send their slaves to Florida and hire them out. Noting that George Whitfield, another Lenoir County cousin and University of North Carolina graduate (1823), was in Tallahassee with a large number of his slaves, Hardy added that the planter liked the surrounding country. In fact, Whitfield soon established a plantation in Leon County. Hardy offered hard evidence that he had become a major planter: "The cotton is not yet picked out. I have sold 100 bales at 14 cts per lb. which is all I have ginned out. I shall have about 100 bales more." The natural increase of his slaves proved inadequate to answer the planting needs of Goodwood. In January 1836, Hardy paid James M. Harris of Tallahassee $1,500 for Silby (eighteen), Hester (eighteen), and Hester's two-month-old child. With Goodwood's agricultural potential beginning to be realized, it was little wonder that Croom concluded, "The winter here has been finer than usual."[38]

In the spring of 1836 Hardy bought more slaves. In April he purchased a twenty-year-old woman named Iamonia and her month-old son from William Wright of Decatur County, Georgia. The sale price was $800. That same month Croom paid $925 for Sam, who was warranted by his owner, Richard Hayward, a Tallahasseean and master of Bellevue plantation, "to be sound in health & limb." In October, Elias, a black of unspecified age, was obtained for $600 from William Hollister of New Bern.[39]

Frances tried not to be a burden to Hardy, and while urging deliberation on major decisions, she supported his Florida ventures. She rarely mentioned her problems, but Henrietta Mary, no less than Hardy, was concerned about her mother. While in school in New York, she corresponded regularly with her parents. Henrietta Mary voiced her worry in a letter to Hardy in March 1836: "I have just received a letter from mother. She was in a cheerful tone, but I am sure, by something in the style, that she was not well. . . . How sorry I am that she cannot enjoy better health, and I hope that her health will improve when she changes her place of residence."[40]

Hardy was pleased with the land his brother had bought. Acquiring it gave him a stronger tie to Florida, and Bryan had long since made the territory his home. Even if Hardy and his family did not settle in Leon

County permanently, sound business sense dictated a not-too-distant residence. Hardy would have to continue spending a considerable part of each year in Florida, and 1835–36 was no exception. As he explained to Frances, "I have made a very good crop and the greatest difficulty is to get it ginned and carried to market. I am however proceeding with it but cannot finish until late in March, by which time my preparations for the ensuing crop will be made—and I shall be able to leave for Newbern." [41]

It was completely rational that "on reflection," as he wrote Frances, he concluded that New York was too cold and too far from their business: "[I] think that we will settle in Charleston where the winters will not be too cold for me, nor the distance from Florida too great—The society in Charleston is equal to any in the United States. Bryan is willing to go there also and perhaps Dr. Bellamy and other of our friends may follow." Still, Hardy's commitment to Florida meant that he had to have some kind of dwelling there. But he did not want the Leon County home to be on a grand scale: "I shall therefore only build a temporary House in Florida to give us shelter when we visit the plantation during winter months." [42]

With his decisions made, Hardy moved in February 1836 to make the Lafayette Grant purchases permanent. Croom made final his possession of Section 27, obtained two years earlier from Nuttall, Braden, and Craig. By 1836, the land sold for $9,570, with $4,785 due January 1, 1842, at 8 percent interest. [43] In March, a month later, Hardy finally obtained clear possession of Section 26, the tract he had negotiated for in 1834 with Count Laporte. Along with the section, he inherited a rustic cabin located on the western edge of Lake Lafayette. Built by Laporte, the cabin was no doubt improved and made more comfortable by Croom. Still, Hardy had not obtained Section 23 or Section 34 from the Frenchman. Following Nuttall's death, the partnership of Braden and Craig continued to operate. Cash was rarely involved, as most sales in the Lafayette Grant were by promissory notes, and the partners probably had been unable to meet the purchase terms of the grant. In any event, the Lafayette heirs had appointed Robert W. Williams, a Tallahassee attorney and leading planter, as their agent, and he sold Section

26 to Hardy for $7,540.50, considerably more than the North Carolinian had bargained for earlier.[44] Section 26 also included a substantial part of the western one-third of Lake Lafayette. Hardy now had made an individual purchase of 1,280 acres and owned another 1,200 acres with Bryan. Goodwood, which so long as Hardy owned it was known simply as the Lake Lafayette plantation, had 2,480 acres.

Once he and Bryan had completed their real estate ventures in 1836, Hardy managed with some difficulty to get eighteen bales of cotton handled. In April he returned to New Bern by way of Augusta and that July went to New York. Bryan remained at Rocky Comfort. Florida was never far from Hardy's thoughts, and he wrote his brother, "I am desirous of renting for the next year [1836–37] Car[r]uthers' place near Tallahassee (both land & house) but particularly the house which I should like to have the use of when I reach Florida. I wish you would take measures to secure it for me—if it can be had."[45] John Carruthers was an old squatter on the Lafayette Grant who had been allowed to buy a quarter section. His residence, located near the Crooms' land, was described by George Whitfield: "A tolerably good house was on the place, calculated for the accommodation of a planter's family, according to the then circumstances of Florida."[46] Somehow negotiations broke down, and the arrangement was never made.

After Hardy left Florida, Bryan and Eveline experienced a tragedy. The Crooms and Harriet, their house servant, were among the fifteen passengers on board the paddle-wheel steamboat *Ohioan*, which left Apalachicola for Columbus, Georgia, on April 22, 1836. Bound upstream with a load of freight, the *Ohioan* made good time. The next morning around eleven o'clock the steamboat was about six or eight miles below Ocheesee Landing when a fire broke out at midships. Flames, driven by a heavy wind, engulfed the vessel within fifteen minutes, but that was time enough for the women passengers to be placed in the vessel's yawl and rowed to safety. The crew and male passengers jumped overboard and swam ashore. Tragically, Harriet was so frightened that she refused to get into the yawl. She panicked, leaped from the deck, and, despite all efforts to save her, was drowned. That the *Ohioan* was uninsured and only a small portion of the cargo had any coverage meant the estimated loss of $25,000 was practically total. The cause of the fire was never discovered.

The passengers' personal effects and clothes, except those they were wearing, were lost. Like the others, Bryan and Eveline were fortunate to escape with their lives. Eveline, who already had a fear of steamboats, was adamantly opposed to any further travel, causing Bryan to ask Hardy to buy a cloak and black suit for him in New York. He also wanted him to purchase a gold waist buckle for Eveline and, while he was at it, one for his niece Henrietta Mary as well.[47] Hardy responded to the news with sympathy, declaring, "[The] loss of your valuable servant Harriet is much to be regretted." He added, "The spectacle and the danger must have greatly affected Sister Eveline, and I fear she will not soon recover from her dread and dislike of Steam Boats."[48]

The accident, compounded by an unnamed but extreme illness, caused the usually stoical Bryan to become despondent. He wrote Hardy on July 8, 1836, "I feel convinced now that I cannot be satisfied with a summer life in Florida. The determination to alter my residence is the only thing that cheers me now . . . ; you nor your family can never be satisfied here." Bryan favored Augusta but was not inflexible. Should the brothers decide to build a home, Bryan wrote Hardy, "You must get a drawing of those buildings at New Haven [Connecticut] that you admired so much or some other buildings that please your fancy." As a person of common sense and given to sober reflection, Bryan advised Hardy, "Think seriously of this for I must go some where and should like for us not to be separated. We have been a good deal harassed by Indian alarms but have never regarded them and shall not."[49]

Later in July 1836, Bryan reported more bad news to his brother. One of Hardy's overseers at Goodwood, a man named Parker, had died. Parker's death was sudden, and on short notice Bryan hired another overseer, one less skilled, but the crop had already been made. The corn and cotton looked good, and Hardy's slaves, who had been sickly, were much better, having discovered "a new spring that [gave] them very good water." While it pleased Bryan to ask Hardy to have two fashionable dresses made for Eveline in New York and to buy her a hat or a bonnet, his melancholy was plain. The series of unfortunate events, plus the recent July heat that made the August sun seem even more relent-less, caused Bryan's irritation and despair to increase. With uncharacter-istic truculence, he wrote Hardy, "I am pleased to hear of the good health of your children; would it not be prudent for them to spend the next winter South—Augusta or Charleston? I have had a sad time of it this summer; I am perfectly worn down with ennui and disgust, (per-haps you would say worn out); 'a plague on sighing and grief; it puffs a man up like a bladder.' You did not seem to sympathize with me enough—the object nearest my heart is to live hence in some decent place and have your family near us and others of your friends who would like."[50]

Continuing his mordant letter, Bryan pointed out, "You have never spent a summer here and can form no idea of the poverty of the country. There is not one barrel of good Flour in the whole of Middle Florida; I have sent to Quincy, Mount Vernon, Tallahassee and St. Marks, and have returned without any; five hundred barrels sour Flour in Tallahassee—not a Bacon ham, no fruit, not a bottle of lime juice; we are living now upon black bread and stinking shoulders and wire-grass beef, and if you have the wealth of Croesus, why you could look at it. Besides a man rusts here as well as rots." Bryan concluded on a philosophical note, "I am full of spleen, you see, but it is because I am dwelling on the pros-pect and reality; place your family here and you have the picture before you—we are all apples."[51]

Bryan's dissatisfaction was temporary, and although it was based pri-marily on personal problems, it was also caused by the general situation in Florida. The Second Seminole War, begun in the mid-1830s by Na-tive Americans who rightfully felt betrayed and resisted giving up their Florida lands, raged on. Isolated settlers in middle Florida, including Leon and Gadsden Counties, feared attacks. The critical financial situ-ation was another problem. Florida's territorial Legislative Council had chartered more banks than the population could sustain. Some of them, such as the Union Bank in Tallahassee, used land and slaves to secure stock and would collapse in the late thirties and early forties. The notes of Florida banks were hurt by a lack of specie, not to mention wide-spread mismanagement, and President Jackson's "specie circular" of 1836 helped plunge the nation into a severe financial panic. Florida suffered especially because Jackson's action forced public lands to be paid for in metal coin. As speculators and planters demanded that the state banks redeem their paper money in hard cash, many of the specie-shy institutions were forced to close. Jackson's successful war against the Second Bank of the United States removed that national agency as a point of control over shaky banking practices. There was little legislation to restrain state banks from making loans without sufficient collateral.

Exacerbating the situation was Jackson's "distribution bill" of 1836. Intended as a means of reducing the national surplus, the measure succeeded all too well. It made federal money available for internal improvements projects and encouraged states to embark on grandiose schemes. Ever the Whig, Hardy interpreted events: "*Jackson is no doubt the root of the evil, tampering, as he has constantly been, for several years, with the currency.*" The Florida Territory was further injured by the extremes of weather—hurricanes and droughts—as insects and pests ravaged crops. Florida's economy was a long time recovering from the Panic of 1837 that followed.[52]

Even so, the Crooms persevered and continued their plans to create the kind of private world that would please them. With Hardy coming to Florida in October 1836, the plan was for him and his family to meet Bryan and Eveline at Augusta.[53] Hardy's family returned from New York to New Bern, and he made arrangements to ship his furniture to Charleston, buying horses and a peddler's wagon to carry "our servants" out. The plans were changed when Hardy received word that William's school situation was intolerable. As a concerned parent, he pondered whether to go to New York and investigate the situation. It was mid-October, and since Bryan and Eveline were already waiting in Augusta, Hardy told them to go on to Charleston. First, they were to obtain letters of introduction, and he mentioned several names. He requested of Bryan and Eveline, "Ascertain (if you like the place) the practicability of *renting* good dwelling houses, the prices &c. If you like Charleston I give you *carte blanche* to act for me in engaging a house &c."[54]

Charleston was an ideal place for a man such as Hardy Croom. That was made clear in a letter he wrote from New Bern to his friend Dr. John Torrey in New York: "We arrived here in safety nearly two weeks ago and I have since been much engaged in making preparations for my departure South. I am about to break up my establishment here and transfer my family farther South. I do not propose to settle there in Florida, but probably in Charleston where I can more easily visit my plantation in winter, and where I shall enjoy a more cultivated society and greater literary means than I can elsewhere find at the South." The risk was small: "If I should find the climate oppressive during summer I can easily transfer myself and family to the North for two or three months in each year or two. Here too I can have my children with me and the means of educating them at home, which you will allow is no small consideration."[55] Hardy closed his letter with a romantic poem that he had written in praise of Florida. The imagery was good, but the effort indicated that his talents lay with botany, and there is no evidence that Torrey urged its publication.

During much of October 1836—while Fanny and Hardy were in the midst of their complex preparations to move—the crisis, whose details were not revealed, between Will and the brothers Peugnet continued. In general the boy became unhappy with his tutors, and they were no less displeased with his performance as a scholar. In the classic role of an aggrieved parent, Hardy wrote to John B. Carroll (the husband of Frances's sister Henrietta) requesting him to withdraw William Henry from school and put him under the care of Henrietta Smith, who was in New York. If his mother-in-law did not send the boy home, Hardy wanted Carroll "to select a good school for him where he [would] be kindly treated." That same day he wrote the Peugnets a letter of authorization for Carroll to take Will out of school.[56]

In his letter to Carroll, Hardy brought up other business, including the news that he would be receiving the bill for a portrait of Hardy that had been painted recently. Without doubt, Carroll did not mind being inconvenienced, since Croom added that he was shipping his cotton from Magnolia to the New York businessman. Hardy also requested Carroll to send him a keg of buckwheat flour, a keg of soda crackers, a canister or caddy of gunpowder tea, and a keg of lard. Writing from Goodwood plantation, where almost anything could be grown, Hardy also ordered a barrel of Irish potatoes.[57]

A few days later Hardy had second thoughts about the school situation. He wrote Carroll that should William Henry be removed, he wanted the businessman to handle the logistics. If Will remained, Hardy wanted him to learn Latin, French, reading, and writing. The difficulty was finally settled, and the boy continued with the Peugnets. Hardy also mentioned to Carroll his desire to convince Bryan that Charleston was preferable to Augusta. As for other business, "I am about to buy a negro man and therefore may increase the draft upon your [commercial] house to seven or eight hundred dollars." [58]

Additionally, he asked Carroll to ship all the things his family had left in New York, including his newly ordered coach, directly to Charleston. Hardy would shortly ship his household goods in New Bern to the South Carolina port. "I think also of sending my woman Tempe and her children in the same vessel, and if I do so I will write to you to [arrange for] insurance on both." [59] As it turned out, nothing was settled that fall. Bryan and Eveline went to Augusta but, hearing of cholera in Charleston, returned to Rocky Comfort. Hardy was made current when he reached Augusta and found a letter from Bryan waiting for him. Hardy was in the company of their first cousin George Whitfield, who was also going to Florida, and the party, which included two "servants" (Edward was doubtless the driver), was traveling in Hardy's four-horse carriage. [60]

When Hardy finally arrived in Florida, he was probably surprised to receive a letter from Elizabeth Armistead in New York. He had continued to urge Henrietta Smith and Elizabeth to settle in Florida, or at least send their slaves there. Hardy had offered to handle all the details. His sister-in-law, who was concerned about the war with the Seminoles, responded to his efforts: "Ma received a kind satisfactory letter from you . . . ; she will answer it soon. I have delayed replying to my part of the letter, from the wish of first getting home to see how things were there and to receive the letter you promised to write to me on your arrival in Florida, respecting the Indians." Elizabeth thought delaying a decision until summer would be advisable, though she felt "very much flattered" by his "gratifying offer": "If I knew how, should be glad to avail myself of it. How much I wish me and my belongings [were] in Florida with you at this moment you cannot know, but as soon as I reach home you shall hear from me concerning the negroes; I shall certainly send them if I can make arrangements for their going. We got a letter from sister Fanny last week—they were all well and in good spirits."[61]

It is unknown if Hardy considered the letter no more than sugar-coated prevarication, but the communication may have persuaded him to make a final decision. Hardy reached Florida in late November and paused briefly at Rocky Comfort. He was in time to witness the wedding of his half brother William to Julia Stephens. William had recently moved from North Carolina to Gadsden County, and his bride's family had migrated there from New Bern sometime in 1833.[62] After the wedding, Hardy went to Goodwood, where he was caught up immediately in picking, hauling out, and ginning his cotton. Occupied as he was, a few days after hearing from Elizabeth he finally convinced Bryan that Charleston should be their future home.

"We intend to go there some time in January [1837]," Hardy wrote Fanny, "to procure dwellings, after which I will proceed on to New Bern to move you . . . thither. I am looking forward to this period with a great deal of pleasure and with some impatience. I shall however have the intermediate time so much occupied as not to feel it so sensibly as I otherwise would." Hardy's letter spoke the truth of his involvement: "I put the men to cutting new ground in order to enlarge the crop next year. Negroes are very high now and land has risen considerable. So that I made my purchase in good time."[63]

In January the Croom brothers left Florida, taking the usual route. "Bryan and myself arrived here last evening," Hardy wrote his wife from Augusta, "and will proceed this evening to Charleston where we will arrive tomorrow evening. We have fully made up our minds to settle there and I am looking forward to a great deal of happiness and enjoyment when we get settled . . . especially when we get all our dear children once more around us, which will soon be the case after we get to Charleston." Hardy explained that the plan was to rent houses for a year or two and afterward to build. Once they found places, Bryan would return to Florida and bring his family to Charleston. Hardy would go to New Bern and do the same.[64] The Crooms looked forward to enjoying the results of their careful plans.

3 *A Passage to Charleston*

The brothers reached Charleston in late January 1837. "I have now the satisfaction of informing you," Hardy wrote Frances, "that we have been quite successful, both of us having got very good houses in pleasant and healthy situations"; the mild winter weather made believable some less than accurate stories by local boosters. According to Hardy, "We have ascertained from the experience of families residing here for a long time that Charleston is remarkably healthy throughout the year, there being no occasion to leave it in summer unless we choose to do so." He expected to be in New Bern by mid-February and make the arrangements to move.[1] Bryan returned to Rocky Comfort, but Hardy remained in Charleston several more days.

Hardy reflected on some details of the city's activities in a letter to Dr. Torrey: the house he rented was formerly occupied by a "Mr. Poinsett." Hardy described the property as "very pleasant . . . in the healthiest part of the city, encompassed by two or three acres of beautiful shrubbery." The home, Poinsett's Grove, was owned by Joel R. Poinsett, a prominent South Carolina politician who was interested in horticulture, botany, and the arts. On returning from service as ambassador to Mexico, Poinsett introduced the flowering shrub that was named for him and by 1837 had moved to Spartanburg, South Carolina. The Charleston place rented by the Crooms was on Rutledge Street in a suburban area outside the city limits known as the "Neck." Living there were planters and some merchants who built grand town houses on large lots, allowing for "healthy breezes." The Reverend John Bachman, who lived nearby, had Hardy to dinner and introduced him to John James Audubon, his house guest and lifelong friend. Of German descent, the Lutheran minister wrote in the fields of science and theology, was a dedicated naturalist, and shared Audubon's passion for ornithology. During the evening's conversation, Croom, to his great satisfaction, was in his intellectual element.[2]

Hardy experienced the best of the city's social life: within three days he went to a public ball ("well attended by the fashionables"), accepted an invitation from a General Hayne for dinner, and dined at the home of a Miss Lightwood.[3] Yet for all his approval of Charleston's social and cultural advantages, Hardy did not lose his objectivity. While he praised the city library, philosophical society, and museum of ornithology and geology, he remarked to Torrey, "I see many proofs in Charleston that they are not free from the vice so general in all southern climates, that of *indolence* [and] want of energy and perseverance."[4]

Still in February, Hardy wrote Bryan about a house in Charleston that his brother might prefer and told him of his plans to have the Hamlins (originally from Maine, the family prospered as merchants and shippers in the St. Marks—Magnolia—Newport towns south of Tallahassee) forward his Florida "things" to Charleston. He dispatched a similar letter to Carroll in New York asking him to have Hedenberg of Newark, who was making him a carriage, ship it to J. & C. Lawton of Charleston.[5] In March, Croom wrote Elizabeth Armistead in New York regarding her decision to remain there. He assured her that she and his family could exchange frequent visits. Hardy renewed his suggestion that Elizabeth and her mother sell their holdings in New Bern and send their slaves "to Florida, where [mother and daughter could] either carry on a plantation or hire them out to great advantage." He added, "I think you need have no fear of the climate for I have not lost one [slave] of *bilious* disease in the six years they have been there."[6]

Fanny and the children—by now Justina Rosa had developed her personality and was the frequent recipient of dolls and books from her parents—wanted to take advantage of Elizabeth's invitation and spend the summer with her in New York. Hardy accepted the offer. His wife's current health was still an issue, but as Hardy wrote Elizabeth, Fanny's latest attack had passed over without any bad symptoms, and the trip would help her. Croom would visit his Florida plantation, attend to business in Charleston, and join them all in New York in the summer. In the fall the move to Charleston would be made.[7] An added pleasure to visiting New York was the prospect of seeing Dr. Torrey. He wrote the botanist outlining his plans, and added, "If I can escape the bad effects of those sudden changes in your Summer atmosphere which nearly killed me last year, I hope to be well enough to join you in some of your botanical excursions."[8] About the time of Hardy's letters to Elizabeth Armistead and Dr. Torrey, Henrietta Carroll (sister of Elizabeth and Frances) died. Her death on February 11, 1837, occurred shortly before Hardy's departure for Florida. Although she was buried in New Bern, he did not attend the funeral. Henrietta Carroll had not executed a will, and the disposition of her estate would soon increase family tensions.

By this time Hardy's main interests in Florida were at Goodwood plantation. Before reaching the territory, he wrote his wife from Augusta. True to his botanical bent, Hardy had spent his time there "very pleasantly" with a friend, Dr. Wray, a botanist who had "many handsome and rare flowers in his garden." Croom added, "We have good news from the war. The Indians are surrendering and the war will soon be at an end."[9] The amateur botanist was overly optimistic—fighting would not wind down until 1842. Hardy's letter to Frances was written in April and headed "Lake Lafayette near Tallahassee."

Hardy reached Rocky Comfort on March 28, and on April 3 Bryan and his family departed for their new home in Charleston. They were accompanied by Ann Hawks and her son, Benjamin. Eveline's sixty-year-old mother was under the strong impression that the move would be a temporary one and that both her son-in-law and Hardy would settle permanently in Florida.[10]

Bryan and Eveline had been busy with their preparations. The drawn-out Gadsden County case among the Crooms, Mills, and others over the rental of slaves had gone against them in a court of appeals. Yet it was really a victory because the adverse judgment amounted to approximately $200, much less than they had anticipated. Bryan had sold some of Hardy's cotton and made final arrangements. "I wish to pay off every thing I owe before I leave here and it will take all the money that I can command," the cautious brother wrote Hardy. Bryan asked Hardy to borrow $1,000 for six months for them, which would relieve him "from a good deal of anxiety." Beyond that, the less cosmopolitan Bryan wanted his brother to come to Charleston as soon as possible: "I should hate to be there without money and without friends." [11]

Perhaps Hardy was a guest of the Baltzells and rode out to Goodwood in the mornings to inspect his five hundred acres in cotton and two hundred more in corn. More likely he stayed in the Laporte cabin on Lake Lafayette. On the day his brother left, Hardy started building the house he had spoken of earlier. He selected Lot 29 as the site for the dwelling. He wrote his wife, "We finished raising the frame to our house today (32 feet square). So that by next winter I hope to have a comfortable house." (The structures on Goodwood plantation are discussed in detail in chapter 6.) Hardy left for Charleston a few days later and notified Frances to write him there. In the meantime his wife had boxed her recently purchased rosewood piano, stool, and cover for shipping. Frances and her family members left before daylight to take the stage to Plymouth, North Carolina. After a brief stop at her mother's home, the remainder of the journey to New York was made by ship. [12]

While in Florida, Croom met Dr. Alvan W. Chapman (1809–99). A native of Massachusetts who had come south to Georgia before migrating to Florida, Chapman was living in Quincy in the fall of 1836, when he met Hardy. Although he was a medical doctor, Chapman placed botany above all else, and in 1860 he published his classic *Flora of the Southern United States*. The young Chapman, who was just developing his scientific interests, was impressed by Hardy's knowledge and by what he represented as a man. According to Chapman, "Of [Croom's] personal traits it is needless . . . to say more than that he belonged to that class of wealthy and intelligent southern gentlemen, whose homes, renowned for their unostentatious hospitality, were the abode of all that is charming in the refinements of domestic life." [13]

Writing to Dr. Torrey, the admiring Chapman declared, "[Florida] is most certainly a remarkable field for a Naturalist. Mr. Croom, I am happy to state is now in the Territory. I was favored with a call the other day." Croom reported to Torrey that he and Chapman left Quincy and visited "the Apalachicola river, the habitat of the Torreya and the Croomia." In typical Victorian prose he informed his New York friend, who had never been to Florida, "You would be delighted were you [here] at this time, where Flora displays the beauties of her realm and the groves are vocal with the songs of birds." [14]

As April drew to a close, Hardy prepared to leave Florida. Henry J. Gaskins, young and married but with no children, had become his main overseer at Goodwood, and his salary for 1837 was $600. Croom was much concerned about the construction of his house and sent Gaskins a letter from Tallahassee to "Lake Lafayette," only a few miles distant. "Frank [a slave of Hardy's who was a carpenter] must not make the windows 7 feet 8 inches high," he wrote Gaskins. "That will be too much. He must make them only 6 feet 8 inches high and three feet wide—so as to take in 18 panes of glass (10 inches by 12)." Hardy wanted his overseer to inquire of the Hamlins if anything had arrived for him—probably supplies or building materials. [15]

In late April, Hardy reached Charleston, where he stayed with Bryan and Eveline and her mother and brother. [16] The severe economic Panic of 1837 had set in, and Croom was worried on a personal level about conditions in Tallahassee. He wrote to Gaskins and included "the bill of lading for the molasses": "You had best carry a little money with you to pay the freight or ask Messrs Hamlin to pay it for you. . . . 2 barrels were intended for my brother Bryan but he does not want it and you may take it all for our use—and give *some* of it out in part of the rations to the negroes." A few days later Hardy wrote Gaskins, "I hope you will make a good corn crop and raise some hogs. Times are dreadful here. It is impossible to get any money. I am going in a day or two to look at the *horse mill* [a power source combining belting and machinery that allowed horses to operate it] I spoke about and if I like it I will buy one as soon as I can."[17]

In early June 1837, Hardy left Charleston and went to New York. Bryan, who was getting settled in Charleston, received a communication from Hardy that he "found things bad enough, but not worse than [he] expected." Their New York factor had not disposed of Bryan's cotton. For his part, Bryan was to try to sell Hardy's horses and carriage. "I believe we shall be obliged to consult economy in all our arrangements for the next year," Hardy concluded. No sooner would encouraging economic news arrive from England than worse revelations would follow.[18]

The best thing was to put as good a face on circumstances as possible. Hardy wrote his half sister Betsy's husband, Dr. Samuel C. Bellamy, at Marianna, "The disappointment has been great (i.e., the fall of cotton) but it is a misfortune that none of us could foresee and our only remedy is to economise, and another crop, I hope, will relieve us from our embarrassment. I expect to remain here [New York] until October and to be in Florida in November. The embarrassment of the commercial class here is beyond all precedent."[19]

The economic hard times were caused by the Democrats, according to Hardy, who was losing some of his philosophical complacency. "Such a reverse as our country has suffered, in a time of profound peace," he wrote Sam Bellamy, "is probably what never before happened to any nation under similar circumstances; and is, in a great measure, clearly traceable to the madness and wickedness of our national administration. Still I fear that the people are too ignorant and prejudiced to see it."[20]

Hardy did not neglect his Florida interests. On June 26, he wrote Gaskins that he expected to come to Goodwood by early fall. "I wish you to carry on the House as well as you can. You can hire Mr. Shine [Richard A. Shine was a civic leader and Tallahassee's leading builder] to make the chimneys when you are ready for him, say in August or September. I will have the window sashes made and sent out. I hope the negroes will behave themselves and that I shall find all things right when I reach Florida. . . . My health is at this time tolerably good."[21]

Throughout the summer of 1837 Hardy was busy. On June 11, his eighteen-year-old half-sister Betsy died in Jackson County. The cause of the young woman's death is unknown, but it may have been a contagious disease, because shortly afterward, Alexander, her eighteen-month-old baby and only child, also died. Hardy wrote Dr. Samuel Bellamy a letter of sympathy. If Bellamy were to visit Lenoir County, Hardy wanted him to build a brick wall around the family cemetery.[22] In a follow-up letter Bellamy was informed that Hardy's children were in good health and that their educational arrangements had improved. Hardy said that his own health problems had been relieved by a visit to Saratoga, and he expressed approval of Bellamy's plan to take the bodies of his wife and child to Lenoir County for burial in the Croom family cemetery. Hardy expected to return to New Bern from New York in early October and go from there to Charleston. Bellamy was unable to carry out his intentions, and his wife and child were buried in Jackson County.[23]

In June 1837, Hardy wrote Gaskins that the window sashes, ready glazed, eighteen lights to a window, 10 x 12, had been shipped. By late July and early August there was a respite from economic gloom, and as Hardy informed Gaskins, "Our bales and cotton of [the] last crop that I sent here were much liked and I hope you will not fall behind the last year's mark." He added, "Myself and family are all well. I am very desirous of seeing you all and also the plantation. I will go out as early in the fall as I can."[24] News from Bryan that he liked Charleston pleased Hardy and increased his desire to settle there.[25]

In New York, Hardy met Comte Francis de Castelnau, who was about to set out on his own trip to Florida. The two men shared many common interests, and the Frenchman was much taken with the intelligence and beauty of young Henrietta Mary. On reaching Florida, the foreign naturalist and talented artist visited Tallahassee and went out on the Crooms' property at Lake Lafayette. There he made a sketch of Hardy's cabin that he later included in his book *Vues et souvenirs de l'Amerique du Nord* (1842).[26] Ann Hawks, privy through Bryan to Hardy's plans, said that he "was building a very good dwelling house, not merely temporary, and as good as any about the country, and calculated for permanent residence."[27] The Croom family's need for a home that was "not merely temporary" was obvious. Writing from Lake Lafayette in March of an unnamed year and referring to the Laporte cabin on Lake Lafayette, Hardy informed Bryan, "If you and Eveline or Benjamin should come down I could entertain you. . . . We do pretty well except in the [way] of beds & bedsteads." [28]

Ellen Call Long, who was born in 1825 and grew up with Tallahassee, remembered as a young girl (she would have been eleven or twelve) going out to Lake Lafayette in the spring. The daughter of Richard Keith Call wrote, "We were received by a genial host, and a botanist, in Mr. Hardy Croom. He gave us strawberries and cream on his flower-covered porch, and promised even better things (as if they were possible) the next season, for then he would bring his family to Florida." [29] Ellen Call's visit would have been in the spring of 1836.

George Whitfield saw the Laporte cabin (and Hardy's improvements) on Lake Lafayette and described it as being practically a new structure. He remembered that in its early stages the cabin was a double log-pen dwelling begun by Hardy in 1836. According to Whitfield, the house "contained, after it was finished, two large rooms below, and two small ones in the attic. It was a one-story house. There were no piazzas to it. . . . There were no chimneys to it, or plastering." Even so, Whitfield said, "It was neatly put up; he had a good carpenter. I do not think it then had window sashes. It was unfinished; nothing but the frame was up." [30]

Hardy furnished the Lake Lafayette cabin with inexpensive bedsteads, cots, and chairs. There were two tables, one pine and the other cherry. Trunks substituted for nonexistent closets, and the china, pitchers, and utensils matched the other spartan furnishings in their lack of elegance. Even so, Hardy placed his books in the rustic house. The cabin and its setting, nestled close to Lake Lafayette, were a microcosm of frontier Florida. As described by Hardy, it was bordered by live oak and magnolia trees. "It is frequented," he wrote a friend in 1835, "by an immense number of water birds, consisting of ducks, the Brent goose, several species of cranes &c., and is inhabited by trout, perch, the soft shell turtle, and finally the hideous *alligator*. We have here also a species of chameleon, and it is said a species of *scorpion*. [31]

Whitfield also remembered that there was a dwelling "building at the time of his [Hardy's] death on the place. It was afterwards completed by Bryan Croom, who lived in it for some time."[32] Whitfield's statement was corroborated by Gaskins. Deposing in 1840, the overseer said that the house was intended for Hardy's family and would have been better than the original structure.[33] The second house was obviously not built on the same site as the log-pen cottage. As discussed below, the authors believe that it, like the Goodwood mansion, shared the common location of Section 29.

That Frances wished to make a good impression in Charleston was seen in July when she visited Elizabeth Muller, her New York dressmaker. Choosing black silk, black muslin, and brocade, she was fitted for four dresses—each having a lined cape. Such shopping was expensive but not extravagant: the bill for the dresses, including cloth, findings (supplies), and labor, amounted to $59.43. The ensembles, although in the latest fashion, were also for mourning and were chosen to acknowledge the recent deaths of her sister and of Hardy's half sister and her son.[34]

In September 1837, Hardy, keeping Bryan informed, noted that he had been to Newport, Rhode Island, and was making final plans to come to Charleston and proceed from there to Florida. He also revealed some facts that helped explain future events, and he envisioned some ominous possibilities as to his fate. Comment has been made that relations between Hardy and his mother-in-law, while not hostile, were not always harmonious. He explained to Bryan that when Fanny's sister married John Carroll, a contract had been made. It provided that should she die without leaving a child and without making a will, her property would go to her family as though she had never been married. All those circumstances obtained when Henrietta died. "I mention it to you now," Hardy wrote, "that in case I should not live to see it settled, you may know the claims of my wife and children. Mrs. Smith and Mrs. A[rmistead] having been instrumental in making the contract, seem now disposed to avoid it for the purpose of preventing my wife and myself from a share, the purpose being to divide the property between them and Mr. Carroll. I see no reason why I should assent to such a course." Hardy closed by noting his intention to leave a last will and testament under seal with James Donaldson "before [he] set out for

Charleston to provide for any accident on the passage."[35] Donaldson was a trusted New York merchant with whom the Crooms had dealt for years. If Hardy drew up such a will, it was never discovered. Later, claims were advanced that the will existed, but others denied that the document was ever drafted. The question was of crucial importance and would be sharply debated in subsequent trial testimony and depositions.

Hardy delayed departure until the health of Fanny's Aunt Camack improved enough for her to travel with the family. Everything was now in place, and he wrote Bryan, "You may therefore with certainty expect us by that boat which shall arrive at Charleston on the 8th October." Always concerned about Florida, he noted, "I am very glad to hear that you have the prospect of a good crop. The report from mine was very favorable up to the time of the *last gale*. . . . Still the injury may not be so considerable as first impressions led [Gaskins?] to suppose. On the 6th Sept. we had out about 20 Bales ten of which were *bagged*. My own health is unusually good at present."[36] Croom's expectations were no less than those of many Leon County residents. The *Tallahassee Floridian* reported in October, "[The] last few days our city has assumed quite a lively appearance. . . . The fall business has already commenced. New cotton is coming in briskly, and notwithstanding the difficulties in the commercial community, we understand that a good business will be done this season."[37]

Beyond his natural compassion, Hardy understood that the well-being of his slaves enhanced his capital returns. In 1837 he had shipped to Goodwood slave supplies that included five dozen wool hats, kerseys (coarse, lightweight woolen cloth, ribbed and with a cotton warp), red linseys (or linsey-woolsey — coarse cloth made of linen and wool or cotton and wool), and twilled blankets. Osnaburgs (heavy, coarse cloth originally linen and later cotton) were regularly ordered.[38] No less than his concern for economic profit in Florida, Croom longed to pursue his scientific interests there. Aside from the blessings of peace and the stopping of bloodshed, Hardy wanted the Second Seminole War to end so that he could include in his studies the flora of south Florida. "Another idea," according to a friend, "was the formation of a botanical garden at his plantation near Tallahassee for the cultivation of rare plants and shrubs." That intention was remembered and remarked on later by several acquaintances. His friend added that "Hardy's principal amusement was conversation and botany."[39] The planter-scientist had little regard for games such as cards, although he played backgammon with Frances. "He was fond of literary pursuits," according to Ann Hawks. "His favorite amusement was the study of botany." As Hardy put it himself, "My only interest is botany."[40]

Departure schedules were slightly altered, but Hardy posted a letter to Bryan on October 5: "I write to say that I have taken my passage in the steam boat *Home* which is to go on Saturday the 7th and you may expect us in Charleston on Tuesday 10th. If convenient send your carriage to meet us at the Boat when it arrives."[41] The Croom family anticipated a pleasant voyage, and the head of the household looked forward to spending his fortieth birthday (October 8) steaming down the Atlantic coast.

The Croom party had every reason to think that selecting the *Home* was a wise choice. The paddle-wheel steamer was owned by the Southern Steam Packet Company, whose principal officer was James P. Allaire of New York City. He headed the Allaire Iron Works and had established the first steam packet lines between New York and Charleston. Allaire was a businessman, not a boat builder. In 1835 he contracted with the firm of Brown & Bell of New York to construct a strong and substantial ship. The price was $100,000. The keel was laid, and the work proceeded safely and slowly—there were no defects in the materials or the workmanship. The *Home* was launched April 16, 1836, but hard economic times delayed completion until the following April. By the spring of 1837 the *Home* was fitted up for the southern trade.[42]

While the 220-foot-long ship was under construction and lying in dock in the North River, crowds of people visited it. According to the *New York Herald*, "The Home steam ship was remarkable for her beauty. She sat like a swan upon the waters. . . . [Visitors] admired her symmetry—praised her proportions—her fitting up—her noble appearance. . . . She was too beautiful, too finely, too delicately proportioned. In smooth weather—in calm weather—in the pleasant summer, she did well, and acquired a reputation."[43] Before beginning regular commercial runs, the handsome side-wheeler made a short public relations voyage, demonstrating its qualities to a large number of guests. The result, as reported by a New York newspaper, was that the metropolitan journals "for a day or two, were as profuse in admiration of the model and construction, as they were to the crackers and champagne of the captain. A company of three hundred giddy persons, under the influence of novelty, and in a calm summer sea, pronounced her the *ne plus ultra* of naval architecture."[44]

The *Home* became the fourth steamer in Allaire's fleet and made three round-trip voyages between New York and Charleston in the summer and fall of 1837. On its second trip in September it completed the run from New York to Charleston in only sixty-four hours. An admiring *New York Star* noted that it was "a quicker passage than was ever before performed by any steam or other ship. She . . . thereby established an admirable record as a packet ship."[45]

A few days before departing, Hardy saw his old friend and fellow North Carolinian the learned Francis Hawks, and on the day the vessel left New York, Croom said goodbye to John Torrey. Elizabeth Armistead and her daughter pronounced their farewells, and Alexander McConochie, James Donaldson's bookkeeper, acting in the absence of his employer, came down to the dock to see the Croom party off.[46] The Crooms and Mrs. Camack boarded the *Home* along with 80 or 90 other passengers (including James B. Allaire, the owner's nephew, who went along as a technical observer, and 30 or more women). The diverse group included people from Georgia, New Hampshire, Connecticut, Alabama, New York, Massachusetts, and New Jersey, although the largest number were returning home to Charleston. No doubt the Crooms admired the interior appointments that equaled those of a fine hotel. The passenger list was uncertain because 6 or 8 people came on board just before sailing. The 43-man crew brought the total to 120–30. Captain Charles White (his first name was also listed as Carlton) commanded the vessel. He was an experienced seaman, having risen from the lowest ranks to the position of commander. He had been a captain for more than ten years, had an excellent reputation, and was a part owner of the *Home*, having invested all of his money in the venture (the ship was insured for $40,000). Beyond that, White's reputation for sobriety was unsullied. This last characteristic would soon be called into sharp question.[47]

Almost immediately the Croom family, especially William Henry, who was in and out of everything, impressed several of the passengers with their courtesy and bearing. Henry Vanderzee, a twenty-eight-year-old clerk in a Charleston dry goods store, conversed with Will and liked him "for his smartness and affectionate and engaging manner." Mathilda Schroeder, thirty-five, a fancy dry goods store owner from Charleston, warmed to the youth because he reminded her of her own son.[48]

The *Home* departed from its East River dock at the foot of Market Street at shortly past four in the afternoon and soon encountered difficulties. According to the testimony of several passengers, the captain dismissed the pilot before reaching the Narrows. Then about 5:20 the steamer ran onto the bank off Sandy Hook lighthouse and grounded. Captain White was obliged to take on another pilot, and it was four or five hours before high tide finally freed the *Home*. After consulting with Allaire, Captain White did not return to port and have the vessel examined for damages in dry dock. His failure to do so would bring him harsh criticism for dereliction of duty (one newspaper had "no words sufficiently strong to express the gross culpability of his conduct").[49] Captain White and his staff, believing that the *Home* was sound, resumed the voyage.

On October 11, the schooner *Mary* docked at New Bern, and its captain reported that a steam packet bound from New York to Charleston had gone ashore between Cape Hatteras and Ocracoke Island. There was speculation that the vessel might be the *Home*. Then, more as an informative note than as a sound of concern, the *Charleston Mercury* of October 13 reported that the *Home* had not arrived. More disturbing, there was confirmation that besides being three days late, the steamer had not put in upcoast at Beaufort or Smithville, North Carolina.[50] Bryan and Eveline must have read the notice with mounting apprehension. There was, in fact, cause for real alarm. Once in the open sea, the *Home* had experienced normal wind and weather until Sunday night (October 8), when it was hit, according to Captain White, by "a heavy gale of wind" from the northeast. It was a time of uncertain and unscientific weather information, and without warning the *Home* had encountered a tropical hurricane known as Racer's Storm. The hurricane had traveled from Jamaica to the Yucatan and Texas coasts only to double back across northwest Florida, sweep through Georgia and South Carolina, and enter the Atlantic Ocean off the North Carolina coast.

The high winds continued, and on Monday afternoon the boat began leaking. At that time the *Home* was just north of Cape Hatteras, North Carolina, where uncertain currents and shifting sandbars had made the area grimly famous as a graveyard for ships. The vessel's pumps were put into operation and at first functioned adequately, but under the storm's force they soon failed. As the ship took on more water, both crew and passengers—men, women, and children (Hardy Croom among them, although he tired and had to stop)—began bailing desperately with buckets, kettles, pails, pans, and any other kind of containers that were available. The passengers also helped throw the vessel's supply of coal overboard. Various travelers and crew members would remember that, momentarily, calm prevailed. Yet panic could not be suppressed when about eight o'clock that night the water rose to the ship's furnaces, putting out the boiler fires and causing the engines to fail. The ship's movements became increasingly difficult to control.

At some point Captain John Slater, a passenger from Portsmouth, New Hampshire, who had already confronted White about his seamanship, assumed partial command of the attempts to save the steamer. Another passenger, Captain Alfred Hill, who was on his way to Charleston to take command of a ship, responded to pleas from the passengers and aided in working the pump and organizing bailing efforts. Like Slater, Hill was highly critical later of White's lack of leadership, noting his absence at critical stages.

Meanwhile the hurricane continued, its winds churning waves that tossed the *Home* wildly about. Captain White resorted to the use of emergency sails, but it became obvious that they were of little use (one was bent and another blown away by the storm's fury). By then water was flooding the cabin floors, and White, perhaps with Slater's advice, determined that the only chance was to run the ship head-on to shore. By then the steamer was south of Cape Hatteras, six or seven miles from the Ocracoke Island lighthouse at the inlet to Pamlico Sound. With its bow at an angle, the ship floundered toward shore, and the passengers were ordered to assemble on deck. Many of the women had gone forward to be nearer the beach. The moon was at first quarter, and at times its light broke through the scudding clouds, although visibility remained poor. So much water had been taken on that the steamer was stopped in the outer breakers some one hundred yards or more from land. The water depth was about twelve feet.

Everything seemed to happen at once. There was a constant roar, as Andrew H. Lovegreen of Charleston, forty-two and a dry goods merchant, stood on the upper deck tolling the ship's bell. Lovegreen would survive, although his bell-ringing efforts, whatever their purpose, went unheard amid the din. At the moment of striking, waves made a breach over the boat, sweeping many of the women into the sea. The *Home* then swung around heading slightly northward and bringing the larboard (left) wheelhouse next to the shore. The strong current was moving diagonally toward the beach. The ship had sunk until the deck was nearly level with the water. One of the three lifeboats was stove in, and no sooner was a second small boat launched with two or three persons than it capsized. Then a long boat was filled with twenty-five passengers and lowered to the water. It had scarcely progressed fifteen feet before being upset and all its occupants washed away. The smokestacks began tottering, and the port stack crashed, killing a woman carrying her baby. The *Home*, designed for speed rather than strength (the twenty-two-foot beam was inadequate for its length), was helpless before the battering of gale winds and powerful waves. The hull broke into three parts. Within twenty-five minutes or less the ship was smashed to pieces.[51]

Young Allaire was among the victims, but about forty of the passengers and crew were more fortunate. Some managed to swim to safety. Mathilda Schroeder, who had been charmed by William Henry, was lashed to one of the ship's timbers by another passenger. In this manner, and unfashionably attired in a nightgown and wearing a handkerchief around her head, she floated safely to shore. Another Charlestonian, Mrs. Lacoste (or La Coste), a large woman who was in her seventies, survived by using a settee as a buoy. They may have been the only women who did not perish, and of the several small children on board only one, a twelve-year-old boy, avoided drowning. Captain White and seven men were washed to safety on the companionway of the forecastle after it snapped off. One man saved his life by clinging to a spar, while Hiram Anderson of New York, who could not swim, owed his survival to an Indian rubber life preserver that friends had persuaded him to buy before leaving. Life preservers were just coming into use, and Anderson was the only passenger who had one. In the calamity's post-mortems the importance of such devices was widely discussed. Considering the relatively short distance to land, had life preservers been provided, many more passengers would have been saved. As a result of the wreck there were widespread demands to require life preservers on all steamboats.[52]

The Crooms, according to several witnesses, spent much of the day near the dining cabin. Distinctive in a white hat that had a high crown, wearing a black dress coat, and holding a handkerchief to protect his mouth and face, Hardy aided intermittently with the pump and bailing. About the time the *Home* grounded, Hardy was seen with Frances (wearing a black and white straw bonnet and dressed in dark clothes) and a similarly dressed Mary Camack on either arm. Justina Rosa stood in front of them. Clad in a rounded, dark blue jacket but without a cap or hat, William Henry followed behind. Henrietta Mary, reported by one passenger as wearing a light dress and by another as wearing a dark dress, was not with them. Once the waves swept people off the deck, no witnesses recalled seeing Frances or Mrs. Camack again. Thirty-five-year-old Benjamin B. Hussey, a Charleston bookseller who lived through the ordeal (his wife perished), remembered noticing Hardy and William Henry standing in the gangway. The young boy was crying and pleading with his father to save him. Following recurrent waves and winds, Hardy was not sighted again.

Two passengers, John Bishop, twenty-four and a gardener from West Ferry, New York, and the already mentioned Henry Vanderzee remembered clinging to a piece of the ship with William Henry. As they neared the shore, the boy lost his grip and was washed back out to sea and his death. Earlier, Conrad Quinn, a fifteen-year-old barber-hairdresser from Jersey City, New Jersey, remembered talking with Henrietta Mary on the wheelhouse before it was swept away. He did not observe her afterward. Based on the recollections of passengers who saw the family, no one was able to pinpoint the circumstances or time when Frances, Mary Camack, and Justina Rosa died. Less vague but far from precise were the conditions of Hardy's final moments. More was known of the two oldest children, and it seemed that Henrietta Mary died before William Henry. In all the confusion and terror people were concerned with self-preservation, and crises were occurring so fast that recalling the fate of others was difficult. Yet determining the last Croom to die would be crucial to future events and the ownership of Goodwood plantation.[53]

Survivors later described the wreck of the *Home* in anguished terms, and newspapers recorded the tragedy in the melodramatic but utterly sincere style of the day. The *Charleston Mercury* declared, "What a horrible death! To die in the midst of wreck and dismay—the howl of waters mixed with the shriek of [a] hundred victims all strangling in the same flood—to give this cherished body up to the loathsome creatures of the serf [*sic*] and shore—to be buried where humanity can never drop a tear or plant a flower—Thus feeble and delusive are the threads which hold us, and thus suddenly do the little jarrings of nature snap asunder connections."[54] Southern lamentations were matched by those in northern newspapers, such as the *New York Star*'s reaction:

> The fearful raging of the hurricane—the foam of the sea and the white caps of the billows breaking on the rocky shore—the light bark dashing her ribs on the pebbled beach, and rent asunder by repeated shocks— the screams of despairing souls shut out from hope—the uplifted eye to heaven—the silent prayer—the clinging of mother to daughter and father to child—the roar of the tempest—the pale gathering of the full moon shedding its rays on the appalling sight—the hoarse voice of the mariners "piercing the night's dull ear," and the last shriek of the dying as the mountain billows swept them into the deep—closed this dreadful scene, terrible to think upon, much more to behold. The will of God be done.[55]

Some of the victims were carried out to sea, and their bodies were never recovered. The beach was strewn for six or seven miles with the debris of the *Home* (trunks, some closed, others open with their contents scattered, were much in evidence) and people both drowned and alive. Most of the survivors spent the remainder of the night on the beach, although at least half a dozen made their way to the lighthouse, several miles away. Daylight revealed a scene of horror, and under the direction of William Howard, who lived on Ocracoke, a number of the dead were expeditiously buried.[56] Frances Croom was among the seventeen or so persons buried by Howard in his cemetery; others were interred at Ocracoke as well. William Henry's body was found three weeks later on the south side of Ocracoke Inlet, and he was buried there. Later both the son and mother were taken to New Bern for burial, as was the recovered body of Justina Rosa. Hardy, Henrietta Mary, and Mrs. Camack were never found.[57]

In New Bern the *Spectator* held out hope that the city's prominent residents had survived, but as more details were received, the paper bordered its columns in black ink. Reporting the deaths of the Crooms, the *Spectator* remarked, "Endeared to the community by the warmest ties of friendship, by the exercises of those courtesies of life which flow from a kind disposition and a cultivated mind, it is not surprising that the sad fate of this amiable gentleman and his family has cast a gloom over a town in which he so long resided."[58] In its subsequent issues the *Spectator* ran detailed accounts gleaned from other journals, and in December it printed a long poem entitled "The Wreck of the 'Home,'" by "B."[59]

Down the coast at Wilmington the *Advertiser* commented, "Never has it devolved upon us to record so heart-rending a catastrophe; so serious a dispensation has never afflicted the Southern people." In Alabama, where one of the survivors was from Montgomery, a paper regretted the "frightful calamity." The *New York Herald* singled out the Croom family as a special object of sorrow and misfortune. Hardy, "a gentleman of the highest respectability in North Carolina, and in Florida . . . , was in the prime of life and in the midst of happiness." The *Herald* added that Henrietta Mary, "an accomplished young creature, was hardly out of her teens, and was returning to the south." Tribute was paid to the entire family, including the bereaved Henrietta Smith, who in a matter of months had lost two daughters, a sister, her son-in-law, and three grandchildren.[60]

The survivors left as soon as they could. Some were provided with accommodations in North Carolina towns and cities before finding transportation back to New York or on to Charleston. Captain Ivy, whose steam packet *Boston* carried a number of survivors to Charleston, refused to accept any fares, and those who reached the city by train also traveled free of charge.[61]

Repercussions were predictable and inevitable. The wreck attracted so much attention that within less than a month James W. Hale, a New York dealer in books and newspapers, published a brief, error-filled book entitled *Authentic Account of the Loss of Steam Packet Home, from New York Bound to Charleston. Compiled from Various Sources: Together with Many Facts, Incidents, and Anecdotes Never Published Before.* The *Charleston Patriot* lent its columns to the cries for a searching inquiry. "We demand an instant investigation," the *New York Herald* editorialized. "The disembodied spirits of one hundred victims to cupidity and avarice demand it."[62] In Tallahassee, the *Floridian,* which noted Hardy Croom as a resident of Leon County, carried descriptions of the wreck taken from other newspapers. According to the Florida paper, "A fearful responsibility, moral as well as legal, rests on those who controlled her movements; and a full investigation into the facts of the case will, we trust, be made." Because the *Home* was a new packet, the *New Orleans Picayune* believed, "Something wrong may be fairly imputed to her builders."[63]

In Charleston on October 19, eleven survivors met at Shelton's Hotel. There they issued a statement praising the conduct of the *Home*'s engineers, mate, and crew but declaring, "We believe the boat was unseaworthy, and that the captain became incompetent from intoxication." Additional remarks thanked the various benefactors who had provided them with aid and comfort.[64] Going beyond the Shelton Hotel statement, some Charlestonians demanded further action. According to "Humanity," the *Home* was not seaworthy. Other steamboats put in to safety or rode out the storm (among them the *Charleston*, the *Mincken*, and the *Philadelphia*), which was less violent than other hurricanes. A modern study has rated the hurricane at the "intensity minimal" level.[65] At the least a public meeting was called for, and in response to such proposals, a gathering was held at City Hall at noon on October 21.

Henry L. Pinckney, mayor of Charleston, presided over the well-attended meeting that unanimously adopted resolutions introduced by various individuals. The preamble to one set of resolutions noted that the "reckless disregard of human life" by the profit-driven owners and officers of steam vessels required a statement of protest. Accompanying resolutions extended sympathy to the victims of the *Home* and called for the appointment of a twenty-one-man committee to investigate the disaster and make recommendations. Its findings were to be reported to the city council and published. In compliance, Mayor Pinckney appointed Joshua W. Toomer to head the committee. A separate resolution called on passengers to refrain from the popular practice of publishing cards praising a particular ship or captain. Still another resolution asked for state or federal laws requiring all arriving ships to be inspected for their seaworthiness.[66]

Bryan and Eveline remained in Charleston until late October. According to Ann Hawks, Bryan had grown to dislike the city, finding it hot and unhealthy.[67] Adding to Bryan and Eveline's horror and sadness and shock was the memory of their recent narrow escape from the steamboat *Ohioan*. It seems likely that they would have attended the public meeting.

Toomer's committee met and heard testimony from five survivors of the wreck and others who had been on an earlier voyage of the *Home* from New York to Charleston. The consensus of the survivors was a serious questioning of White's competency. They charged that he had been drinking and declared that the *Home*'s structure—weakness of the frame, insufficient bracing for the keel's length, and concentrated heft of the machinery—rendered it unseaworthy. In its report the committee agreed with the witnesses, placing equal blame on Captain White and the "unfaithfully built" steam packet.[68] In general, more newspapers condemned White than defended him. For example, an angry

New York Herald (October 25, 1837) wanted him marked as a monster: "As to the Captain, if he was intoxicated, there should be no delicacy in saying so, that travelers may be put on their guard against ever trusting themselves with such a man." His action displayed "inexcusable carelessness or want of knowledge of navigation," according to the New Bern newspaper.[69]

The committee in Charleston had no punitive authority, and Captain White was not without his defenders. The testimony of the five witnesses before the Toomer committee was refuted by "A Friend to Capt. White" in a letter to the *New York Gazette.* "Friend" pointed out that the witnesses were not sworn. They were not only hostile to White but had interfered with his command of the ship. Nor were White's friends permitted to cross-examine or call other witnesses, such as John D. Roland. The knowledgeable twenty-seven-year-old Roland, a steamboat captain from Columbus, Georgia, was a passenger who praised the captain's conduct.[70]

D. L. Milne, the steward, admitted that the ship's bar was broken open by some of the passengers but insisted that the liquor was confiscated and thrown overboard. Those who thought the captain was drunk were guilty of mistaken identity. In fact, Milne declared, from the time the ship left port, to the best of his knowledge, Captain White did not "leave his post at the wheel . . . all that night, nor until he was called to breakfast the next morning." Milne continued, "He did not, to the best of my knowledge and belief, eat anything until the day after we were wrecked on the Ocracoke Island, and did not sleep from the time we left New York until around 5 o'clock P.M. on Monday." As for being drunk, Milne said, "I do believe that all Captain White drank during the whole time on board was not more than two glasses of Absinthe Cordial, both of which I gave to him, one in the morning and one in the afternoon, both of which was [*sic*] from the bottle from which I had been giving some to the ladies, some of whom were sea sick. He (Captain White) was completely worn out with fatigue and [was] entirely drenched with water the whole time, from Sunday noon until the vessel struck. I think that Capt. White did everything he could to save the vessel and lives." [71]

William Wright, the beleaguered captain's former employer, wrote the *New York Journal of Commerce* that White had sailed for him for seven years on the Old Line fleet of packets to Liverpool, England, and for the last four years had been captain of the packet steamer *Natchez.* "I have never, till now," Wright stated, "heard a whisper against him in any form; nor can I credit it now. His conduct, from his youth, has been in my estimation without reproach."[72] The *New York Gazette* agreed that public inquiries were needed and explanations called for, but it stated, "No blame can . . . be fixed either upon the builders or the captain. . . . Their duties have been faithfully performed, and . . . the *Home* was as well fitted for the voyage as a steamboat can be, and from the first moment of danger, every exertion was made to save the lives of her passengers."[73]

Captain White and three members of his crew made a sworn "Protest" (report) to John Pike, the Port of Ocracoke notary, on October 13, 1837. The protest objectively recounted the voyage's events from New York to the sinking and its aftermath. In clear prose White claimed that when the storm hit he sought a safe harbor, but circumstances prevented his finding one. At only one point in the report did the captain become less than precise and objective: at the last moment, "the passengers and crew of the vessel, men, women, and children, became intermingled in confusion and horror, clinging to any fragment they could seize hold of, and each succeeding wave [swept] numbers at a time into the ocean." The captain and crew placed the blame on no one, including themselves. The culprit was the hurricane Racer's Storm. The protest was reprinted later in 1837 as a small book and included a longer recital by White of events surrounding the accident. Statements and affidavits supporting White by various passengers were also added. The two documents were compelling and convincing arguments.[74] The exact number of deaths was never known, although ninety was the most generally accepted estimate. Apparently, no criminal or civil suits were brought against Captain White, Allaire, or Brown & Bell. Yet the loss of the *Home* caused the collapse of Allaire's Southern Steam Packet Company. Within a short time, the line's other steamers were sold to a Charles Morgan, who transferred them to New Orleans and engaged them in a packet service to the Texas gulf ports.[75]

There was no public demand that steam packets be removed from ocean service and confined to river traffic. In the twentieth century, airline crashes that killed large numbers of passengers were investigated and existing regulations made tighter. Whatever the cause of a plane accident, no one suggested confining travel to land vehicles. So it was with the *Home.* "This is but one of a thousand disasters," according to the *Pensacola (Florida) Gazette,* "known and to be heard of, occasioned by the late extraordinary gales; and should by no means be taken as evidence that the sea may not be safely navigated by steam."[76] Yet the *Home* tragedy undoubtedly influenced a major congressional act in 1838 upgrading safety standards for steamboats.[77]

The Croom kin were hard hit by the tragedy, but grief had to be sustained, even as the settling of Hardy's large estate became necessary. Bryan, the relative most closely associated with Hardy economically, physically, and emotionally, took charge. The plan to reside in Charleston was abandoned, and Bryan set about tying up some loose, uncertain, and, as it turned out, volatile ends. "B," the New Bern poet of the *Home* disaster, was a friend and admirer of Hardy. Shortly after the wreck, a tribute to Hardy by "B" was published in the local *Spectator.*[78] Included were some speculations about the complications of dividing his friend's estate. Since the family had died in a common disaster, determining who died last would be difficult—perhaps impossible. The way to litigation was wide open: who now would inherit what? Whether Bryan read "B"'s article is unknown, but it did not matter. Hardy's brother was fully aware that gaining lawful possession of Goodwood plantation would be complicated. He settled his affairs in Charleston, returned to Florida, and geared his activities toward achieving that goal.

4

"The Issue Joined"
and the Croom Network

Following the loss of the Croom family, two related and important questions demanded immediate attention: did Hardy leave a will, and if so where was it? Logic made the answer to the first question seem academic: surely Croom — unwell, a man with four dependents, a man about to undertake an ocean voyage — would have made legal provision for his estate's final distribution. Ann Hawks would testify that it was always Hardy's habit to draft a will before making a trip and that he often left it, along with his other important papers, in her care. She maintained that her son, Benjamin, was one of the witnesses. Yet Bryan's mother-in-law did not claim to have seen a will drafted in 1837, and her statement about Hardy's habits was made fifteen years after the *Home* disaster. She did nothing to clarify the immediate situation.[1]

Note has been made that on September 18, 1837, shortly before debarking from New York, Hardy wrote Bryan angrily complaining about a plot by Henrietta Smith and John Carroll. Their plan, he averred, was to deny Frances a part of the inheritance left by her recently deceased sister Henrietta Carroll. In the same letter Hardy remarked that before leaving for Charleston he would probably deposit his will under seal with James Donaldson, his cotton factor.[2] On October 19, after Bryan received confirmation that Hardy and his family had perished, and once the immediate shock had abated, he wrote Donaldson seeking information about his brother's will. Bryan was still in Charleston, where he remained until late October. The New York businessman replied on October 26, 1837: "With reference to your inquiry, I am sorry to say that there is reason to suppose that your brother's will was in his trunk on the ill-fated vessel. He told Mr. McConochie [Donaldson's bookkeeper] that he would probably leave it with me, but he has not done so, and he had previously informed Mrs. Armistead that he had made a will and that it was in his trunk."[3]

Elizabeth Armistead and her mother would both state that while Hardy was in New York they heard him speak "of having made a will which he carried or had carried about in his trunk and remarking on the folly of so doing, said he had a thought of enclosing it to some one. On no other occasion did [they] hear him speak the subject and then he said no more than in substance above stated." In fact, the women "solemnly declare . . . that they never saw any will or paper purporting to be a will of the said Hardy's, that none such was ever deposited with them nor, as far as they have any knowledge, information, or belief, with any other person and therefore [they] have no reason to doubt that . . . Hardy died intestate." The two women added that they had "never seen any will or paper purporting to be a will of [Hardy's] and [had] never heard of the existence since his death."[4]

Collectively, Hardy's blood relatives declared that they—his full brother Richard; half brother William; other half brother George Alexander, who was the ward of William; and his half sister Ann and her husband, Dr. Edward C. Bellamy—consented to have Bryan take charge of Hardy's estate. But what about the missing will? With the question unresolved, how could Bryan apply for a letter of administration whose wording required the sworn statement that the deceased left no such document? There was strong evidence that one existed or had existed. Hardy had written about his intention to draft one and deposit it with Donaldson. Although Donaldson denied receiving it, the merchant believed such a document had existed and that Hardy had informed Elizabeth it was in his trunk. Elizabeth and her mother admitted that Hardy told them of the testament's existence (Bryan did not know this last fact). Still, Bryan was aware of most of the circumstances. After discussing the situation with his lawyer, he made a decision.

Bryan went to Tallahassee on December 19, 1837, where he signed two documents that gave him control of Hardy's estate. In one of them Bryan stated that to the best of his knowledge Hardy died "without a will" and that he would faithfully administer the estate, prepare an inventory, pay the various debts, and make a fair distribution. D. M. Rainey, the court clerk, affixed his signature to the declaration. The second document was also signed by Rainey and witnessed by Leslie A. Thompson, judge of the county court of Leon. Thompson's signature made Bryan's role as administrator official. Edward C. Bellamy and William Croom served as his sureties in the amount of $100,000.[5]

Bryan justified the ethics of his actions. By law and out of personal honor he was bound to try to discover a will if one existed and on discovery surrender his administrative authority. Hardy's will, Bryan reasoned, might well have been in his trunk and been lost in the storm. He had no proof that Henrietta Smith or any of her family had destroyed or suppressed the document. Nor, according to Bryan, did he foresee that any rival claim would be made to Hardy's estate. Bryan's family disagreed with him, convinced that the will existed. Yet it had not surfaced. The estate could not be left in limbo; it had to be settled. The Crooms believed that even if the will were found they would be the sole beneficiaries, and for those reasons the family agreed to let Bryan become the administrator. The planter was satisfied that he had followed the honorable course, abiding by the spirit, if not the exact letter, of the law.[6]

On February 12, 1838, just over four months after the *Home* tragedy, Henrietta Smith was made administratrix of Hardy's estate in North Carolina. Elizabeth Armistead and John Carroll provided her with $10,000 bond. She was granted permission to sell Hardy's personal estate to pay off certain debts owed to her.[7] Activating her authority, the widow Smith held an auction two months later, on April 3. Well advertised in the *New Bern Spectator,* the sale attracted a large crowd to the

Front Street home in New Bern, where buyers selected from a bewildering variety of household goods. In addition, six slaves—a man, three women, and two children—were sold or hired out. The orderly auction went well and was accomplished in six lots. Not counting the slaves, the sale brought in the large amount of $3,115.93. None of the books that Hardy kept in North Carolina were placed on sale, possibly because not many buyers were anticipated, but whatever the reason, the disposition of his library is unknown.[8] Henrietta also took possession of the Crooms' house servants in New Bern. As the most direct descendant of Mary Camack, Henrietta inherited her sister's estate. Included were the lands in Ohio, although the Camacks had made no property improvements and had let the taxes lapse. Much of the land had been foreclosed and resold, and it is doubtful that she derived much of value from Mary's holdings.

Despite the finality of Henrietta's official status as custodian of Hardy's North Carolina estate, and despite her auction of the Croom couple's personal property, Bryan went to New Bern to investigate the situation. His journey included a search of the Craven County Courthouse for pertinent documents. As a result, Bryan filed a notice on April 12 (only a few days after Henrietta's sale) to the next of kin of Hardy's widow: he would make application before the Craven County court for letters of administration to Frances's estate.[9] Misgivings set in, and he never made the application. Bryan explained later that it did not seem the proper thing to do.

Almost nine months after the partial dispersal of the Croom estate in North Carolina, a smaller sale of Hardy's property was held at Goodwood. On January 26, 1839, farm equipment, agricultural produce, and a limited number of livestock, as well as household goods (but no books), were auctioned off. The sale netted $2,861.75. The only purchasers were the Croom family, one kinsman, and Henry J. Gaskins, the overseer.[10]

It was not long before the question of Hardy Croom's estate turned into a bitter and extended legal struggle. The litigation pitted Crooms and their kin against Smith, Armistead, and their kin. The affair was a classic example of families engaged in acrimonious dispute over issues of slaves, land, crops, and buildings; and, not least, there were the dual matters of pride and guilt. The lengthy civil case (or cases, since there were several) would finally result in a landmark legal decision of enduring significance. The ruling came from the Florida Supreme Court and affected the litigants profoundly. Beyond that, it also had a far-reaching and important impact on how future courts would interpret presumption as to order of death in a common calamity.

Even so, the controversy did not start out that way. In the late spring of 1838, Bryan wrote Henrietta leaving his address and promising his "immediate and personal attention to any proposition she might wish to make." John Carroll, who had been to New Bern, learned of Bryan's letter and forwarded to him an offer drawn up in May by Will Haywood Jr., Henrietta's counselor. Carroll wrote Bryan that the proposal was one "she [hoped might] meet the views of all parties." [11]

Henrietta's offer maintained that Hardy and his family were legal residents of North Carolina, where state laws provided that the personal property and personal estate of a deceased person descended to the surviving heir or heirs regardless of domicile. William Henry was the last to die in the *Home* disaster, and upon his death Henrietta Smith became the sole next of kin and was the legitimate heir to the whole of Hardy's personal estate. She expressed her unfamiliarity with Florida's real estate laws but had been informed that they provided for an equal division between paternal and maternal relatives. Thus, Henrietta's family was entitled to one-half of Hardy's real estate. Such was Smith's view of the situation, but, anticipating that the Crooms might have a different interpretation, Henrietta agreed to compromise.

Once Hardy's debts were paid, she proposed dividing his personal property equally between herself and the Croom family. She offered to divide the real estate in a similar manner: one-half to her and Elizabeth Armistead and one-half to the Crooms. If her proposition was unacceptable, Henrietta was willing to consider any reasonable suggestions by the Crooms' counselors. She also expressed a willingness to submit the whole subject to neutral arbitrators. Playing a strong trump card, Smith added that she had already initiated interviews with various passengers aboard the *Home*. The passengers' accounts, she contended, clearly established William Henry as the last survivor. In fact, statements by the survivors had prompted Henrietta's claim to Hardy's estate and, she added, might persuade the Crooms to accept her offer to compromise.

Of course the Crooms had every right to reject all the offers and go to court. If so, she hoped "that they [would] concur in the opinion that any suit made necessary by their declining [to compromise] [would] be conducted with mutual kinship and without disturbing those amicable relations heretofore mutually cultivated." To guard against any unnecessary delay, Henrietta hoped an early reply in writing would be convenient and suggested on or before August 1, 1838.[12] If one accepted the legitimacy of Smith's claims, then her offer to compromise was both fair and generous.

The Crooms had two months to reply. Their answer to Henrietta was a polite but unequivocal no. Her proposals had emphatically disturbed "those amicable relations heretofore mutually cultivated." But if an out-of-court settlement was impossible, neither the duration of what became an ordeal nor the scars it left were known, or probably predictable, when Smith and Armistead's lawyers—Joseph M. White, William P. Duval, and William H. Brockenbaugh—initiated the proceedings on January 24, 1839. That day they (or one of them) mounted the steps leading from the basement of Leon County's new courthouse and walked across a four-columned porch to enter on the first floor. Built in 1838, the handsome Georgian building was a point of civic pride. One of Tallahassee's few brick structures, it symbolized justice in a land whose citizens were still struggling to form an orderly society. Located on the north side of Park Avenue (then known as 200 Foot Street, the capital's northern boundary), the large edifice had two main floors, a high attic, and a cupola. Within its chambers the attorney or attorneys filed a bill of complaint on behalf of Smith and Armistead.

The document was addressed to Judge Thomas Randall of the Superior Court of the Middle District of Florida sitting in chancery. Because Florida was a territory, superior court judges were appointed by the president and confirmed by the United States Senate. Randall, like his fellow judges, served a four-year term, and his court had original jurisdiction in civil and criminal cases. Superior courts and judges were the equivalent of the circuit courts and judges that came into existence in

1845 with statehood. If nothing else, the Croom case was a welcome diversion for the small, thin, quick, and restless Judge Randall. The sharp-featured jurist usually dealt with people accused of such crimes as gaming, assault and battery, dueling, and less genteel forms of fighting.

The bill of complaint was filed against Bryan and the other Crooms as individuals and additionally against Bryan as the administrator of the estate. The bill had a major contention: Henrietta Smith and Elizabeth Armistead, as the legal heirs of Hardy Croom, were entitled to all of his personal estate (which included slaves) and a part of his real estate.[13] In its details the complaint was both broad-ranging and specific. First, the solicitors reviewed the "melancholy accident," claiming that because of his physical condition, Hardy died first, followed by Frances, Justina Rosa, and Henrietta Mary. The last to perish was William Henry, who almost reached the shore safely. The lawyers noted that for a long time and up until his death, Hardy resided in New Bern, where he benefited greatly from Frances's inheritance. Hardy's operations in Florida were carefully reviewed but with the insistence that he never changed his residence or domicile or that of his family from North Carolina.

Bryan's role as administrator of Hardy's Florida estate was acknowledged—with the statement that he should pay whatever debts Hardy had incurred. But Henrietta Smith (Elizabeth Armistead's name was woven in and out of the complaint, but Henrietta's was primary) was not only "entitled to the whole of the slaves, and other personal estate" left by Hardy but to any profits or increase in the holdings since his death. The Smith-Armistead lawyers contended that title to Hardy's personal estate was regulated by the law of the deceased's domicile. Because North Carolina was the home of Hardy and his children, the plaintiffs were entitled to the personal estate as next of kin to the person dying intestate.

Besides the personal estate, the plaintiffs laid claim to one-third of Hardy's real estate. They now admitted that the law of the Territory of Florida required the distribution of one-third of a deceased person's real estate to the next of kin, in this case the Crooms. But Florida's laws provided further that the remaining two-thirds of his or her real estate be divided equally between the next of kin on the father's and the mother's side, which meant one-third to Henrietta and Elizabeth. The plaintiffs also insisted on entitlement to one-third of any profits (less necessary expenses) accruing to Hardy's real estate since his death.

In justifying the bill of complaint, the lawyers pointed out that Henrietta and Elizabeth had attempted to obtain their just rights without resorting to law. They had offered to relinquish a portion of those rights, had agreed to compromise them on reasonable terms, or to refer the matter to arbitration by disinterested parties. Yet all their attempts had been spurned, and they were left with no choice. They now wanted the court to award them all of Hardy's personal estate and one-third of his real estate. Because the other parties had defrauded the complainants by claiming Hardy's entire estate, both personal and real, they asked Judge Randall to make the Crooms admit or deny the charges against them. Finally, they wanted the judge to require Bryan to provide a full account of his handling of the estate.[14]

The Crooms were not a family to surrender easily what they considered indisputably theirs—theirs, as they saw it, by any and all criteria of justice and law. Whatever doubts they might have had concerning Smith and Armistead's intentions were dismissed by the particulars cited in the bill of complaint. Aside from Hardy and Bryan, who the Crooms were and the course of their lives up to the early 1840s bore directly on the legal proceedings. Hardy and Bryan—because they owned land jointly, including part of Goodwood, and were together often—had the closest relationship of all the Crooms. Susan Matilda and Betsy were dead, but the other siblings kept in touch by visits and occasional correspondence. Their familial ties extended to economic relationships. The Crooms were a confederation of relatives knit together by common threads of loyalty that could be loosened or tightened as circumstances required. The *Home* tragedy and the impending legal battle rallied the family into close alliance and gave it sharp focus.

Bryan wanted to go beyond the role of administrator of Hardy's estate and assume individual ownership of Goodwood. To do so he had to clear title to the plantation with the other Crooms. The family members agreed that Hardy's full brothers should receive larger shares.

Thus, Bryan was entitled to two-sevenths of the estate, Richard to two-sevenths, and William, George Alexander, and Edward and Ann Bellamy to the remaining three-sevenths. Bryan dealt first with Edward and Ann Bellamy. On March 27, 1838, he paid the couple $2,478 for all their "interest, right & title of every kind in and to the lands of . . . Hardy B. Croom in Leon County." In 1847 Bryan would make an additional settlement with the Bellamys, paying them $5,250.[15]

Ann Bryan Croom Bellamy was born in 1812. Ann and her sister, Elizabeth Jane (born March 28, 1819), who was known as Betsy, inherited three plantations in Lenoir County, as well as slaves, from their father's estate. The land in North Carolina was divided equally between the sisters.[16] On December 8, 1829, the year of her father's death, Ann married Dr. Edward C. Bellamy of Nash County, North Carolina. The marriage took place at William Croom's Newington plantation in Lenoir County and was a prominent social event. It would have been important if no one but the numerous Crooms had attended. But there were others present, and Hardy described various dinners honoring the couple. As for the ceremony, "There were about fifty or sixty persons present—though not half the *kin* were here."[17]

Dr. Bellamy was a member of the class of 1822 at the University of North Carolina, although he did not graduate. Five years later, on July 15, 1834, Betsy married Samuel Crowell Bellamy, Edward's brother and also a physician. Where either of the Bellamys received his medical degree is unknown. Like her older sister, Betsy was married at home.[18] The Crooms and Bellamys were distantly related. Edward and Hardy were friends, and on one occasion in North Carolina, the doctor gave Croom some good advice on buying a horse.[19] The story of the Bellamy families was one of economic, political, and social success but also one of failure, family feud, and tragedy on the Florida frontier. The discussion that follows takes their story through the first phases of the contest over Hardy's estate. Approximately the same time frame is used to place the other Crooms in historical context.

Both Bellamy families settled in west Florida's Jackson County, where the seat of government was Marianna, and both migrated largely because Hardy convinced them that the new territory was a land where fortunes could be made. Samuel and Betsy arrived first, and Bellamy bought public land as early as 1836. Later, he purchased public land on five occasions.[20] Samuel, or Sam, abandoned medicine and established himself as a successful man of the soil at Rock Cave, his large and productive plantation along Baker Creek. He also frequently engaged in selling land.[21]

Life was not easy in the Territory of Florida, not even for a man of wealth such as Bellamy. By December 1836, both he and Betsy were suffering from chills and fevers (possibly malaria), and their only child fell ill as well.[22] They recovered, and the industrious Bellamy soon became an important man in the rich cotton-producing area of Jackson County and the fast-growing and prosperous town of Marianna. An active social life could be enjoyed there (Sam built a large home in town but never lived in it). The novelist Caroline Lee Whiting, who moved to the town from neighboring Gadsden County, wrote later, "I do not like Marianna hours. To go between nine and ten, take supper at two or half past two is entirely too fashionable for a little county village. There is a great deal more show here than at Quincy, but I like the spirit of the place better."[23]

Among other things, Samuel served as an appraiser for the local branch of the Union Bank and was one of Jackson County's delegates to Florida's constitutional convention of 1838–39. At the convention, Bellamy, a loyal Whig, represented the wealthier classes. He was a leader in a losing effort to provide constitutional safeguards for banking in Florida. The victorious Democrats, following Andrew Jackson's example, sharply curtailed government participation in banking activities. Locally, Sam sponsored a school on his plantation and built a bridge across the Chipola River.[24]

Bellamy enjoyed his affluence. In their close relationship, Croom and Bellamy sometimes mixed business with friendship. Sometimes Hardy helped market Bellamy's cotton in New York, though not always with success. In 1836 Sam learned that Hardy was planning his usual trip to New York and persuaded his brother-in-law to purchase him a carriage. He wanted a four-horse vehicle (but one light enough for two horses to pull) with green harness. The conveyance was to be dark with green trimmings; the mounting for the carriage and harness was to be of silver. "But I will leave that to your good taste—let it be in the most fashionable style and the most splendid article you can purchase . . . [for] *seven hundred to one thousand dollars.*"[25] Bellamy wanted delivery as soon as possible to New Bern or Washington, North Carolina.

The good life for Sam Bellamy was shattered by the death of Betsy on May 11, 1837, followed by that of their son within a few days. Hardy wrote Bellamy a letter of consolation: "To the husband and parent these are afflictions to weigh down the stoutest heart." It was a time of great sorrow, but Hardy reminded him, "It is the duty of us all to struggle against our griefs and to bear our lot in this world whatever it may be."[26] On a more impersonal level, the disruptions of the Second Seminole War and economic depression brought Bellamy increasing debts, and he sought escape in excessive drinking.

Edward C. Bellamy, called Ned, and Ann moved to Jackson County in the late 1830s. Ann had relinquished her dower rights, which, combined with Ned's own resources, gave him the means to become a planter without having to practice medicine. Even so, Ann retained title to some of her property, especially slaves. Ned bought public land at four different times, although he sold property more often than he bought it (one sale in 1854 brought him $20,000).[27] Ned and Ann had seven children: William Croom, Charles Edward, Eugene, Hardy, Harold, Ann Elizabeth, and George Whitfield. Their selection of names, as a matter of course, was bound to complicate the family tree. Several of the sons attended the University of North Carolina and later served in the Confederate army. One son, Charles Edward, was an outstanding student at Chapel Hill and later became a doctor. He married his first cousin, the novelist Elizabeth Whitfield Croom, of Quincy, and died during the Civil War while serving as a surgeon.[28]

The Edward Bellamys were among Jackson County's leading families. Ned, in the tradition of his Croom in-laws, was a leader in establishing the mission in Marianna that in 1838 became St. Luke's Episcopal Church. His interest extended to sporadic service as a lay deputy to the general convention of the Episcopal Diocese of Florida.[29] Hickory

Hill, Ned and Ann's 2,240-acre plantation along the east bank of the Chipola River, was a showplace and the center of much social activity.

Caroline Lee Hentz, a prolific romantic writer and a transplanted native of Massachusetts, had family connections in Jackson County. She used the Bellamys' Hickory Hill in her novel *Marcus Warland; or, The Long Moss Spring* (1852) to refute the charges levied against the South by Harriet Beecher Stowe's *Uncle Tom's Cabin*.[30] Novelist Hentz defended her motives by noting, "The description of Mr. Bellamy's plantation is drawn from the real, not the ideal." In vivid prose she described Hickory Hill: "Far as the eye could reach, his magnificent cotton and corn fields rolled in snowy opulence or waved in golden splendour."[31] When Hardy came to Florida for his annual work visits, he always contacted his Jackson County half sister and her husband, while Bryan and Eveline maintained relations with Ned and Ann from Rocky Comfort and later from Goodwood.

After settling the Bellamy claim to Goodwood in March 1838, Bryan next contacted Richard, the only remaining Croom sibling with whom he shared a common father and mother. According to Richard, he made an agreement with his brother to surrender his claims to Goodwood. Whether the agreement was verbal or registered as a legal document is unclear. It was not recorded in the deed records of Leon County.[32] The agreement between the brothers settled the matter of Hardy's estate sufficiently to answer the Smith-Armistead bill of complaint, but it was less than a permanent arrangement. Besides being intelligent and innovative, Richard was nothing if not obdurate and disputatious, possessing inventiveness, feistiness, and tenacity in equal measure.

Richard was born on September 20, 1805, in Lenoir County, the fourth child of William and his first wife, Mary Bryan. Richard was a handsome man with a medium build. He had a broad forehead, heavy eyebrows, a long nose, wide mouth, and thin face. His story paralleled and was interconnected with those of his brothers, and he shared the planting and intellectual talents common to the Crooms. Like them, Richard and his family were faithful members of the Episcopal Church, and he became a major figure in the history of Goodwood plantation.

Growing up in Lenoir County, Richard attended the University of North Carolina, and in the twenty-one-member graduating class of 1826, he was one of seven seniors to deliver an "intermediate Oration." At some point Richard became a physician, but it is doubtful that he ever practiced medicine. He never used the title.[33]

On April 9, 1829, Richard's marriage to Winifred Bryan Whitfield confused the family tree more than that of any Croom before him. Considering the record of his predecessors, extra confusion was quite an achievement. Winifred was seven years younger than he (born October 17, 1812) and a native of Spring Hill in Lenoir County.[34] She was the daughter of General Bryan Whitfield and Winifred, who was the general's second wife as well as his first wife's niece. Unraveling the relationships is further complicated by another fact: Elizabeth "Betsy" Whitfield, one of the general's daughters by his first wife, was the senior William Croom's second wife. Having William and Richard, father and son, marry half sisters was perplexing, even for the Croom family.[35]

The year of Richard's wedding (1829), his father died, leaving him a comfortable inheritance to start married life: slaves and five different farms or places in Lenoir County.[36] In 1831 Richard purchased Hardy's North Carolina lands, freeing Hardy to invest in Florida. In that same year Richard sold 350 acres in Lenoir County for $2,000.[37] The year that Richard and Winifred came to Florida is unknown, but it was sometime in the early 1830s. There is no record of his buying land immediately, and the couple probably lived temporarily at Rocky Comfort with Bryan and Eveline. They had six children: Winifred Bryan, Nicholas Pavolich, Mary Whitfield, Bryan, Susan Matilda, and James (born October 14, 1843, but died in infancy).[38]

The Alabama frontier, much of it surrendered by the Creek Indians in the Treaty of Fort Jackson (1814), was opened before that of Florida. The area was booming, and its fertile lands had interested Hardy and Bryan, while various North Carolina kinsmen—Crooms and Whitfields—had migrated there and become planters. Richard and Winifred were similarly attracted and moved to Sumter County, Alabama, about 1835. Despite the move, neither Richard nor his family ever severed their connections with Florida. Later, Richard would maintain a plantation in Leon County even though his permanent residence was in Alabama.

Sumter was a rich Black Belt county created on December 18, 1832. It was bounded on the west by Mississippi, on the east by the Tombigbee River, and to the north and south by Choctaw and Pickens Counties. The Noxubee and Sucarnatchie Rivers and a number of large creeks cut across the county's one thousand square miles of rolling black prairie lands, alluvial and interspersed with ridges and hills. Livingston, the county seat, was laid out in 1833 and named for Edward Livingston, prominent politician and friend of Andrew Jackson. Most of the settlers were families from Virginia and the Carolinas. Many were yeoman farmers, but there were a number of large planters such as Richard Croom. Cotton was the basis of the county's wealth, and slave labor was the force that drove the economy. By 1860, Sumter's population of 5,519 whites, 28,091 slaves, and 25 free persons of color gave it rank among the state's top fifteen slaveholding counties.

Joseph G. Baldwin, a brilliant contemporary writer of picaresque novels and stories, lived in Sumter County and gave a classic description of how the Southwest, as the lower South was then known, was developed. In his book *The Flush Times of Alabama and Mississippi* (1853), Baldwin wrote, "Emigrants came flocking in from all quarters of the Union, and especially from the slaveholding states. The new country seemed to be a reservoir, and every road leading to it a vagrant stream of enterprise and adventure. Money, or what passed for money, was the only cheap thing to be had. Every cross-road of every avocation presented an opening,—through which a fortune was seen by the adventurer in near perspective." According to Baldwin, "Credit was a thing of course. To refuse it—if the thing was ever done—was an insult for which a bowie-knife were not too summary or exemplary a means of redress." [39]

On June 24, 1836, Croom first bought land in Sumter County. The 81.57 acres were located in the county's southwestern section along the Tombigbee River. The purchase was made directly from the government. Richard built his home in this area, which later became known as Whitfield. Located directly on the river, Whitfield was first known as

Black Bluff and was eleven miles east of Gaston, a substantial town.[40] From the mid-1830s until the late 1850s, Croom steadily acquired and sold land.[41]

Richard probably took the slaves he had inherited from his father to Alabama. Natural increase raised his workforce, and he also bought bondsmen. In 1842 he made a major purchase of sixteen chattels; ten were aged twelve or less, making them, in strict economic terms, a good investment for the future. He paid Calvin Davis $6,500 for the blacks, and Davis warranted "the said slaves to be sound in body and mind and slaves for life."[42]

The transplanted North Carolinian made money in land because he engineered more sales than purchases—and at higher prices. At least eleven times he received cash, mortgages, or promissory notes from grantees.[43] Everything was going well for the Sumter County Crooms when their close family ties were suddenly disrupted in the fall of 1848. On October 1, the devout Episcopalian Winifred died suddenly while on her knees in prayer.[44] Completely occupied with his planting interests, Croom had relied heavily on Winifred to manage the household and raise the children.

Richard continued his farming in Alabama, but he turned increasingly to Florida. It was logical that the widower would send some of his children to Goodwood to live with their Aunt Eveline and Uncle Bryan for various periods. The recently completed Goodwood mansion was large, and without doubt the childless master and mistress welcomed having their young relatives as extended guests. Ned and Ann lived nearby in Jackson County, and, as will be seen, Richard's half brother William and his family resided even closer, in Quincy. George Alexander, another half brother, also lived in Gadsden County and was in the process of moving his ever growing family to the Tallahassee area. Nor could Richard, being a true Croom, resist expanding his landholdings (which he had never completely given up) in Leon County, especially in the Lafayette Grant.

As of October 1839, Bryan had cleared title for Goodwood with Edward and Ann and with Richard. Continuing to administer Hardy's estate and to defend the Croom family's right to it, Bryan moved to settle the claims of his two half brothers. William Whitfield Croom, who was George Alexander's guardian, remained a legal heir until January 18, 1843. At that time Bryan paid him $5,000 for his interest in Hardy's holdings. Two days later, George Alexander accepted a like amount and released his part of the estate to Bryan.[45] Both had agreed to surrender their claims to Goodwood by the time that the family answered the Smith-Armistead bill of complaint.

Born in 1814, William W. Croom got his first name from his father, while Whitfield was his mother's surname. With a much stronger physique than his three half brothers, William had dark brown hair, a high forehead, a large nose, and a strong mouth and square jaw. When his father died, William inherited slaves and Tower Hill plantation in Lenoir County. He received a sound secondary education and, when not engaged in his studies, helped his mother operate Newington plantation until her death. No haughty scion of wealth, snapping his fingers and issuing commands, the young boy plowed in the fields. He also helped a resourceful slave named "Smoker John" at various tasks. The black got his nickname because he was once caught stealing turkeys by suffocating them with smoke. Whatever his foibles, "Smoker John" was proficient at the difficult and essential job of digging wells. William and Smoker were friends, and Croom recalled later that the bondsman "dug many a well" for his father. "I stood by ready to give him a dram when he got chilled in the well—and he got chilled very often."[46]

At the urging of Hardy, his half brother moved to Gadsden County sometime in the early 1830s. Scarcely twenty, William seems to have missed the college education that Hardy, Bryan, and Richard received. Yet he may have received some college training. It was not at the University of North Carolina, but his correspondence clearly is that of an educated man. He had a good command of French, and it would be of advantage to him later in life, a life that was plagued with bad luck. Without question, he had in full measure the Croom family sensitivity, insight, and intelligence. He realized how not having a mother and father affected him as a young man and years later wrote his son, then a student at the University of North Carolina, "I had never found (on account of my seclusion) or been taught the *habit* of looking at peoples['] motives, but judged every body by myself, a most pernicious habit in a man who is conscious of the rectitude of his own actions. This is a habit that I find difficult to shake off. I hope you shall be more fortunate in acquiring a juster estimate of human nature."[47]

His future wife, Julia Stephens, was born in 1814 and lived in New Bern with her family until they followed the lead of the Crooms and other North Carolinians and, by the mid-1830s, migrated to Gadsden County. Julia's features were attractive and in proportion. Her kind face was given character by a strong chin. One of eight children, Julia was part of a family headed by Marcus Cicero Stephens that helped build Gadsden County. Although they knew each other in North Carolina, William and Julia were married in Florida.[48] It was a union of two aristocratic families. William, like his brothers and half brothers, had egalitarian instincts but, like all of them, realized his position as part of the upper class. That was true even when applied to certain family members. Once when his son mentioned some remote relatives, William told him, "The Crooms you speak of are distant kin of ours & we never cared to recognise them, at the same time they *are* kin and I have always met them cordially but have never cousined them."[49] After his marriage, young Croom did not follow the usual family pattern of becoming a planter. Instead, he settled down in Quincy as a merchant, probably with initial aid from Bryan and Eveline at nearby Rocky Comfort. By 1840 William resided in the county seat with a household of eleven that included five slaves. In 1841 he paid $2,000 for three town lots and one-third of three others.[50]

Some time after selling his rights to Goodwood, William and Bolling Baker formed a partnership (Croom and Baker) as merchants. They bought part of Lot 89 in Quincy, and two years later Croom gained sole control of the property.[51] The closest William came to farming was in 1848 when he paid $500 for eighty acres in Gadsden County. Thoughts of planting turned to those of speculation, and he sold the land in 1850 for $640. The original owner, Nathaniel D. Zeigler, had paid $200 for the land and thus made $300, indicating that he was a good businessman or that Croom was a bad one, or, more likely, that William considered a profit of $140 preferable to working the land.[52] By 1850, William owned eleven slaves, had an estate valued at $10,000, and was engaged in business and property sales in Quincy.[53]

As George Alexander's half brother and neighbor, Bryan had an affectionate relationship with him. The young man and, later, his wife and children were frequent guests at Rocky Comfort and Goodwood. Born in Lenoir County on October 7, 1821, George Alexander was William and Betsy Croom's fifth child and youngest son. Just ten years old when his mother died, the young boy was placed under the guardianship of William, his only full brother. The latter saw to it that George Alexander received a good education at the highly regarded Pittsboro Academy in Chatham County. Chartered in 1787, the academy attracted students from across North Carolina and produced two governors, as well as other state leaders.[54]

William handled the estate, including slaves inherited from his father and adjoining plantations, Newington and Red Hill in Lenoir County, that George Alexander received after his mother died.[55] Mindful of his own experience, William made it possible for his brother to attend the University of Georgia in 1841.[56] George Alexander lacked the scholarship (certainly the incentive) of his half brothers, spending only a year in college, but his time in Athens was not wasted.

While there he met Julia M. Church, three years his junior and one of university president Alonzo Church's winsome daughters. A transplanted Vermont Yankee, Church was a schoolmaster and Presbyterian minister who had come to Georgia in the 1820s to teach in Putnam County. There he met and married Sarah J. Trippe, member of a leading planter family. Church became president of the University of Georgia in 1829 and held the post until he retired in 1850. Any thirty-year tenure, let alone an academic one, would be bound to produce controversy. Church's did, and the time span also produced a large family. Several children died in infancy, but eight survived both parents.[57]

Georgia undergraduates courted the Church girls because of their charm and attractiveness; nor did it hurt to get on the good side of President Church. Between 1841 and 1843, George Alexander probably returned to Florida and lived with his older brother in Quincy and also spent some time with Bryan and Eveline. Julia was attracted to young

Croom's light brown hair, gray eyes, and fair complexion, as well as to his personality, and their relationship deepened into love. They became engaged, and the wedding took place in Athens on February 13, 1843, and was performed by a Presbyterian minister, the Reverend Francis Bowman. A New Englander himself and family friend, Bowman was the preacher at the nearby town of Greensboro.[58]

In preparation for his married life, George Alexander bought extensive property in Gadsden County from Bryan. In fact, he purchased nothing less than Rocky Comfort plantation. On January 21, 1843, only a month before the wedding, he paid the bargain price of $12,000 for the 2,000-acre place. Witnesses to the transaction were Dr. Edward C. Bellamy of Jackson County and George Whitfield.[59] The couple probably moved to Gadsden County sometime in late February. In March, George Alexander bought another tract, this time a smaller one of 79.72 acres, from Bryan. The price was only $100, and Bryan may have considered it something of a wedding present.[60]

Bryan's dealings with George Alexander in 1843 indicated that he felt secure about his title to Goodwood. Even with his title uncertain, Bryan moved his family to Leon County in late 1838 or early 1839. They lived briefly in Tallahassee while the second house was completed at Goodwood. Larger and more elegant than the cottage on Lake Lafayette that had been so appealingly sketched by the comte de Castelnau, the second home was located in Section 29. Richard A. Shine, whom Hardy had recommended to supply the brick, probably put the finishing touches on the residence and within the next few years began construction on the big house. Like Bryan and Eveline, George Alexander and Julia settled into a prominent place among the planters of Gadsden County and began raising a family. Similar to Hardy and Bryan before him, the young married man would later obtain land in Leon County and move there.

In the meantime the opponents in the pending trial were busy. Henrietta and Elizabeth sought the advice of Joseph M. White, who was a capable attorney and Florida's territorial delegate to Congress. After considering the issues, but without going into details, White told the women that if it was established that William Henry survived his father, they would inherit equal shares in the estate. Hiring White as one

of their lawyers was a shrewd move for the complainants—a word, together with plaintiffs, that Smith and Armistead would hear as synonyms for themselves hundreds of times in the future. White's colleagues
in the case, William P. Duval and William H. Brockenbaugh, were also
leading solicitors. Duval had resumed the practice of law after his term
as territorial governor ended in 1834, and Brockenbaugh would shortly
become circuit judge of the Middle District of Florida. Unaware of the
opposition's maneuvers, Bryan also sought White's advice and courtroom expertise. Florida's delegate complied with the first request but
had to refuse the second. Even so, Bryan and the other Crooms were
powerful constituents, and White apologized that his skills were already
engaged. He advised Bryan to compromise rather than lose the case.
Anticipating such an arrangement, White made a remark that was
memorable for its total inaccuracy: "[I] think there is not room for a
judicial controversy."[61]

Led by Bryan, the various family members answered the particulars
contained in the bill of complaint, or at least the particulars they felt
obligated (on advice of counsel) to answer. Bryan and William, together
with Edward and Ann Bellamy, filed a joint reply. Later, William, acting for George Alexander, and Richard made separate answers.[62]

On May 27, 1839, Bryan's foursome appeared before Isaac R. Harris,
a justice of the peace, at the courthouse in Quincy and filed their rebuttal to the claimants' bill of complaint. There was no need to go to
Tallahassee to deposit the document prepared in consultation with
Thomas Baltzell and James D. Westcott Jr., their lawyers. Baltzell and
Westcott had fashioned a careful and well-reasoned reply for their
clients.

The defendants contended that when Hardy died he was a resident
of Leon County, a citizen. That meant his wife and children had the
same legal residence as he: Florida. Even if one or more of the family
had survived Hardy, which the reply did not admit, the laws of the
territory, not North Carolina, governed the disposal of the estate. All of
Hardy's personal estate was regulated, the defendants insisted, by the
laws of Florida, Hardy's lawful domicile at the time of his death. They
argued further that because Hardy died intestate, all his real estate
was also regulated by Florida laws. Bryan's group noted that he had in

no way meddled with the settlement of Hardy's real estate anywhere outside Florida, leaving such matters to the proper courts in North Carolina.

If, as the defendants believed, Hardy survived his wife and children, then Florida's laws entitled them to all the deceased's real estate in the territory and all of his personal estate wherever it might be. They claimed that even if Frances survived Hardy, she acquired no title to his real estate in the territory. Nor did she to any of his personal estate except as dower, which, because she died before making any assignment of it, became extinguished and void. In addition, slaves and other personal property that Hardy acquired by and during his marriage became his exclusive property, and following Hardy's death, it had the same status as his other personal estate. They averred further that if the children survived Hardy, their claims to his personal and real estate ended with their deaths. The argument was based on Florida's descents law of 1829. Hardy's estate automatically descended to the paternal side of his family, the Crooms, in the same manner as if there had been no maternal side.

While admitting that the entire Hardy Croom family perished in the wreck of the *Home*, Bryan and the others denied that when the steamboat left New York Hardy was ill. Instead, they insisted that he was in good health and cited a letter from Hardy to Bryan dated September 28, 1837, as proof. The defendants noted that they had no personal knowledge of Hardy's physical condition on board the *Home*. Yet they dismissed the bill of complaint's assertion that the prolonged strain caused by the hurricane had debilitated him. That claim, they declared, was mere conjecture and was unsubstantiated by evidence.

The Crooms' response went into detail, not only about Hardy's being "well nigh restored" and "having become comparatively robust and strong" but also about his personal qualities. Hardy was "naturally possessed of more than an ordinary share of moral courage, energy of mind, and fortitude in times of difficulty, danger, and peril; and always in such emergencies acted with great coolness, prudence, and discretion." Because of the wild disorder and the panic and terror that accompanied the destruction of the *Home*, the defendants believed that "no certain credible testimony as to who was the last survivor of [the] family [could] be obtained or exist[ed]."

Activity by the complainants to secure testimony from passengers on board the steamboat was acknowledged. Such "extraordinary pains and great exertions" had produced and would produce, they agreed, no more than "ex parte and one sided statements." The Crooms revealed that copies of such statements had been sent to Bryan with the intention of causing him to accept a compromise. The efforts were dismissed because they did not "detail and exhibit the true facts." The defendants made a convincing point: how could passengers, who had known the Crooms only casually and briefly, have been able—in the dark, during the chaos of a hurricane—to identify Hardy "or the members of his family, much less . . . have noticed and borne in mind so as to have detailed with minuteness, certainty, and accuracy the various particular incidents" of their deaths?

To the Crooms, the circumstances of William Henry's floating to shore on a piece of wreckage before being swept back out to sea and his death offered no proof that he survived his father. Hardy had equal opportunity to do the same thing. Before the complainants could establish that any of the children survived their father, they "should be required to prove when [Hardy] actually died." The presumption had to be that Hardy Croom "in the prime of life being but forty years of age . . . in his then improved state of health and strength was able to take care of himself and so preserve his life longer" than his children and ill wife. Thus, in the concise words of Baltzell and Westcott, Hardy "was the last survivor."

The answer to the bill of complaint related how Bryan had established himself as administrator of Hardy's estate and upheld his stewardship. The Crooms also claimed that administering the estate of Frances and the children had to be done through the courts of Florida. Their answer further explained the disposition of Hardy's property in Florida. It asserted that when he died Hardy owned Goodwood plantation in Leon County, livestock, and "sundry slaves and personal estate of considerable value." Goodwood had been only partly paid for, and the estate owed debts amounting to $50,000. Bryan, as administrator, had not "as yet been able to pay [them] without sacrifice to said estate which he ha[d] sought to avoid." Administering the property according to Florida laws, Bryan had filed an inventory and appraisement of Hardy's personal estate with the county clerk. Bryan's reports, vouchers, and accounts of his administration were on file, and he had dealt with the various Croom family members regarding the estate's distribution. Bryan contended that the complainants had no claim to Hardy's real or personal estate and no right to demand an accounting of his administration. He referred them to his reports at the county clerk's office. Unless otherwise ordered by the court, the defendants stood by their refusal to cooperate further. They asked the court to dismiss the bill of complaint and award them their reasonable costs.[63]

On September 6, 1839, some four months later, William Croom, speaking for his ward and half brother, seventeen-year-old George Alexander, replied to the bill of complaint. Once again William returned to Justice of the Peace Harris and the Gadsden County Courthouse, where he had appeared earlier with Bryan, Edward, and Ann. The second statement was long and had been prepared under the supervision of Walker Anderson, Croom's lawyer. It reviewed the involved story of Hardy's life in North Carolina and Florida. The statement explained how Hardy, not only a resident of Florida himself, had persuaded family members and others to move there. Croom emphasized how all Hardy's legal documents—deeds, purchases, contracts—referred to him as a citizen of Florida. Also rehearsed were the various complaints that Hardy had against Smith-Armistead. To keep the peace, George Alexander was willing to give up his legitimate claims to Hardy's estate outside Florida provided the complainants retreated from any demands in Florida and paid their share of costs already entailed by the controversy.[64] As noted earlier, not until 1843 (William on January 18, and George Alexander on January 20) did the two heirs relinquish their claims to Hardy's estate to Bryan.

On September 13, 1839, a week later, the combative Richard became the last Croom to respond. Crafted with the aid of his counsel, Charles S. Sibley, the reply was filed with Richard G. Wellford, clerk of the Superior Court of the Middle District of Florida for Leon County. Adding issues of his own, Richard presented the same basic case made by the others: Hardy was the last Croom to die; he was a legal resident of Florida; he profited little economically from his marriage to Frances; his sick wife was dominated by her mother; there was ill will between Hardy and his mother-in-law and other members of her family.

Richard believed strongly that Hardy had made a will but that the complainants had suppressed or destroyed it. Henrietta Smith had not produced any of Hardy's personal letters in her possession because she knew they were harmful to her case. Moreover, Richard's reply continued, Henrietta cheated Hardy and Frances out of their just inheritance from the estates of Frances's brother, Nathaniel Smith, and her sister Henrietta Carroll. Richard was far from being satisfied with the Smith-Armistead offers to compromise. He knew some offers had been made to Bryan, but none had been tendered to him. If they had been, he would have refused.

Without furnishing any details, Richard noted that he and Bryan had made an arrangement about Goodwood and the remainder of Hardy's estate. Still, on principle, Richard declared himself "not willing to relinquish to said complainant one cent of any part of Hardy's estate however derived" that he was entitled to by law. As he would later tell his daughter Mary, "Sometimes I may have acted passionately & imprudently with the impulse of constitutional irritability & bad advisors, [but] my conscience does not accuse me of any *fixed* or intentional desire to injure any person in [his or her] character and reputation." Richard was adamant in asserting that Hardy's estate was governed by the laws of the Territory of Florida. Even if some of Hardy's children survived him, any and all of Hardy's siblings were entitled to his personal estate in Florida and elsewhere.[65]

Once the replies from the Crooms had been made, the Smith-Armistead lawyers moved, on November 23, 1839, to file their general replication to the answers, and the case was put at issue. With the lines drawn, the litigants' lawyers continued the business already begun of taking depositions from witnesses scattered from Florida to New York. The families and their counsels planned strategies and set themselves for the struggle. The parties on both sides had much to gain, but Bryan and Eveline had more to lose.

5 "Too Feeble to Concede the Artifice"

The case would have begun shortly except for what, on the surface, seemed to be a curious maneuver by Richard Croom. He was, in fact, acting with the obvious collusion of Bryan (and the probable consent of the other family members). After the Crooms had filed their several replies to the bill of complaint, Richard and Bryan signed and deposited in the Leon County Courthouse a formal agreement on October 11, 1839. By its startling terms Richard purchased all of Bryan's Florida holdings, both acknowledged and claimed. The arrangements were to be handled by the Manhattan Bank of New York. The younger brother agreed to pay Bryan $160,000 for Goodwood (2,480 acres) and Rocky Comfort (approximately 2,000 acres). In addition, Richard was to obtain ownership of 128 slaves in Florida. Six more slaves in Hardy's estate were in North Carolina and were included in the transaction. By deliberate oversight Henrietta Smith was not consulted about giving them up. Bryan further agreed to transfer to Richard all his mules, oxen, cattle, hogs, goats, sheep, corn fodder, peas, wagons and carts, plows, harnesses, and farming equipment, but not the present cotton crop on the land. The agreement was an amicable one, as evidenced by the payment schedule: annual installments of $16,000 that were interest-free. Bryan was to relinquish his own two-sevenths of Hardy's estate, the two-sevenths he had received from Richard, and the one-seventh he had obtained from Edward and Ann and abrogate the agreement that had given him the one-seventh claimed by William. Richard would bargain with George Alexander for the remaining one-seventh.

The unusual agreement mentioned the Smith-Armistead claim but dismissed it as invalid. In the event that Hardy's will was discovered, then the agreement between Bryan and Richard would become inoperative. In the meantime, Bryan was to continue as administrator of the estate, and if he and Richard had a dispute over management policies or other issues, they agreed to appoint an arbitrator and abide by his decision.[1]

What had happened? Were Bryan and Eveline giving up all that they had struggled for, and if so, what were their motives and future plans? There are no certain answers. It is possible that the Crooms, needing more time to secure witnesses, decided to try a different legal maneuver. The fiery Richard wanted to attack the Smith-Armistead forces more aggressively, and the agreement with Bryan put him in a position to re-enter the controversy (he had removed himself by relinquishing to Bryan his claim to Hardy's holdings). Richard's next tactic gives credence to this theory. On February 10, 1840, Charles S. Sibley, whose legal services Richard had retained, followed his client's instructions and filed a cross bill of complaint against both the complainants and the defendants to the original bill. He added the name of John Carroll to the list.

The Circuit Court for Middle Florida sitting in chancery was informed that Richard, after providing an answer to the original bill that took him out of the case, had annulled his arrangement with Bryan. In addition, the Alabama planter declared he had made and would make certain arrangements with the other family members that entitled him to take over Hardy's estate. The clear import was that now he was a major participant in the dispute. That Richard filed a cross bill of complaint against Smith-Armistead was not unusual, but having done so against his own family assuredly was and lifted the controversy to a new level. The long bill occupied twenty-five legal pages in the record. As for Smith-Armistead, Richard repeated many of his original statements and levied charges that John Carroll was conspiring with them and acting as their agent. He wanted the original case halted until the complainants gave an adequate accounting of how they had handled Hardy's property outside Florida. The complainants should be forced to surrender all of Hardy's letters and papers in their possession, and they should, as non-Florida residents, be compelled to provide monetary security should they refuse to abide by an adverse decision. In particular, Richard wanted them to supply much more information about Hardy's will.

Sibley's draft of Richard's instructions accused Bryan of colluding with the other family members to surrender their legitimate claims to Hardy's property outside Florida. Such action had resulted in "manifest detriment, prejudice, injury, and loss" to Richard. The Crooms should also present to the court whatever information they had about Hardy's will and, no less than the complainants, supply the court with the deceased's personal correspondence and documents. Richard wanted the judge to halt the original dispute and subpoena all the parties to appear before the court and answer his cross bill of complaint.[2]

The specifics of Richard's agreement with Bryan on October 11, 1839, and the former's filing of his cross bill four months later suggest a Croom family battle plan. Their claim to Hardy's estate could be enlarged and strengthened, and the complainants would be placed on the defensive. When forced to reply to Richard's charges (known in the official records as Case 237), the Smith-Armistead forces interpreted his action as no less than a collective conspiracy by the Crooms. They answered with a deposition taken in New York on September 9, 1840. According to their lawyers, "The attempt to make up an issue between the now plaintiff [Richard] and his said co-defendants in the original suit is too feeble to concede the artifice."[3]

The reply, couched in bitter language (both sides abandoned their earlier polite phrases and courteous asides), asserted that despite making a new arrangement with Bryan, Richard had no claim and no right to bring the suit. Henrietta and Elizabeth argued that the new Croom design was to have Richard declare that Hardy left a will. The move would relieve Bryan of the appearance of lying under oath, since to become administrator he had sworn that Hardy died intestate. They added that so long as Bryan remained administrator, the Circuit Court of Leon County could not decide the issue of a will. Only a court of probate could do that.

The Smith-Armistead lawyers produced twenty-seven of Hardy's personal letters and quoted from them to establish that he considered New Bern his home. The reply detailed the issue of a will, stating that neither Henrietta nor Elizabeth had seen such a document and making an "indignant denial of the gross and indecent charge" that they had suppressed or destroyed it. The allegation, they protested, was "unqualifiedly false."

John Carroll did not believe that he should be a defendant. He denied being the business agent of Henrietta and Elizabeth or that he had drawn their original bill of complaint. Yet he admitted having read it and proceeded to deny the existence of a will, that any animosity existed between Hardy and the Smith family, or that there was any duplicity in the settlement of his own wife's estate. Carroll affirmed that Hardy benefited greatly from his marriage to Frances; New Bern was Hardy's domicile, although he planned to move to Charleston; and at his death Hardy was indebted to Carroll in the still unpaid amount of $1,300. He accused the Crooms of suppressing statements from witnesses whose testimony was unfavorable to their cause. Carroll was not technically the agent of Henrietta and Elizabeth, but he was clearly and deeply involved as a close adviser in the case. Having made their replies, Henrietta and Elizabeth asked the judge to dismiss Richard's cross bill of complaint.

Smith-Armistead and Carroll had responded on September 9, 1840, but the Crooms did not reply until January 9, 1841. In their response, the Crooms accused Carroll of gathering evidence and obtaining favorable statements and depositions for Henrietta and Elizabeth. Bryan used the opportunity to explain how he became the administrator and why the course he had followed was the honorable one. Bryan had now come to accept Richard's view that the opposition forces had "destroyed, suppressed, or withheld" Hardy's will.

The other Crooms explained how Bryan had been chosen as administrator. The family members repeated specifically and in detail earlier statements buttressing the argument that they were the legitimate heirs to the estate. They produced a number of Hardy's letters as exhibits and expressly denied suppressing the statements of any witnesses as charged by Carroll in his "scandalous and defamatory imputation, so unnecessarily and recklessly made." They charged that Smith-Armistead had not produced pertinent documents and letters in their possession or accounted fully for Hardy's estate outside Florida and that such an accounting should be forthcoming before the case proceeded.[4]

The records showing what happened to Richard's cross bill of complaint cannot be found. Later events indicate that it was dismissed. As what might rightly be called "Richard's Sideshow" unfolded, the two sides continued to build their cases for the main trial. The Crooms concentrated on deposing people in Florida and North Carolina. As has been seen, the family had two major objectives. First, they wanted to prove that Hardy was a legal resident of Florida at the time of the *Home* disaster. Second, they wanted to prove that Hardy was the last Croom to die in the tragedy or, almost as important, establish that it was impossible to prove who perished last in the common disaster. The Smith-Armistead forces collected sworn depositions from passengers on the *Home* and from people acquainted with Hardy and his family. Curiously, at this stage of the controversy they did not depose many residents of New Bern. Like the Crooms, Smith-Armistead expected to win their case by proving legal residence: North Carolina, they contended, was Hardy's domicile; their second objective was to prove that William Henry survived his father and was the last family member to die. Because the trial became so strung out and included an appeal to the Florida state supreme court, many of the witnesses were deposed or testified several times. As time passed, the original list of witnesses was expanded, especially those called by Smith-Armistead.

As consuming as the litigation was, the principals had their private lives to lead. Henrietta Smith and Elizabeth Armistead went about their daily activities in New Bern. Theirs was a predictable, routine pattern and in sharp contrast to that of Bryan and the other Crooms. Bryan and Eveline, along with her mother and brother, had moved to Goodwood, completing and settling into the second and more commodious house that had been started. Bryan's obligations as administrator meant running the plantation and seeing to it that the slaves were working and that the cotton and corn crops were cultivated. The sale at Goodwood in 1839 of Hardy's household goods and other personal property has been mentioned. At that auction, or, more probably, a second one held the same year, the Croom heirs had a combination hiring out and sale of some of the Goodwood slaves.

By any standards of efficiency and profit, the auction was unsuccessful. Yet it revealed something about the Croom family. The sale was open to the public, although the family had done little to promote it, and the Crooms outnumbered the others who attended. Also present to bid were Dr. Edward Bellamy and George Whitfield. Among the other bidders were George Fisher, a tempestuous man who had once paid a fine of one cent and costs for assault and battery, and Michael Sedwith. The latter, who remembered a few others in the small crowd, made a successful bid of $155 to hire for the year Cornelius, a "boy not grown." Sedwith also bid $5.68 per stack for five stacks of fodder. Pleased that he had obtained such a bargain, the bidder quickly realized that the family did not want to separate the slaves. The Crooms' desire to keep the workforce at Goodwood was seen by their offer to return Sedwith's $155. He refused at first but finally agreed when he was given the stacks of fodder free. Since hiring out had none of the wrenching permanence of selling, the Crooms let Sedwith hire another young black for $250. He was to work in a brickyard owned by Colonel Wyatt (probably William Wyatt, best known as a civic booster and the owner of Tallahassee's Planters' Hotel). "The negroes appeared to be a likely lot," Sedwith said.

Had they chosen, the Crooms could have realized a large sum from the sale. Fortune, the slave driver whose abilities were well known in Leon County, and the others were valuable. Field hands brought high prices and specialists even higher. At the time, black carpenters such as Frank were worth $400 to $450 per year, and Ted, Fortune's brother, was a wagoner as well as a field worker. As it turned out, the Crooms sold or hired out only a few of their slaves and for less than their value. The family did most of the buying. By keeping the bidding low they caused the auction to fail. Because they could continue to use the slaves profitably, the Crooms took no major loss, but as Sedwith explained, the family could not bear to see the slaves separated.[5]

Amid the problems of litigation, settling Hardy's estate, and operating Goodwood, the Crooms moved to erect a monument commemorating the memory of their brother and his family. Pages 580–81, Case 1214, in the Leon County Courthouse are only a small section of Bryan's detailed year-by-year accounting of how he administered Hardy's estate. Yet they reveal the sale in February 1840 of a marble monument by the New York firm of R. I. Brown. The details—purchasing, insuring, and shipping—were handled by the Crooms' longtime commission merchant James Donaldson. Once the monument reached Florida, Richard A. Shine took charge and had it brought to the capital on the Tallahassee–St. Marks railroad. From there he drayed it to St. John's Episcopal Church on Monroe Street. Shine placed the monument in front of the church on the southwest corner and built an iron railing around it. Total expenses from the purchase in February to the installation in May were just over $575.

The memorial named Hardy, Frances, and the three children and noted the time and circumstances of their deaths. A moving paragraph paid tribute to Hardy:

> Amiable without weakness, learned without arrogance, wealthy without ostentation, and benevolent without parade. He sought not the world's admiration, but noiselessly pursued his path through life, finding his purest earthly pleasure in the bosom of his family, the society of his friends, and the companionship of his books. The best tribute to his worth is to be found in the affectionate remembrance of those, who having known him from boyhood, loved him while living and deplored him dead.

No matter how immediate and demanding their everyday existence, the Crooms realized that losing their case meant losing Goodwood. Crops follow an undeviating cycle of planting, cultivation, maturation, and harvesting. In response, Bryan carried out the necessary operations, but he was aware of how active the complainants were and that he could not afford to neglect the litigation. The acting master of Goodwood was pragmatic about his priorities. Determining the last survivor relied heavily on information offered by the Crooms' fellow passengers on the *Home,* and that testimony favored the plaintiffs. Hardy's physical condition was also an important factor in deciding which Croom perished last, and, again, the testimony, both in number of witnesses and in their points of view, aided the Smith-Armistead cause. Additionally, there were numerous witnesses who gave testimony or depositions that were neutral. That is, their information set the record straight (or straighter) concerning historical background, certain facts, and the sequence of events. The skill of the lawyers and the believability of the plaintiffs and defendants were equally important in affecting the superior court judge's decision (there was no jury).

The Crooms dug deep and in 1839 and 1840 produced a group of individuals who gave impressive evidence that Hardy was a bona fide resident of Florida when he died. The pro-Croom witnesses usually stressed that Florida's climate greatly benefited Hardy's health and was an important reason why he made the territory his permanent home. They also reached and articulated the rational conclusion that because Florida was the source of Hardy's income, economic self-determination argued that Florida would be his main residence. Beyond that, many Croom witnesses pointed to Hardy's commitment to enlarging his scientific research in Florida and establishing his experimental botanical garden at Goodwood. Nor did they fail to comment on Hardy's active dislike of New Bern's climate, his concern about the city's economic decline, and his sense of frustration at having his Florida plans thwarted by Frances's family.

Those points and more were made by George Whitfield, who lived in Florida himself. Whitfield added that Hardy considered himself a citizen of Florida. Benjamin B. Hawks, Bryan's brother-in-law, made a brief declaration supporting the defendants. Unfortunately, the thirty-eight-year-old Hawks became ill and died of unexplained causes in Tallahassee, on December 12, 1840. Other Croom relatives spoke to the residence argument.[6] Thomas S. Singleton, collector of the Port of New Bern, was the uncle of Eveline Croom on her mother's side. His testimony in 1840 echoed the points made by Whitfield. Singleton remembered Hardy's comment that he would not bring his slaves back for the best plantation in North Carolina.[7] A number of New Bernians who testified in 1840 were unrelated to the Crooms but shared the views of Whitfield and Singleton. They included Francis Lamotte, a merchant; George Wilson, a farmer; Robert Primrose, a merchant; John Harvey, an inspector of naval stores; and Peter Eustis, a doctor. A New Bern merchant named Michael Sente, like many of the others, stressed that Hardy considered North Carolina's climate injurious to his health. By contrast, he was reinvigorated and restored by his yearly visits to Florida.[8] Most of the New Bern witnesses remarked that Hardy was absent from the city much of the time, took little interest in local affairs or local and state politics, owned no property other than through his wife, and had long since sold his holdings in Lenoir County and removed his slaves to Florida.

Having established Hardy's Florida domicile through the testimony of New Bernians, the Croom lawyers shifted their focus to the territory itself. John Miller, a forty-year-old planter in Leon County, swore that Hardy considered Florida his residence and told him he was building a house for his family there. Henry J. Gaskins made the same points but with greater authority. As Hardy's overseer, he offered personal knowledge about the cottage at Goodwood and the second house under construction. Noting how Florida had improved Hardy's health, Gaskins stated categorically that the deceased Croom viewed Florida as his official residence. Stephen T. Miller, who knew the Crooms in North Carolina and had himself moved to Tallahassee, where he became a successful lawyer, declared that Hardy considered Florida and nowhere else his home. Miller said that Hardy spoke with bitterness about how Henrietta and Elizabeth had prevented his family from leaving North Carolina. Noah Thompson, a young planter who became one of the county's leading cotton producers, explained that he had been persuaded to migrate to Florida by Hardy because Croom liked the territory and lived there himself. Robert H. Berry of Leon County, who had given Hardy letters of introduction to use in Charleston, said that Croom only intended to make the South Carolina city a summer residence. Hardy told Berry of his dislike for New Bern and that in the winter of 1837 he planned to bring his family to live in Florida.[9] In addition to depositions, the Croom lawyers had numerous personal letters written by Hardy to Bryan. Henrietta and Elizabeth's counselors also produced some of Hardy's letters, especially those addressed to Frances. Yet the correspondence offered by the complainants did not match in volume or vividness that of the defendants. Other documentary evidence used by the Croom lawyers were poll lists showing that Hardy voted twice in Florida elections and various examples of deeds describing him as a resident of the territory.

With the aid of Carroll, who helped locate witnesses and handle logistical problems, the Smith-Armistead lawyers emphasized that Hardy's physical condition rendered him incapable of being the last Croom to survive. Dr. Hugh McLean of New York City testified in March 1840 that he knew the Crooms socially and occasionally prescribed medicine for Hardy. He saw the Crooms shortly before the *Home* sailed. It was Dr. McLean's opinion that the children were physically fit, while Frances "appeared to be in ordinary health." As for Hardy, "When I last saw him he was in a state of utter prostration and incapable of much physical exertion beyond a short walk." [10]

Dr. Francis Hawks, Hardy's lifelong friend, was deposed at the same time and place as McLean. Although he was not a physician, Dr. Hawks outlined Hardy's medical history. Hawks's diagnosis was that his early law partner in New Bern may have been consumptive. The eminent cleric was under the impression that the Crooms planned to leave North Carolina and settle in Charleston. Hawks had never heard Hardy refer to Florida as his home. [11]

Added to the testimony of McLean and Hawks, which was made more convincing by its impartiality, were remarks supplied by Dr. John Torrey. The longtime correspondent, intimate, and scientific colleague of Hardy was also deposed in New York City. Dr. Torrey saw Croom shortly before his departure for Charleston and believed that Croom planned to live there. The botanist also objectively recounted Hardy's health problems and stated that his planter friend was particularly weak in October 1837. [12] Impeaching the statements of McLean, Hawks, and Torrey would not be easy.

Whatever their reasons, the Smith-Armistead lawyers did not use the first stages of the dispute to depose many citizens of New Bern. Instead of establishing Hardy's North Carolina citizenship (which they would do later), the plaintiffs concentrated on which Croom was the last to die. To do so they depended primarily on the recollections of various passengers aboard the *Home*. The depositions of individual survivors and the cumulative effect of their statements hurt the defendants' cause. For example, young Conrad Quinn of Jersey City, New Jersey, was deposed in New York City. Quinn remembered Croom's feebleness, and, while declining to make a definitive statement, he believed that William Henry survived his father.[13]

John Bishop, a gardener who lived in New York, gave his deposition in Athens, Georgia, in September 1839. His testimony was important because he was on the piece of wreckage that William Henry clung to before losing his grip and drowning. After stating what he knew, Bishop speculated that when Hardy was swept overboard he might also have seized some means of support and survived for a time. Then early in March 1840, Bishop received a letter from Carroll in New York telling him that he was to testify again and to come by his office. Apparently Bishop did so, and his second deposition was less tentative. Bishop said that the feeble (the word most often used to describe Hardy) passenger had become exhausted by his bailing efforts. Asked about the order of survival, the witness was now firm in his belief that Hardy died before his son.[14] The defendants could not prove that undue influence had been exerted on Bishop to change his testimony.

Henry Vanderzee, a clerk from Charleston, had also shared the piece of wreckage with William Henry. He corroborated Bishop's statements but had no opinion about who survived last. Indeed, no passenger was precise about the time of Hardy's death. Even so, Vanderzee offered more positive evidence about the exact time when William Henry died. Andrew A. Lovegreen, a Charlestonian, described how he swam five or ten minutes before riding a piece of wreckage to shore. From his own experience Lovegreen believed that a strong swimmer might have lasted twenty minutes in the powerful surf, and he concluded that Hardy's physical prowess was crucial to his survival in a hurricane.[15] Benjamin B. Hussey added to the image of Hardy as a man too frail to battle a raging storm. He remembered, as did others, seeing and hearing William Henry crying to his father to save him.[16]

Mathilda Schroeder, the Charleston storekeeper who was impressed by William Henry, further strengthened the Smith-Armistead case. Among other recollections, she saw Justina Rosa washed overboard, saw

William Henry after her last glimpse of Hardy, and believed that only a powerful man and a good swimmer could have reached shore without support. Specific about time, she believed William Henry survived the others by half an hour.[17]

The witnesses mentioned here and others established that Hardy, Frances, Justina Rosa, and William Henry (until he got separated) were together as a group and were swept overboard within minutes of each other. Henrietta Mary was in another part of the *Home*. Without doubt the plaintiffs benefited from the information provided by surviving passengers. Still, not one witness actually saw Hardy perish. No matter how weak he might have been, the defendants' contention that Croom was a strong swimmer was not contested. It was possible that once in the sea Hardy could have grabbed a piece of debris and kept afloat. That was the rebuttal the defense planned to offer at the trial.

All the time-consuming and expensive preparations by the Crooms and Smith-Armistead were finally completed. The lawyers were ready with their depositions and their witnesses, and the trial should have been held in 1841. That did not happen. Instead, the entire controversy went into legal limbo. Had Richard Croom's cross bill of complaint stalled the Smith-Armistead case? Did both sides, each fearful of the other's evidence, agree on a delay? The adversaries reached no out-of-court settlement, and the bitter feelings remained intense. Answers to why the trial was not held are speculative and unclear, but it was put on hold for well over a decade.

Trial or no trial, Bryan moved from administrator of Goodwood to owner of the plantation. As noted, with the legal dispute postponed and with the possibility that it might never take place, Bryan and Eveline (along with her mother and brother, Benjamin, who continued to live with them until his death) gathered their five house servants and moved from their temporary quarters in Tallahassee out to Goodwood. Once there, they began refining and expanding the plantation, and by 1840 Bryan had established a routine at Goodwood and was taking an active part in local affairs. Religion was and would remain an important part of Eveline's life, and in short order she was christened in St. John's Episcopal Church.

An accepted and popular way for a citizen to show concern was to sign a petition taking a public stand on some issue. Although he never had sought and never would seek elective office, Bryan joined some fellow Whigs in 1840 in petitioning President Martin Van Buren. They informed the Democratic chief executive of their feelings: his appointment of Robert Raymond Reid as territorial governor did not represent the true sentiments of Tallahassee's citizens. In the well-established tradition and spirit of partisan politics, they ignored the native South Carolinian's past services as a congressman and judge in Georgia and as a judge in Florida. Reid's renowned oratorical talents were also lost on them. More positively, in 1841 Croom signed a nonpartisan petition recommending the appointment of a man named Minor Walker as United States marshal.[18]

With no immediate crisis facing him, Bryan renegotiated his agreement to sell Goodwood and Rocky Comfort to Richard. On October 4, 1842, the brothers signed a new document announcing that they found it "mutually satisfactory to cancel said agreement & dissolve the bargain in reference to said land & negroes so that they [were to] stand to each other as if the [agreement] had never been made."[19] Exactly one month later Bryan paid Richard $15,000 for his two-sevenths—including real and personal—of Hardy's estate.[20] It seems safe to infer that the agreement in 1839 for Richard to purchase Goodwood and Rocky Comfort from Bryan was a legal tactic and never intended to go into effect.

Then, as noted, in January 1843, Bryan formally purchased the parts of Hardy's estate owned by William and George Alexander and that same month sold Rocky Comfort to the youngest Croom brother. In the 1840s and 1850s Goodwood emerged as one of Leon County's largest and most productive cotton plantations. Few Floridians or southerners owned more slaves or ginned more bales of cotton than Bryan. The Second Seminole War ended by 1842, and the effects of the financial panic finally dissipated. Like Bryan, the other Crooms also prospered, and their numbers increased. Family members maintained the unwavering Croom tradition of bestowing on their children names favored since the eighteenth century. The following chapter updates the lives and times of the Crooms and describes how Goodwood became the nexus, the vitalizing center, for the family.

Hardy B. Croom. Cofounder
of Goodwood plantation.
Portrait done about 1835.

Bryan H. Croom. Brother
of Hardy Croom and cofounder
of Goodwood plantation.
Daguerreotype made about 1845.

Frances Smith Croom.
Wife of Hardy Croom.
Portrait done about 1835.

Henrietta Smith. Mother
of Frances Croom. Portrait
done about 1858.

William Whitfield Croom. Half
brother of Hardy and Bryan.
Photograph taken about 1855.

Julia Stephens Croom. Wife
of William Whitfield Croom.
Photograph taken about 1850.

Elizabeth Whitfield Croom
Bellamy. Daughter of William
Whitfield and Julia Stephens
Croom. Photograph taken
about 1860.

Stephens Croom. Son
of William Whitfield and Julia
Stephens Croom. Photograph
taken about 1860.

Richard Croom, brother of Hardy and Bryan, and two of his children,
Mary and Nicholas. Photograph taken about 1855.

Front view of Goodwood mansion. Photograph taken in 1885.
This is how the house looked in the 1840s.

South and west sides of Goodwood mansion. Photograph taken in 1885.

Comte de Castelnau's rendering of Hardy Croom's cabin on Lake
Lafayette in Leon County, Florida, 1836.

The wreck of the steamboat *Home*, October 9, 1837, which claimed the lives of Hardy and Frances Croom, their three children, and Frances's aunt. Illustration courtesy of the Outer Banks History Center, Manteo, North Carolina.

Memorial monument at St. John's Episcopal Church, Tallahassee, Florida, dedicated to Hardy Croom and his family.

6

Brick and Mortar and
"Very Likely Slaves"

The home begun by Hardy Croom and completed and occupied by Bryan and Eveline was located in the northwest corner of Section 29. It faced west and was set on a hill whose 150-foot elevation (lofty by Florida standards and the highest in Tallahassee) permitted welcome breezes to engage in combat, no matter how unequal, with the heat and humidity. The incline sloped southwest for an eighth of a mile toward the road connecting Tallahassee with rural Leon County and communities such as Miccosukee. North of the home were clear springs that assured a supply of fresh water for the Crooms and their slaves.

The house whose construction was directed by overseer Gaskins and whose chimney and other brick were supplied by Richard A. Shine is still extant. It has gone through various changes and is currently known as the Guest House. Without doubt Gaskins utilized the labor skills of Frank, the expert carpenter, and other Goodwood slaves for the construction work. Originally the first floor had two rooms and was a double unit with front and rear entries. There appears to have been a stair in the middle of the house that led to the living area on the second floor and to the basement. How the basement was used is uncertain, but

113

most likely it was kept habitable rather than being utilized as a warming kitchen.

The kitchen was located a few feet south of the house and was built
at the same time or added by Bryan and Eveline shortly after they
moved to Goodwood plantation. Still standing, the kitchen, like the
Guest House, has been altered and remodeled several times. As built by
Gaskins or Shine, it was a single room, a simple rectangle with doors
located on the south and west elevations. The kitchen faced west and
had a basement that was used as a root cellar. A third contemporary
structure, a two-room building facing east, was constructed across from
the kitchen. The two buildings were no more than fifty feet apart. The
small, unfloored structure was apparently constructed in part to shelter
a spring and was probably used as a place to keep milk and other
perishables cool. The Croom complex consisting of a home, kitchen,
and cooling room was, as described by various people who knew it, comfortable and adequate. There were also slave quarters, as well as barns,
stables, and other outbuildings.

Despite the soundness of its construction, the home was clearly un-
suited as a permanent dwelling for a major planter. Having selected
Goodwood plantation as their residence, Bryan and Eveline set in motion the construction of a home suitable to their station. The legal challenge by Henrietta Smith and Elizabeth Armistead to their ownership
of Hardy's estate still loomed. But assuming that possession was nine-
tenths of the law and trusting in the legality of their claim, the couple
hesitated no longer.[1]

There has been speculation about when Goodwood was built and who
the architect or contractor was. It seems likely that construction was
begun in the mid-1840s and that the builder was the aforementioned
Shine. Without a formal title or degree, he was an architect and engi-
neer and an important but largely unheralded early settler in Florida's
capital. A person of impressive height and weight, Shine had links
to New Bern, and his wife was also a North Carolinian. The couple
had migrated to Leon County about 1830 and were longtime friends
of Bryan and Eveline. As a contractor-architect, Shine built private
homes—his own on 200 Foot Street (Park Avenue); that of William and
Martha Williams Bloxham (parents of future governor William D.

Bloxham) on Calhoun Street; and probably the Brokaw-McDougall house, which closely resembled Goodwood, on North Meridian Street.

As a public builder, Shine undertook and completed his largest project: the new state capitol, completed in 1845. When he finished the Catholic church in 1854, the church's members were unable to pay all of his fee of $2,562.70. The obliging Shine undertook to collect $400 in unpaid subscriptions and credited it to the church's debt to him. In 1857 he directed the work of building the Pensacola and Georgia Railroad through Tallahassee east toward Alligator (Lake City), where it connected with another line to Jacksonville. Tallahasseeans marveled at Shine's engineering feat: a deep and dramatic railroad cut through the eastern part of town that symbolized an opening to a larger world for the provincial capital.[2]

A shrewd and active businessman—Leon County deed books recorded at least sixty-six of his real estate and other transactions—Shine profited from his brickyard. Located on the eastern outskirts of Tallahassee near Goodwood, Shine's yard manufactured bricks that were notable for their deep brown color dotted with darker specks of an ironlike substance. His largest profits came in 1843 following a disastrous fire that destroyed much of downtown Tallahassee. Most of the rebuilding was accomplished with bricks from Shine's yard. Unfortunately and unknown to him, time proved that the clay used to produce the bricks was soft and crumbly.

Shine and his wife raised a large family. Not content with economic activities, he was an active promoter of public education and the proud captain of the Leon Riflemen, a local militia company. Active in politics, he was a longtime Whig representative, serving continuously from 1844 (one term in the territorial Legislative Council) to 1855 in the state House of Representatives (four terms). By 1860 Shine was a wealthy man, owning thirty-one slaves and possessing a personal estate worth $26,000 and real estate valued at $40,000.[3]

Testifying in 1857, Shine said, "About eight years ago I was engaged in building a large house for Mr. Croom on his place."[4] He was talking about Goodwood. The home was an aesthetically appealing three-storied structure located only twenty or thirty feet south of the other buildings. It was flanked on the east by the kitchen and the occupied house and on the west by the cooling room. Goodwood faced toward the south. The building had features that were essentially Greek Revival in design, but it was one of the first homes in Florida to be built in the Italianate style just becoming popular in the United States.

Southerners found the style, which was a facet of the European-based romantic movement of the nineteenth century, particularly attractive. Like Italy, the South had a hot climate and was a region of broad landscapes and vistas. Goodwood's Italianate "look" was effected by its exterior features and ornamentation: the floor to ceiling windows; the handsome lantern (a square cupola on the roof that, while ornamental, served the more utilitarian purpose of admitting light and air and improving ventilation); the hipped roof, bracketed cornices, cast-iron columns, and grilles; the broad veranda (like most southerners, the Crooms did a lot of front porch sitting); and the use of color—Goodwood was probably finished in a fieldstone hue with contrasting trim.

Bryan and Eveline spared no expense in building their home. The mansion's main portion was fifty-five feet square with exterior-bearing walls and two longitudinal interior-bearing partitions that formed a central hall on the ground floor and defined circulation space on the upper two floors. The home was made with Shine's brick scored with stucco to simulate stonework. The exterior walls were two feet (three in some cases) thick. Hand-hewn and saw-sawn timber was the wood used in the construction—the floors were of wide heart pine. The original design was square with five bays and had a low overhanging pyramidal roof and decorative brackets. The front roof peak had a Gothic-style window, while the front facade had cast-iron trim. Goodwood's well-used main entry was a pair of six-panel heart pine doors with fixed glass top panels and a fixed glass transom. The doors' silver-plated hardware was probably imported from England. The rear entry was similar in design.

A visitor to Goodwood would immediately notice the first floor's almost symmetrical plan: a wide center hall with two principal rooms or parlors (with ceilings of fifteen feet) on either side. There were frescoed ceilings in the north and south parlors (the images in the south parlor were based on Aesop's fables and the four seasons). Elaborate chandeliers in the parlors and elaborate plaster trim and ceiling medallions reflected the Italianate influence. A ten-foot pier mirror, more often called a looking glass by mid-nineteenth-century Americans, was located in each parlor and added to the sense of symmetry. Beneath each mirror was a thirty-inch marble-topped console table. A mirror eight feet high and six feet wide was hung over the mantle in each parlor, and all four of the mirrors were in the French rococo style.

Other striking features were the sixteen sets of French doors, each containing eight panes of glass, around the entire first floor. The quality of construction was evident in the large panes of glass used in the windows. New ways of making glass sections bigger were coming in and were expensive. Each room on the first two floors contained a fireplace. Family lore has it that the marble used in the eight fireplaces was imported from Italy. Whether the story is true or not, the stone was of fine quality—six of the fireplaces (five white ones and a single black one) were plain, while the remaining two were white and highly carved.

Located between the east rooms, a mahogany staircase with semicircular flights rose to the second floor, which duplicated the plan of the first. The stairs continued to an attic on the third floor that was divided into one large room and two smaller rooms. A wood circular stair led from the attic to the lantern. There was a basement, used primarily as a warming kitchen, that could be entered from the outside and was connected to the nearby kitchen by steps protected by a small portico. A service stair from the basement opened east of the main stair and may have extended to the second floor. The large home's 7,588 square feet were not too many because the Croom household of three was frequently enlarged by the visits of family members and their children. It was not uncommon for their guests, particularly if they were family, to remain for weeks.[5]

The attractive site had Florida's profuse natural vegetation and trees, and although Bryan did not install the botanical garden that Hardy planned, flowers and shrubs were planted. The house itself combined function and beauty; nor did the ornamentation intrude on the simple form and the pervading sense of quiet.

The Croom family furnished their home with new furniture. The pieces that survive are heavy mahogany and mahogany veneer in the Empire style—also known in England and in Charleston and Savannah as Regency or Pillar and Scroll. An outgrowth of Grecian styles, Empire was considered both suitable and desirable for Greek Revival or Italianate homes. Leon County plantation mistresses and their counterparts in antebellum middle Florida liked Empire furniture. Eveline and others were attracted by the style's overall boxy shapes and its flat and polished surfaces with rounded ends and gentle curves. Most of the Crooms' furniture was later distributed among relatives, and a large part of it was destroyed by fire.

Shine built a home for the Crooms that increased in appeal with the passage of time. It was furnished fashionably, and the grounds were dotted with live oaks and other trees. The natural vegetation and grasses blended with planted flowers and shrubs, and the overall result would have pleased Hardy and Frances Croom.

With his own experience and that gained working with Hardy, Bryan became a prosperous planter on a scale that matched the grandeur of his home. The Goodwood that he obtained from the Croom family members comprised 2,480 acres. Final settlements were required, and between 1844 and 1850 Bryan made payments totaling $11,558 to the heirs of Lafayette for Sections 27, 28, and 29. Robert W. Williams negotiated the settlements. Goodwood, including Section 26, lay on an east-west line in the southern part of the Lafayette Grant.[6] In 1847 Bryan added Sections 11, 14, and 23 in the township. They adjoined each other immediately north of Section 26, so that what had been horizontal holdings became vertical as well. Bryan paid Dr. John A. Craig (member of the original firm of Nuttall, Braden, and Craig) $30 cash and $10 an acre.[7]

Goodwood, like other southern plantations and farms, did not benefit from scientific agricultural practices. Land planted yearly in cotton without lying fallow or without crop rotation became depleted. No commercial fertilizer was available. George T. Ward, owner of Southwood plantation, leading Whig politician, and Union Bank officer, testified, "I knew the [Croom] lands well before any part of them was cleared and since. They were first rate lands." The respected Ward, a staunch

Presbyterian, said of Bryan, "[He] has been considered a very successful planter and has been understood to make large crops." Still, after a number of years the lands were "very much worn."[8] Leon County planters, the Crooms included, mistreated the soil. Bryan's real estate activities were not unusual. He simply followed the standard practice of southern planters: secure more land to maintain and enlarge crop production. Goodwood now had 4,400 acres and resembled a reverse capital letter *L*.

Bryan's property had become so large that he split it into two farming operations and, in effect, into two plantations, each with its own overseers and slaves. According to Richard Saunders, who had lived in Florida since 1828, "The lands were considered the best in the county."[9] Gaskins, who was either replaced or joined in 1838 by C. C. Kyle at a salary of $700, left Goodwood by the mid-forties to farm on his own. Dead by 1852, Gaskins was succeeded by Hinton J. Saunders (no relation to Richard Saunders), who became the overseer on Hardy and Bryan's older property, and by Francis Hyman, who served the same function on the lands newly acquired by Bryan.

The slaves were basic to Goodwood's operation, and their well-being and productivity were fundamental to success and profit. Bryan had his own slaves, who were brought from Rocky Comfort plantation. Like Hardy, he was solicitous about the welfare of his bondsmen. In 1839 one of the slave women from Hardy's estate became terminally ill. Bryan described bringing her into his house, where a young slave woman took care of her for more than two weeks. His "white family attended her regularly for sickness and administered medicine & such things from the table [as] she was able to eat during her sickness." Bryan added, "I provided her with a coffin and winding sheet & had her buried." The expenses came to $16.[10]

Goodwood's owner was concerned with more than the desire to protect an economic investment, although Croom assembled his labor force with the idea of profit in mind. On January 11, 1847, he paid James E. Bettner of Leon County $2,500 for eight slaves. In purchasing Jenny, Julia, Peggy, Robert, Fanny, Minerva, May, and Dallas, Bryan concentrated heavily on women. He expected to benefit from the contract's standard terms guaranteeing to him "the present and future issue and increase of the females."[11]

Bryan also had the use of Ann Hawks's slaves. His hiring of her chattels in return for a money payment and furnishing room and board for her and Benjamin has been discussed. Then in 1837 Bryan and his mother-in-law made a new arrangement. The residence setup was retained, and Bryan agreed that $800 a year was a fair payment for the hire of her nineteen slaves. The new settlement lasted until 1856, although three or four slaves were withdrawn from Bryan's possession when Benjamin married, and a like number were hired out in 1840. Bryan used the labor of Ann's slaves (only one death among them was recorded) to his advantage, and by 1856 they had increased to forty-eight. Even better, Ann did not insist on any annual money payments from Bryan, and none were made.[12] Clearly the ministrations that Eveline and Bryan unhesitatingly provided for Ann Hawks were not one-sided.

The slaves who had been Hardy's property were a major part of the laborers at Goodwood. In 1857 Hinton J. Saunders, who served as overseer on the older part of Goodwood for the years 1846–47, left important testimony about some of the slaves. As he put it, "I cultivated good land. I was paid $350 the first year and $400 the last year I stayed with Mr. Croom." During those years, he ran about twenty plows. "The negroes on the place were very likely, and the force ought to have increased from that time to this [1857] (by) twenty hands."[13]

Overseer for an operation that included a number of minor crops, Saunders was mainly concerned with 300 acres in corn and, especially, with 500 acres in cotton. In 1846–47 each place on Goodwood produced an average of 300 bales of cotton. Almost without exception and regardless of the slaves' ages, Saunders referred to the males as boys and to the females, unless they were children, as women. His descriptions of the slaves refer to 1846–47, and the direct quotes from Saunders's deposition are cited in a single footnote.

In the last decades of the twentieth century, historical scholarship on every aspect of slavery in the antebellum South has produced a large number of important monographs. Collectively, historians and others have used new sources and new interpretations to reveal the slave world as complex and diverse, with family and religion as major components. No student of the peculiar institution is without debt to Frederick Law Olmsted, the keen observer from New England who toured and wrote about the South of the 1850s. His published works, abridged into *The Cotton Kingdom* . . . (1861), closely documented and analyzed the institution of slavery. Olmsted's observations about slave drivers usually paralleled the situation that existed at Goodwood.

"A good driver," Olmsted wrote, "is very valuable and usually holds office for life. His authority is not limited to the direction of labour in the field, but extends to the general deportment of the negroes. He is made to do the duties of policeman, and even of police magistrate."[14] According to Richard Saunders, the Leon Countian who knew the Crooms and their land, Fortune was exceptional. "A good driver such as Fortune [practices] a trade which a very few negroes have the talent or judgment to acquire, the best mode of his valuation would be to rank him with a blacksmith or a carpenter."[15]

Olmsted noted: "Having generally had long experience on the plantation, the advice of the drivers is commonly taken in nearly all the administration, and frequently they are, *de facto,* the managers. Orders are important points of the plantation economy, I have heard [orders] given by the proprietor directly to them, without the overseer's being consulted or informed of them. . . . [The] overseer consults the drivers on all important points, and is governed by their advice." He remembered one "gentleman [who] told [him] that he would rather, if the law would permit it, have some of his negroes for overseers, than any white man he had ever been able to obtain in that capacity."[16] "Fortune," Richard Saunders asserted, "is a good [driver] & understands his business[;] a year or two ago he had charge of fifteen or sixteen hands outright."[17] Overseer Hinton Saunders said, "[Fortune] was a good planter and driver. . . . It is hard to estimate his value. I think he is [of] more value to Mr. Croom than any negro on the place. He is as good a driver as I ever saw if not better."

The frank and colloquial overseer Saunders revealed Goodwood as having a number of slave families; the unit headed by Fortune was especially close knit. Saunders described the patriarch as "a smart old man 55 or 60 years old . . . a driver and a favorite negro and reliable man." Sarah was Fortune's wife, and one of her children was a daughter named Amy (Saunders did not provide her age). "The young woman was afflicted with fits, and the old woman [Sarah] took care of Amy and cooked for Fortune's family until she became disabled in 1847 from an injury to one of her feet, which resulted in cancer. She and Amy both died as I recall in 1847."

Polly, about twenty-eight or thirty, was Fortune's oldest child. She was "a good field hand." The twenty-five-year-old Abby was "reputedly" Fortune's daughter. "[She was] a small woman and a good hand and healthy. Her eldest child, a mulatto and child of a white man, was a girl seven or eight years old, badly afflicted with white swelling. I think her name was Eliza." Abby also had a younger child, about two or three years old. Milly, next in age to her sister Abby, "was a strong, likely, young woman. She was a full hand and would have hired [in 1846–47] for 80 or 100 dollars per year." She never had any children and died in 1848. Fortune's son Jesse was about twenty-three-years-old. "He was a number one hand, probably the quickest on the place. . . . He was sound & healthy." Mingo, another of Fortune's sons, was more able-bodied than Jesse, and although "not quite as quick," he was "a good hand and a young healthy man, younger than Jesse." Little Fortune was named for his father and was "a very likely plough boy—about sixteen or seventeen years old—active, smart and healthy."

Ted, Fortune's brother, was between forty and forty-five. Saunders considered him "a likely man," who was "a good hand and a waggoner [*sic*]." The overseer did not mention whether Ted had a wife and children. Fortune and Sarah, together with their six children and grandchildren, gave order and stability to black life on the plantation and to Goodwood itself. Within the harsh confines of slavery theirs was a life that was complex, meaningful, and bonded.

Other slaves, including Charles and Mirna and Sambo and Barsheba, were married. Charles was "a one eyed man—about thirty five years old. His diseased eye would sometimes inflame and would prevent his working for two or three days[;] in other respects he was a full hand[,] an ambitious man, and a good ox driver." His wife, Mirna, was "a good woman hand—healthy—and about 28 or 30 years old. . . . She had no children." Sambo, forty-five or fifty, was "afflicted": "I think he was ruptured and had the piles very badly. He took care of the stables, and kept [them] clean and prepared the food for the mules[;] in this respect he answered as well as a good hand, but he would be of little value in the field. He was a pretty good conditioned negro."

At about forty-five, Barsheba, Sambo's wife, was "past the time for bearing children, and was of but little value—did but little work in the field . . . stayed about the quarter [and] took care of the sick & children." The difficulty was that Barsheba had problems with her uterus. Dr. T. H. Holt visited her five times between August 17 and October 25, 1842. After his initial examination the physician treated her with morphine and mustard and fitted her with a pessary. His bill was $16.[18]

Barsheba and Sambo had four children, "the youngest of which, a smart little boy, remained at the quarters and about the stable helping his father." Saunders added, "I think that she and her youngest child were worth their board and clothes." Two of Barsheba and Sambo's other children, Cornelius and Sam, worked in the field. Cornelius "was a good hand and sound," while Sam was "a strong, athletic young man, sound and a good hand, he was about twenty one years old." Sambo and Barsheba's only daughter, Sarah, "probably about sixteen—a very likely girl—did not do the work of a full hand, had no child while [Saunders] was there. She would have hired for fifty dollars probably."

Several blacks described by Saunders were examples of how age, health, talent, and sex determined the duties of most slaves. The fifty-year-old Nanny "did the cooking and washing for [Saunders] and family. She had prolapsus uteri and wore a pessary. She was incapacitated for field work, but was a neat and good conditioned woman and useful for housework and as a cook and house servant was worth fifty dollars a year." There was also Old Mary (she was only fifty), who "stayed about the quarters and took care of the children. She had no young children of her own." Tenah "had a family of children and was a good breeder, but for breeding would have been a good hand—about thirty years old." Frank "was an excellent negro and about 35 years of age. . . . [He was] a good carpenter and did the blacksmith work on the place in 1847." According to Saunders, "[Frank] was and is worth I should say at least $300.00 a year." Frank's importance was seen in his treatment. Shoes were a major item of expense for planters and were usually bought in lots. Croom purchased Frank's shoes by separate order.[19] Will "was a very good hand and sometimes worked in the blacksmith shop[;] he was thirty or thirty five years old. Smart good boy, and a full hand in the field."

Saunders described other slaves:

Sylvester: "a lad—do not recollect his age—[was a] robust healthy boy."

Edney: "[a] pretty good hand when I was there, but getting old—aged probably about forty."

Celia: "a young woman . . . and not very healthy."

Moses: "a likely boy, 18 or 19 years of age, and a good hand."

"Sydia and her daughters Milly and Maria were tolerable women hands. Not the best—they were healthy, but not very likely—the daughters were young women grown, and Sydia was about 38 or 40 years old. Her other children did not work in the field. Washington was the name of one of them, and was a likely boy."

"Ben was a good hand 25 or so years old."

"Amos was a good hand a few years younger than Ben."

"Wat was a good hand—hard to manage, but sound, active & robust, about 25 years old."

"Pompey was about 30 years as well as I recollect—was injured in one arm, or shoulder by rheumatism or some other disease. He was a good disposed negro and for ploughing was as good a hand as any."

Only thirty, Phoebe had six or seven children but was handicapped by "milk-leg" and did not work in the field. "[Her] children were very likely. . . . One of them was named William[,] a smart boy who works in the field, and ploughed while I was there. He was about 16 years old. He was worth about $74 a year. Godfrey was another child of Phoebe, but did not work in the field[;] he carried water for the hands, a smart boy, about 10 years old. . . . I think there was another still younger by the name of Andy or Handy." "Dennis was about 30 or 35 years old—an excellent hand."

Although Saunders's memory was imperfect—"There was a boy by the name of Abram on the place. I do not remember him particularly"—it served him well in evaluating many of Bryan's slaves and recounting their characteristics. Saunders knew some of the slaves who worked under overseer Francis Hyman. Two of them were the brothers Ishmael and Buster. "Ishmael was a very good hand about 25 years old. Sound—good disposed boy." His younger brother Buster was "a likely boy and good hand." Together they "and a boy by the name of Luke, a likely boy, worked under Mr. Hyman." So did Daniel and his wife, Esther. Daniel, who "kept the stable," was "about 50 years old—and pretty deaf—he was a steady hand, [a] vigorous man for his age. His labor was sufficient to support his family, worth $50 per year." "[Esther] was about 48 years old and was weakly. I think she had no young children with her. She stayed at the quarters."[20]

Bryan owned many slaves in addition to those mentioned by Saunders. In 1850 the number had risen to 197, making him one of Florida's and Leon County's largest planters.[21] The agricultural census of 1850 for Goodwood (statistics for both divisions may have been combined, but a large amount of Bryan's acreage was not accounted for) revealed a large but not highly diversified plantation. Croom reported 600 acres of improved land and 1,240 unimproved acres. The plantation was valued at $19,200. Corn production amounted to 4,000 bushels. Corn was the basic staple of the slaves, who ate it as cornbread and as a vegetable. Whites, including the Crooms, also ate cornbread and, able to afford the more expensive milling process, ground the corn into white flour to make bread, biscuits, pies, and cakes. Peas and beans were planted among the corn, and Goodwood's 100 bushels provided food for blacks and whites. Fodder (the leaves) and the tops of the cornstalks were fed to the livestock. Oats was another grain planted at Goodwood, and the yield in 1850 was 150 bushels. Like other planters, Croom probably used the oats as special feed for his fourteen riding and carriage horses.

Sweet potatoes were eaten by the slaves at almost every meal, while their consumption by the Crooms, though less often, was regular. The plantation produced 1,000 bushels in 1850. The year's total of cane sugar was four hogsheads, each weighing 1,000 pounds. Even so, Croom regularly purchased sugar from commercial merchants. The rice crop's yield of 900 pounds provided variety for the slaves but was incidental. Rice was cultivated like other row crops. Since no irrigation system was available, its production bore no resemblance to the elaborate process employed along the coast and sea islands of Georgia and South Carolina. Farm machinery was probably undervalued at $500, and the nine mules and three oxen reported could not have sustained the plantation.[22]

Considering the Croom family and their numerous guests and the large number of slaves, the census statistics regarding cattle and hogs seem unusual—at first glance. No cattle, milk, or beef was listed (probably to escape paying taxes on them), and there were sixty-five hogs. The value of livestock was $1,310, most of it represented by horses, and the value of animals slaughtered was an insignificant $200. Because cattle and hogs ranged freely, planters had to keep their cultivated fields fenced. The fences were wooden rails set in zigzag fashion; they were expensive, and their maintenance, requiring much time and effort, was usually accomplished during the off-season winter months.[23]

Just keeping up with unrestrained cows and hogs was difficult, but even more important was the problem of thievery. Hogs were stolen and eaten by slaves (and to a lesser extent by whites). The pilfering was considered fair game and was on such a scale that Croom and other planters sometimes found themselves purchasing pork. Overseer Saunders reported, "[There] was no meat bought while I remained on the place, and I raised meat enough while I was there." The small value of slaughtered animals told a different story, and, in fact, Croom often imported large amounts of prime pork and bacon. "Supposing no meat [was] raised on the place," Saunders calculated, "the expense of buying meat would be about $1000 a year, if pork was at $20 per Bbl." Not that much was spent. Yet Croom elected to supplement home production, including butter, eggs, and lard, with market products and concentrate on cotton.[24] The considerable population of Goodwood relished the food supplements caught or shot in the nearby woods, lakes, and rivers. Fish, wild animals, and birds were in abundant supply.

Cotton was the money crop, and on Goodwood 236 bales were ginned in 1850. The number, although impressive, was greatly reduced from previous years. The significant decline for the crop year 1849–50 was felt across the South, and in Florida the number of bales dropped by almost 20,000. "The excessively hot weather which prevailed for several days after the heavy rains has stripped [the planters'] cotton of a large portion of its forms," the *Tallahassee Floridian and Journal* reported in August 1849. "The stalks in many places are almost bare of fruit except that which has already matured." The paper noted, "The showers for a day or two past may arrest the further falling off, but these came too late to save anything like a full crop." Beyond that, "We have been told also that a few caterpillars have been seen. If they should come now in any large numbers, the crop will be cut very short." Even in a bad year cotton was the basis of Leon County's wealth—16,107 bales were produced in 1850, and at least prices were good, ranging from nine cents to nine and three-quarters cents a pound depending on quality. The fleecy staple was equally important to Bryan Croom.[25] Cotton was the unchallenged monarch, and Goodwood—bustling, productive, graced by a handsome mansion—was a worthy fiefdom.

By 1850 Goodwood was an important part of Leon County's agricultural kingdom. Leon was Florida's only county in which the cash value of farms was more than a million dollars ($1,751,050). No county was within 30,000 improved acres of Leon's 80,952, and it was number one in cash value of farm machinery ($88,578). Leon led Florida in horses, mules, and working oxen. It was ranked first in number of sheep, second in hogs, and had a commanding lead in the value of livestock ($359,623) and value of animals slaughtered ($65,683). Besides being the banner county in cotton production, Leon led in bushels of corn and was second in bushels of sweet potatoes. It was the state's only county with over 10,000 population (11,442) and more than 5,000 slaves (8,203).[26] A small minority within the population, planters such as Bryan Croom dominated the county's economic, political, and social life. The latter 1840s and the following decade were transitional years for the United States, the South, and Florida. The people of the South and North became increasingly distrustful of each other, as tensions grew tighter and the nation stumbled toward war. On a broad scale the sectional crises were subjects of discussion, debate, and action. More personally, the period was both triumphant and catastrophic for Bryan and Eveline and the other Crooms. Their individual fates were worked out or occurred by chance—yet they shared the common and powerful bond of family. Older generations overlapped with newer generations, as the children of William Croom and his two wives saw their own children become adults, marry, and have children of their own. Goodwood plantation played its usual role of both anchor and way station until the banked fires of legal dispute burst into destructive flames that brought a final and bitter resolution.

7

Some Crooms, the Bellamys,
and Their Ventures

Bryan and Eveline maintained contacts with their kin that varied from casual to close. Although relations were more intimate with some than with others, the Crooms, unlike many large families, had no serious generational disputes. Bryan's half brother William and his wife, Julia, lived in nearby Quincy. The Goodwood Crooms visited back and forth with the couple and their two children, Elizabeth Whitfield, born on April 17, 1837, and Cicero Stephens, born on December 12, 1839 (both in Quincy). As discussed earlier, another of Bryan's half brothers, George Alexander, more often known as Aleck, and his wife, Julia, owned Rocky Comfort plantation in Gadsden County. Bryan and Eveline's visits with them and their growing family became even more frequent after they moved to Leon County in the 1850s.

Family ties were revealed in 1853 when Stephens (his first name, Cicero, was dropped except for signing formal documents) was the guest of Bryan and Eveline and Aleck and Julia during the Christmas season. His mother was visiting in New York City and was joined later by William. It is not clear which parent Elizabeth (known in the family as Lizzie) accompanied. Stephens's mother wrote him, "You must spend some time with your Uncle Bryan [and Aunt Eveline] and be polite and accommodating to them. Your Aunt E & Uncle B are very polished and polite and will be apt to notice any rudeness in you."[1] A week later, Stephens received another letter from his mother: "By this time I suppose you are at your Uncle Bryan's and have the pleasure of a whole room and a whole bed to yourself, but no doubt you feel much more lonesome than at Uncle [Aleck's] with all those boys to keep you company. Your Aunt Eveline and [Mrs.] Hawks however are so kind and Uncle Bryan so funny that I expect you get on very well indeed."[2]

Stephens rode his pony over to both sets of uncles and aunts' Leon County plantations. He wrote his mother that his pony was the "wildest" horse at either place, and boasted, "He has never thrown me and never will; he has tried it two or three times but has found his attempts useless & has given up in despair." On Christmas Day Stephens's Aunt Julia gave him a little book of theology as a present. While visiting at Goodwood, he discovered and captured a mouse in his bed and later gave it to a cousin.[3] Young Croom's two weeks' visit was pleasant, and its duration was not considered lengthy.

After Bryan's half sisters, Ann and Elizabeth, married the physician brothers Edward Croom Bellamy and Samuel Crowell Bellamy, the two families moved to Florida's Jackson County. There the Bellamys prospered from their cotton plantations, Sam at Rock Cave and Ned at Hickory Hill. As discussed in chapter 4, Sam Bellamy, like other Floridians, suffered financially as a result of the Panic of 1837 and the difficulties of the Second Seminole War. He might have survived such setbacks but for the illnesses and deaths of his wife and only son. The losses, occurring within days of each other, caused Sam to enter a prolonged period of depression and gradually to develop a dependency on alcohol. What followed were years of physical deterioration and economic ruin.

Sam continued to live at Rock Cave and to claim it as legally his, but retaining possession of the property led to a bitter feud between the brothers. The two men made only one real estate deal with each other, but it was one too many. In 1845, Sam's money problems approached a crisis, and he sold Ned 1,200 acres of land and an unspecified number of slaves for $6,000.[4] The Union Bank, which had a branch in Marianna, held a mortgage on the property (Rock Cave). By the arrangement's terms the plantation would revert to Sam provided he paid off the mortgage.

Inevitably, the question of ownership led to a lawsuit. Desperate for capital and increasingly reliant on whiskey, Sam inserted a notice in the local paper that did nothing to improve his brother's public image. The insult, appearing early in 1848, further strained their relations. Contemporary instead of generational, their dispute had the added bitterness that accompanies an altercation between brothers. Three months later Sam offered his long-neglected medical services to Jackson Countians with a plaintive advertisement: "He has no other means of making his living and therefore solicits the patronage of his neighbors."[5] He had made a will in 1842 (naming his friend and brother-in-law George Alexander Croom as his executor). The document declared, "I wish my remains interred as near as possible to those of my late wife Elizabeth Jane Bellamy." The document was drafted before his rift with Ned, so that being buried beside his wife on his brother's property was a natural request. In a new will made in November 1849, Sam appointed Bryan Croom as his executor. In the will Bellamy acknowledged the ravages of liquor but declared himself "sound in mind and body and wholly free for some months from [his] former vice of intoxications."[6]

By 1850 the beleaguered Bellamy had no slaves at his residence (his bondsmen were probably hired out) and no land in cultivation. Embittered, he drafted a new will in 1851 that gave his estate, after the debts were paid, to his nephews Richard and Alexander Bellamy, sons of his late brother Alexander A. Bellamy. Samuel included caustic statements: "I do hereby most positively declare that none of my estate shall ever, in any event, go to Edward C. Bellamy or one of his heirs." In addition, "I wish my executor to prosecute to the end my lawsuit against Edward C. Bellamy until he is compelled to pay over the last cent he has of mine[;] these damages and future sale of land [are to be used] if necessary to provide for [the] purchase of Union Bank bonds to unlease my estate from the Union Bank."[7]

Even though Rock Cave was in litigation, in 1851 (the same year he made his will) Sam offered it for sale. By then the plantation had been reduced to 880 acres, 550 of them in cultivation. The terms were $6 an acre, but no buyer was willing to risk investing in such an uncertain title.[8] The unhappy events of his last years ended for Sam in December 1853. He had been to Tallahassee but on his return got no farther than crossing the Chattahoochee River into Jackson County. According to the *Marianna Whig*, Bellamy's body was found the next morning near the ferry station. His throat was cut with a razor. As the *Whig* put it, death was by suicide: "The deceased has been exceedingly intemperate for years past, and was most probably laboring under *delirium tremens* at the time."[9] Ironically, the case over Rock Cave plantation was finally settled in 1857 in favor of Samuel Bellamy. Most of the estate's $48,673 was tied up in eighty-three slaves valued at $47,000, and after the Union Bank's claims were paid, only a small amount was left for Sam's nephews.[10]

Ned and Ann and their large family continued to live at Hickory Hill. They maintained good relations with Bryan and Eveline at Goodwood. Twice in 1847, Bryan sold Ann a slave. The purchases were made on the same day, April 16, when she paid her half brother $600 for a sixteen-year-old boy named Abram and another $600 for John Drew, a man of thirty-five.[11] By 1850, Ned was the second leading planter in Jackson County. He owned or controlled 4,000 acres of land, half of them under cultivation, produced 230 bales of cotton, and was master of 170 slaves.[12]

Ned also bought land near Columbus in Muscogee County, Georgia, and established a place there that he named Hopoi. Founded in 1827, Columbus served the people of Muscogee County as their seat of government and place of commerce. Located on the fall line of the Chattahoochee River, Columbus became an important trading, manufacturing, and shipping center for Georgia, Alabama, and Florida. Steamboats left the gulf port of Apalachicola loaded with passengers, manufactured products, and other freight bound upstream on the Apalachicola River. Reaching the confluence in Georgia of the Chattahoochee and Flint Rivers, some packets proceeded northeast to Albany on the Flint. More often they continued north on the Chattahoochee, which formed the state boundary between Alabama and Georgia, to Columbus. The journey from Apalachicola to Albany was 194 miles; it was 262 miles from the port to Columbus. On their return, steamers were loaded at Columbus and picked up additional passengers, cotton, hogsheads of sugar, hides, and lumber at various towns and landings. From Apalachicola the cotton was shipped to American ports and abroad, especially to Liverpool, England, and on to the great textile mills of Manchester. The Crooms often used the steam packets. Columbus was also the jumping-off place for the Southwest—settlers and travelers bound overland for Alabama, Mississippi, Louisiana, and beyond availed themselves of the city's attractions, including horse races, before continuing their arduous journey.[13]

Dr. Bellamy's Georgia land was hardly a plantation. In 1851, he purchased four separate parcels in Lot 69, District 8, a few miles northeast of Columbus. The price, $4,000 for the 131 acres, was high. Deed records do not indicate that there was a house on Hopoi, but there probably was, and mention was made in the transaction of a garden and an orchard.[14] What Bellamy did was to acquire a second home on a pleasant vacation site that could be used by his family and relatives. Hopoi and Columbus became an important part of their lives, and the wives of two of Ned and Ann's sons were from Columbus: William Croom Bellamy married Fannie Lindsay, and Eugene Bellamy married Caroline E. Lewis.[15]

Members of the large Bellamy family of Hickory Hill visited back and forth between the Florida plantation and the Georgia property. Of their Croom relatives the family was closest to William and Julia and their two children, Elizabeth and Stephens. Beyond their kinship, the adults and children of both families enjoyed mutual interests and were together often. On some occasions Bryan and Eveline, as well as George Whitfield, visited Hopoi.[16]

For a number of reasons Ned decided in the late 1850s to leave Jackson County. His motives were economic (after twenty years of cultivation, Bellamy's cotton lands were wearing thin), personal (his difficulties with his brother Sam), and adventurous (the same lure and challenge of a new country that had originally brought him to Florida beckoned again). Ned was determined to move. Somewhere in Mississippi or the Southwest good land was cheap and opportunities limitless.

In the fall of 1856, he and one of his sons, Charles Edward, known as Edward, made a six-week tour of the area. A graduate of the University of North Carolina, class of 1851, Edward took a medical degree at the University of Pennsylvania in 1854, and in 1855 he was awarded a master's degree by his alma mater. The elder Croom was looking for cotton land, and Edward was seeking a place with good prospects for a young doctor. In Bolivar County, located in northwest Mississippi, the Florida planter became acquainted with a large landowner named Charles Clark. The two men bargained, and Croom bought 480 acres.[17]

In the early summer of 1857, Julia Croom wrote to her son, Stephens, that Dr. Bellamy "and the whole family [were] to leave for Mississippi some time in the fall." A few weeks later Stephens's father added that Ned, who was already making progress toward opening his place, planned to sell out in Florida and remove his slaves to his new plantation in Bolivar County, Mississippi. William thought that his brother-in-law had made a good decision.[18]

In November 1857, Bellamy bought 408 acres in the western half and the southwestern quarter of Section 34, Township 22, Range 7 West. He paid Alfred J. Lowery of Madison Parish, Louisiana, $1,080 in three promissory notes.[19] Two months later Ann bought a mortgage from Charles Clark for 1,289 acres that lay in Sections 22 and 27 of Township 22, Range West. The price was $11,262.[20] The Bellamys' land lay about five miles from the Mississippi River and had the potential either to enrich or to bankrupt them. Supposedly, Bellamy also bought a plantation in Tennessee.

Lying about sixty miles below Memphis, Bolivar County was located in the Mississippi Delta. The triangular plain or basin that forms the Delta is in the state's northwestern section between the Mississippi and Yazoo Rivers. Dramatically, almost mesmerically, flat, it begins south of Memphis and extends southwest about 200 miles, ending just north of Vicksburg. Sixty miles at its greatest width, the Delta has sandy loam soil in some places; in other sections it is characterized by a dark, sticky clay known as "buckshot." The sandy loam soil was preferable for cotton cultivation because it drained better than buckshot, although the latter was more ideally suited for rice production.

Bordering the Mississippi River and named for the South American revolutionary hero Simón Bolívar, the county was created from the Choctaw Indian cessions of 1820 and 1822 and was established in February 1836. The fertile land of Bolivar and other Delta counties was even more alluvial than the Black Belt region of Alabama. Yet the area had serious transportation problems. Travel was largely by steamboats, and only gradually were roads built into the interior. Clearing and settling the swampy wilderness was a formidable task. Vines and almost impenetrable cane jungles gave settlers a feeling of isolation and entrapment. Heavy rains regularly transformed the interior into a muddy mass that all but halted commercial and civilian transportation (for heavy hauling oxen were indispensable). Besides its unpredictable climate, the Delta had a widespread reputation for being unhealthy.[21]

The region's liabilities, however, were more than compensated for by its assets. One was the unrivaled hunting and fishing. There was a seemingly limitless abundance of animals, birds, and fish. With few exceptions, the Bellamys and Crooms not among them, southern males were enthusiastic sportsmen. Of all the game inhabiting the woods and swamps of Bolivar County, none rivaled its bear population as tests of a hunter's skill and courage.

The Delta's main attraction, one that made its multiple discomforts worth enduring, was the land. The soil of the "Bottoms," as contemporaries called the Delta, produced cotton on a scale unmatched anywhere. Ned Bellamy was one of the planters who, with their families, swelled Bolivar County's population in the 1850s. In that decade the number of white inhabitants increased by 253 percent and that of slaves by 332 percent. Most of the settlers were born outside Mississippi. By 1860 the county had 1,393 whites (9 percent of the population) and 9,078 slaves. In those ten years cotton production rose by 600 percent, and the average farm was worth $30,000.[22]

Bellamy went about the business of having 400 acres cleared, building some slave cabins, and constructing a large, comfortable home for his family. Sometimes accompanied by his sons, he made several trips back and forth from Bolivar County to Hickory Hill and Hopoi—selling his Jackson County plantation, arranging to have his slaves brought out, and accomplishing the myriad details attendant to a major move.

In September he sold 111 acres of Hopoi but kept 20 acres for himself. He received $6,250, a profit of $2,500 over the original price he paid for 131 acres.[23] All the preparations were accomplished by the fall of 1857.

In early October, Ann and some of the family moved from Hopoi; others had already arrived from Florida, probably taking a steamboat from St. Marks to New Orleans and another from there up the Mississippi River to Bolivar County. The family lived briefly in a log house without a chimney but had great expectations for their new plantation, which they named Hopoi after the Georgia place. Ann's money had paid for most of the Mississippi land, and early in their marriage Edward had sold his wife's property in North Carolina and used her slaves to get started in Florida. Now in 1857, as the family began their Delta venture, Edward put a number of slaves in trust to their son Edward for Ann's separate use.[24]

William and Julia Croom, seeing the boldness of the Bellamys, decided to follow suit. The couple had remained in Quincy, where Croom engaged in business but without spectacular success. In 1850 he loaned John A. Keadle $2,000 to open a grocery store. Croom protected his investment by having Keadle sign an agreement to give the business his undivided personal attention. The document absolved the creditor from any contracts that Keadle made and granted Croom the right to examine the firm's books. The loan was to be repaid out of net profits.[25]

There was ample evidence of Croom's business activities (selling lots in Quincy in 1850 and 1852, transferring rights to a certificate of land in 1856, selling a home and lot in 1857).[26] He owned slaves but rarely traded in human property. One occasion when he did revealed how complicated, even on a small scale, the slave trade could be. On January 1, 1851, William delivered old Lucy (Lucy Logan); her daughter, Maria; Maria's two children, Lucy and Ziphy; and Ziphy's child to William Speight. The purchaser, unable to pay cash, put up three promissory notes (one for $1,050 and two for $1,000 each) drawing 8 percent interest. Later, Speight was unable to make the notes good, so he transferred the contract title to one A. K. Allison. Having little choice if he wished to receive payment, Croom signed the agreement.[27]

Croom was also conscientious in his role as guardian for his younger brother, George Alexander. At least by 1839, and probably earlier, William was Alex's guardian, sending him money and looking after his finances, particularly in 1841, the year his charge spent at the University of Georgia. William filed scrupulous accounts with the Gadsden County judge.[28]

Something happened in 1856 to cause William not only to leave Quincy and Gadsden County but to depart temporarily from the South. On May 24, he wrote from New York listing himself as a resident of that city and giving P. W. White of Quincy his power of attorney. White was to use his own judgment in selling any of Croom's slaves, as well as his lands, lots, and home in Quincy. The reason for Croom's exodus may have been the termination of his guardianship over Aleck. The release of William's guardianship was on the condition that the young man receive $3,500 in cash. That amount represented what was considered the mishandling of the young man's money. It was not a case of the older brother's dishonesty. The difficulty, said George Alexander, was the fault of the court. Even so, William had to pay what was a considerable amount of money. He undoubtedly tried to recoup from this and other financial problems by seeking a position in New York that would provide him with greater income.[29] Certainly Julia made little effort to dissuade him. She was beginning to make her dissatisfaction with Florida known.

Whatever the reasons for the family's departure, lawyer White followed his instructions. The next spring (March 1857), White sold Lot 139 in Quincy to Sarah A. King for $1,100.[30] Then on June 20, 1857, Croom and Julia returned briefly to Quincy. Croom sold Lot 89, which was occupied by his store, to Forman Muse and William Munroe for $3,000.[31] Croom had been gone from Florida long enough to complain that the "hot weather fleas mosquitos & c annoyed [them] not a little." Still, he was relieved because he had succeeded in selling his brick store. "This was the last piece of Real estate I held in Florida."[32]

The Crooms' move to New York was not permanent, and for two years, 1856–57, the family switched back and forth between the city and Columbus, where they rented a place known as the Perry House. They were frequent guests at the Bellamys' Hopoi.[33] Croom continued his trips between Hopoi and New York, and sometimes he went to Quincy, where he tried to tie up loose ends. Now and then some opportunity seemed imminent only to end in disappointment.[34] Elizabeth and Stephens attended good schools in Columbus (better educational opportunities for their children was one reason that prompted the Crooms to leave Florida).[35] In New York the family lived in a boardinghouse. Stephens enrolled in Kingsley's School at West Point, where he "learned little else than mischief," although its location on the Hudson River meant that he "became a first-rate swimmer." Afterward he "went to excellent schools in New York City, and was well prepared for college." Lizzie went to the highly regarded Spingler Institute in New York City, where she acquired writing and verbal skills that benefited her later career as an author and teacher.[36] William was unsuccessful as a commission merchant in New York and did little better in the silk and ribbon jobbing business. Matters went even worse in Columbus, where he became associated with a physician in a business enterprise. Croom accepted notes from the doctor, only to lose all when the bank holding his debtor's money failed. William not only lost his money but went seriously into debt.[37]

Despite his financial distress, the harried merchant had the fortitude characteristic of the Croom family, and no matter the sacrifice, he and Julia were determined to see that Stephens went to college. As Stephens explained later, "Being intensely Southern in my feelings I persuaded my father to send me to the University of North Carolina, where nearly all my uncles, both maternal & paternal & many of my cousins had been educated. I entered the freshman class of that institution in January 1856—my father going with me there from New York." According to Stephens his undergraduate career constituted "the happiest years of [his] life."[38]

In the summer of 1857 Croom's family visited Georgia and at Hopoi learned of Ned and Ann's plans to move to Mississippi. Given their own impecunious situation (William had written his son at Chapel Hill, "Under the circumstances it becomes all hands to live economically for the present"), the Crooms decided to move to Bolivar County and settle somewhere near the Bellamys.[39]

Talk about the fertile Bottoms aroused George Alexander Croom's interest as well. By then he had moved from Gadsden to Leon County, where he was comfortably settled. Still, he reasoned that visiting the new country would do no harm. So in July, William and Aleck, accompanied by Ned and Ann Bellamy's son Edward, journeyed to the Delta. William wanted to find land near that of Dr. Bellamy; his brother examined acreage both in Mississippi and across the river in the Arkansas Delta. Aleck liked what he saw and selected eight thousand acres in Chicot County, a fertile region on the Mississippi's west bank across from Bolivar County. He may have made some arrangement, but it did not include a signed agreement or payment of money. William was equally impressed. He negotiated for one thousand acres about ten miles east of the Mississippi River and near Ned Bellamy's property. The land was acquired from Anthony and Harriet Smith of DeSoto County, Mississippi, and contained parts of Section 1 and all of Section 2 in Township 21 North, Range 7 West. The price was $16 an acre ($16,000), with $400 due on January 1, 1858, and the balance in three payments.[40] For the first time William was willing to become a full-time planter.

Enthusiastic about the area, where land prices were rising every day, William wrote his son, "This is one of the finest planting countries I ever saw and there appears to be no such thing as exhausting the soil."[41] Like Ned Bellamy, Croom had succumbed to Delta fever. Instead of the debilitating physical variety, it was a benign and powerful economic disease. The fever—with its potential for monetary rewards—was a welcome epidemic that raged throughout Bolivar, Sunflower, Washington, and other Delta counties.

Some Croom and Bellamy family members, at least initially, were no less enthusiastic. Fannie and William Croom Bellamy acquired a lot in Prentiss, one of Bolivar County's few towns.[42] In August 1857, Harold Bellamy occupied part of his time at Hopoi, Georgia, camping out and writing his relatives. In a letter to his first cousin Stephens Croom, he described his family's preparations to move. Harold anticipated the Southwest's attractions, advising Stephens, "You will have to go to Louisiana and get one of the pretty Creole girls for a sweetheart, that is what I am going to do, they are as rich as—as—a Mince pie."[43] Julia, who had not been reluctant to leave Florida, relished living in New York. She quickly took to city ways, enjoying the excitement, fast pace, and contact with people. Bolivar County could not have been in greater contrast to New York City, but Julia accepted her husband's decision. Thus she confided to her delighted son, "We will not be Yankees after all, the thing you seem so much to dread."[44] Living with her parents in New York, Elizabeth shared her brother's sentiments and fired off a pack of firecrackers to celebrate the coming move.[45]

In late October 1857, the Crooms, except for Stephens, who was in school at Chapel Hill, followed the Bellamys. Julia, who wrote her son, "I am truly glad that we have cut loose from Florida," and Lizzie rented rooms in Memphis. They found the city "a gay and sociable place," although the inconveniences of being impermanently settled would wear thin.[46] Residing temporarily with the Bellamys, William busied himself readying his place in Bolivar County, where, according to him, the bears were "literally as plentiful as rabbits."[47] The Croom venture was on a smaller scale than that of the Bellamys, but it entailed similar preparations and work. Julia explained to her son, "Your father thinks he has made a good investment[;] says that it is an exceedingly fertile country and will repay cultivation better than any land he has ever seen, but is at present exceeding rough and like all new countries hard to obtain the comforts of life."[48]

Croom brought out most of his slaves, although one family—Manuel, his wife, and children—simply refused to leave Florida. The Delta held no attractions for them, and William honored their request to be sold.[49] The $3,800 that he received was welcome because, as Croom lamented, times were "so hard." He was forced to journey to what Julia called "that everlasting Florida," seeking money to meet his land payments in Mississippi. Some of his slaves' time of hire had run out in Gadsden County, and he brought them back with him to the Delta.[50] William still had not resolved his money problems in Columbus, and there was pressure on him to settle a debt of $5,000.[51] With obvious feeling, he wrote to Stephens, "I hope things will be better soon."[52]

Amid the hurly-burly of moving, young doctor Edward Bellamy and Elizabeth Croom announced their engagement. The first cousins were to be married; as the bride-to-be teased her brother, "Who in the world would have thought it? Would you?"[53] Subscribing to the Victorian protocol of the antebellum South, Edward asked William for permission to marry his daughter and even wrote Stephens explaining the depth of his devotion to Elizabeth.[54] The decision was made in September for a December wedding, but various delays—including some Croom-Bellamy family misunderstandings that were quickly settled and pressing financial problems that were not—postponed the actual ceremony for months. Julia and Elizabeth waited in Memphis, making plans for the wedding, although Lizzie passed part of her time being courted by some male admirers, none of whom she took seriously. Even when the family's large frame house made of hewn logs was ready and they moved in, Julia still would not feel settled. Croom expected the family to spend their summers somewhere else because, as Julia wrote Stephens, "he [thought] the swamp [would] not do to live in the whole year around." Julia and her son were extremely close, and she worried about his future. There was no encouragement from her for him to settle in Mississippi or "in broken down Florida." Perhaps Columbus was best. Georgia was prosperous, and Columbus was a growing city, a place where Stephens would find "more congeniality than in the North," which he had always disliked.[55] Julia notified her son, "We are going down to the swamp as soon as the house is ready," a fact that forced the rueful comment, "I like the society of New York. I mean the good not the fashionable society. Stephens, I am a Yankee. I had rather live there than any where else."[56]

Meantime, Croom traveled back and forth between Bolivar County and Memphis, making occasional visits to Quincy and Columbus. As 1857 drew to a close, Julia and Elizabeth still had not seen the Bottoms, but in mid-December they anticipated their first visit. Julia wrote to Stephens, "[I have] heard that they have some hunters among the ladies down there, but I shant try that." Julia, like Lizzie, had enjoyed going to the theater in Memphis, but she was no longer fond of the city. As for Elizabeth, she pronounced it a dull, "stupid place." It seems unusual that she would declare, "I am sick and tired of this Memphis," when she had such a full social agenda. Lizzie lamented, "I have been to parties and been to parties till I am sick of parties and I never want to go to another."[57]

As the time for moving neared, Julia felt the emotions shared by many southern women who moved from comfortable surroundings to the harsh demands of the frontier. Julia suffered double problems: she had disliked Florida, and now the Delta was worse. She repeated her sentiments: "[I] do not look forward with any satisfaction to a home in the bottoms."[58] Even William, preoccupied with urging family frugality, settling his debts, and getting moved, found the wilderness environment disturbing. "The West is certainly a very rich country," he noted, "but shockingly depraved in morals and manners."[59]

However small the comfort, Julia and Lizzie took satisfaction in knowing that in Bolivar County they would have a permanent mailing address: the small town of Prentiss.[60] Croom was more positive and, in common with the Bellamy men, was already enjoying the opportunities for hunting and fishing. Harold Bellamy liked his parents' new Hopoi and spoke highly of ponds stocked with fish and the presence of wild ducks, geese, deer, wildcats, and bears.[61] Later, a visiting Alabama cousin was startled when he encountered a panther in the yard. Such stories attracted Stephens, who was approaching his final year at the University of North Carolina. He was kept informed about his family's adventures and given news about his relatives. Stephens was inclined to follow his father's advice to train himself in public speaking and read law after graduation.[62]

Julia and Lizzie did not reach the Bottoms until February 1858. They traveled to Prentiss on a Memphis to New Orleans packet and then went inland eight miles to reside temporarily with the Bellamy family at Hopoi. George Alexander Croom was also there. He had made the long trip from Leon County, Florida, for a brief visit before inspecting the land that he liked but never purchased across the river in Arkansas.[63] The Crooms soon moved into their own place, a temporary, hastily built house about 1.5 miles from Hopoi. William had constructed a number of slave houses, and the permanent home was almost complete. It was surrounded by ponds, and the family was serenaded nightly by a chorus of frogs. Ann Bellamy was far more pleased than Julia. At least some of

the family—her son William, his wife, Fannie, and their three children—had come out and settled nearby. Ann also liked the Delta because she believed a fortune could be made from planting cotton. "For
my part," Julia countered, "I think I would rather be where perhaps less
money would be made, but less mud [would] be endured." She told
Stephens, who continued his vicarious sharing of the family's activities,
"This has been a winter of almost incessant rain and the same cause
which makes these lands fruitful, makes them also troublesome. You see
there is a price for every pleasure and a balance for every gift."[64]

By March, William's superintendent was getting cotton planted in
the newly cleared ground and helping his employer plant a garden. Like
everything else, turnips thrived in the dark soil.[65] The family moved
into their permanent home in April. Elizabeth wrote Stephens, "Our
house is not so grand & imposing an edifice as Aunt Ann's, but we find
it quite roomy & comfortable." Julia tried to put up a brave front. Cora,
her house servant and companion, was a reminder of more affluent days.
Julia had a henhouse, and her chickens kept the family supplied with
fresh eggs. She and Lizzie continued to plan the long-delayed marriage.
Yet despite Julia's efforts, the separation from Stephens, the vast soli-
tude, the bothersome mud, the absence of once familiar conveniences,
let alone luxuries, and the weather combined to depress the unhappy
woman's spirits. One scholar has shown how planters' wives on the
Southwest frontier often had difficulty adjusting to conditions so different from those they had known in the upper South. They had limited
geographical mobility in their strange and lonely environment but retained a paternalistic view toward their slaves, treating them well and
possibly identifying with them. Julia had her own family and some kin
living nearby, but she disliked the Delta even more than Florida and,
like some pioneer wives, could not accept the overwhelming sense of
isolation. "This is a wonderful country and very productive," she confided to Stephens, "But I will never be satisfied here[;] it is too remote
from life. . . . There is nothing I more truly regret than that we have
come here."[66] Even their post office had changed from Prentiss to
Rosewood.

Finally, Lizzie and Edward's wedding was set. It was a pleasant interlude but did not approach in scale or pomp what the Crooms would have arranged in North Carolina or Georgia or Florida. Frustrating difficulties such as getting the planting accomplished and an emergency business trip to New York by William were overcome, but there was no Episcopal minister in the Bottoms, and bringing one in would have been expensive. Besides, Julia considered their home too rough to host a wedding reception ("celebration," as she called it). In the end love conquered logistics. The Crooms had attended Calvary Episcopal Church while living in Memphis and had become reacquainted with an old friend, the Right Reverend James H. Otey, D.D., bishop of Tennessee. They had known him earlier when he visited Episcopal churches in Florida. Now the fifty-eight-year-old cleric, sympathizing with the young couple's dilemma, offered his services. The wedding party took a steamer to Memphis and changed their clothes on the boat, and on May 12, 1858, Lizzie and Edward were married by the bishop before a small group of friends and relatives.[67]

After the wedding, Croom went to New York, and Julia visited in Louisville, Kentucky, and Cincinnati, Ohio. The newlyweds returned to the Delta, where Edward deferred starting his medical career to help make the cotton crop. Life had barely settled into a routine when, in July, heavy, extended rains raised the river (already swollen by the wet winter) to flood stage. The Bellamys, Crooms, and others had to use boats to go on the simplest errand. Finally, the levee broke, and the maturing cotton crop was destroyed. During the flood crisis, the Crooms' house servant Cora performed invaluable services. The family was forced to abandon the Bottoms. Ned and Ann Bellamy and their children were also flooded out and retreated to Memphis. Cora, described as "so good & faithful a servant," remained with the Crooms, but, aided by his son-in-law, William was forced to take his other slaves to Memphis and hire them out.[68] The Crooms rented rooms in the Gayas Hotel in Memphis, and, despite all their problems, Julia declared herself glad to be out of "that 'wretched country.'"[69]

Julia's description of the weather was no exaggeration. The Crooms and Bellamys could not have picked a worse year than 1858 to plant crops. Unexpected cold weather produced frost and biting winds in late

April and early May. The cotton crop was damaged, and a shortage of seed prevented replanting. The Mississippi and Yazoo Rivers rose, and recurring overflows or floods were the result. Plantations and planters in the Arkansas and Mississippi Bottoms, as well as others in Louisiana, suffered. In May, the Mississippi River was higher than it had been since 1849, and in June, Memphis newspapers such as the *Avalanche, Daily Appeal,* and *Eagle and Inquirer* were reporting overflows from St. Louis, Missouri, to New Orleans. The *Avalanche* predicted that the waters would "cause incalculable destruction of property." [70]

The worst was yet to come, as July produced rain and flooding, and the network of levees in the Delta broke under the strain. Three-fourths of the cotton crop in Coahoma County, Mississippi, was ruined. Old-timers spoke of cotton prospects as the worst in thirty years, and oats, wheat, and corn were severely damaged. Five hours of rain on July 4 produced flooding in parts of Memphis whose location on bluffs usually made them safe. In Bolivar County two planters, F. B. Lewis and Frank Gadon, had planted 1,200 acres in cotton, but two-thirds of their crops became victim to the overflow. As the *Memphis Daily Appeal* remarked, "The year 1858 will long be remembered . . . as the year of calamities." [71] "Jennie," a correspondent for a Memphis newspaper, observed the flood firsthand and wrote, "How much like some huge aquatic monster the Father of Waters seems! Today he rolls along his course in listless indolence; tomorrow he swells into double his usual size, chases the planter from his banks like an avenging spirit, overflows towns and cities, overturns mighty trees, and goes dashing along his headlong course, as if exulting in mere wantonness of power." [72]

William now had the disastrous loss of his cotton crop to add to his other problems. He soon left for New York searching for some occupation that would bring in money. Despite their economic problems, he and Julia wrote regularly to Stephens, soon to be a dignified senior and already a top student at the university. Elizabeth was only an occasional correspondent, although she crammed her letters with news and opinions. In one communication William wrote his son, "I wish to remind you of many little, not to mention, larger vices, to which young men at your age are liable. Drinking, swearing, gambling,* chewing and smoking, bowie knives and pistols, obscene language, whoring.*"[73] Croom inserted asterisks after the vices he considered most tempting and reprehensible.

Living for a long period in a Memphis hotel was impossible, and the family settled in at Mont Vale Springs, a resort area not far from the city. They even went to Bailey Springs near Tuscumbia, Alabama, but did not like the setting and returned to Tennessee. William found work in New York, although he began suffering arthritic pains. Apparently he owned or managed a store. In September the family, including Edward and Elizabeth, joined him there.[74] The Crooms moved into a rooming house, but their future was uncertain. Edward did not want to practice medicine in New York. Doubtful that he could earn enough to buy a house, he refused to have his wife live in circumstances beneath those of her friends. Yet the flood in Mississippi made planting "no longer pleasant nor profitable," and he and Elizabeth spoke vaguely of moving to Saint Louis. "For my part," Edward wrote, "I prefer [the] South and the Southerners to the Northerners though Uncle William likes the latter the most."[75] More likely, his father-in-law believed there were greater opportunities in the North. For a brief period Edward went to Memphis and lived in a boardinghouse with one of his brothers. Lizzie still liked New York but detested the drawbacks of a boarding-house. She preferred plantation life to such an existence.

Edward was joined later in Memphis by Lizzie and her father, who came down to settle his business affairs. Julia remained in New York and was angry that her husband would have "to go down to that hateful Mississippi this winter to see about his concerns there."[76] Those concerns included the possible sale of his slaves and his property in Bolivar County. William regained some of his vigor but remained in bad health. Despite deep misgivings, Julia soon joined her family in Memphis. From there they returned to Bolivar County. Ned and Ann and the various Bellamys also returned. Ever the optimist, William believed the Delta was destined to prosper and that he could sell his land for twice what he had paid for it. Despite political warfare and growing sectional tension, the nation was enjoying economic good times. America's potential for greatness seemed to justify its optimism. Croom noted that in

New York Cyrus McCormick's invention of the cable was "heralded as the harbinger of civilization and the extension of Christianity."[77] Julia reconciled herself to being back in the Delta, and the day after Christmas 1858, she mused about the joys of housekeeping and being settled. The future was uncertain, but the family's new address was definite: Beulah, Bolivar County, Mississippi.[78]

William faced an unavoidable crisis of economic survival. Could he produce enough cotton in the Delta to pay his numerous creditors and keep his family going? Could he borrow the money necessary to plant a crop? His anxiety was eased in part because Lizzie and Edward were young, intelligent, and healthy. As a doctor, Edward should soon establish a substantial practice. In March 1859, without being able to afford it, William deeded to Elizabeth 480 acres of his Bolivar County land (that December Dr. Bellamy gave Edward six slaves, and Ann gave him one).[79] Nor did William and Julia have cause for concern about Stephens. They took pardonable pride when he finished second in the graduating class of 1859 at Chapel Hill. His future success seemed certain. All that aside, William still faced his debts, immediate and crippling, and there seemed no way to pay them off.

Other than losing his 1858 crop, Edward Bellamy suffered none of William's misfortune. He recouped by borrowing $33,000 from the New Orleans firm of S. O. Nelson and Company. The planter secured the loan by mortgaging his land, cotton crop, and fifty slaves.[80] Ned's crop was good, enabling him to pay off the contract, and by 1860 the owner of Hopoi plantation was a man of place and wealth. The census put the value of Bellamy's real estate at $70,080, and his personal estate was worth $106,000.[81]

8 *The Inner Circle*

George Alexander Croom's primary concerns became and remained his family and his cotton crop in middle Florida. After marrying Julia Church in 1843 in Athens, Georgia, Croom settled in Gadsden County, where he purchased Rocky Comfort plantation from his half brother Bryan. Within a year a son, whom Julia and Aleck named Hardy, was born. Because Julia was only nineteen, she probably went home to have the baby (or the couple may have lived briefly in Athens). Seventeen months later (1846), Julia returned again to Georgia to give birth to her second child, Alonzo Church, who was known simply as Church. After that she was mature enough and she and Aleck were settled enough for the other children to be born in Florida. Because of his growing family, Aleck found that he needed money as much as land. That was probably why, in December 1845, he sold 401.58 acres of his plantation to Richard Haygood.[1]

Young Croom emerged shortly as a successful cotton planter. In 1850 he operated his eight hundred acres of improved land and an equal amount of unimproved acreage with a slave force of sixty-five. The cash value of his plantation was $20,000. He had farm machinery worth

$1,000, while his livestock was valued at $3,000 and included fifteen horses, eight mules, eight cows, six oxen, fifty cattle, one hundred sheep, and one hundred hogs. Croom's farming operation produced 146 bales of cotton, 300 pounds of wool, 1,500 bushels of sweet potatoes, 400 pounds of butter, and 600 gallons of molasses. The value of animals slaughtered was $300.[2]

In contrast to Eveline and Bryan, Julia and Aleck had a large family. By 1850 two more children—William Church, born in 1847 but died in 1854, and Sarah Jane, who was called Sally, born in 1848—had been added.[3] With relatives living in Leon County plus the attractions Tallahassee offered as the state capital, the youngest Croom brother decided to take advantage of a real estate opportunity that arose. In 1850, a Leon County couple, Benjamin F. Whitner Sr. and his wife, Eliza, were looking for property in Gadsden County.

Whitner was a wealthy and cultured South Carolinian who had come to Leon County shortly after 1830 and established Casa de Lago, a plantation of about 1,127 acres. His large home (there was a ballroom on the second floor) north of Tallahassee and west of the Lafayette Grant was built on a bluff on Lake Jackson. It commanded a view of fertile fields stretching along the bending shoreline of the lake's south bank. The mansion's grounds were notable for their large flower gardens. Like many of his contemporaries, Whitner, a staunch Democrat, was interested in politics but not as an office seeker. The planter knew Croom well because one of his children, Benjamin F. Whitner Jr., had married Sarah Church, a sister of Aleck's wife, Julia. The older Whitner and Croom negotiated, and in March Aleck paid him $14,000 for Casa de Lago.[4] A year later Croom sold Rocky Comfort (1,600 acres) to Whitner for $10,000.[5] Both parties were pleased with the results, and Whitner became a prominent cotton planter in Gadsden and well known as a booster of Florida's contemporary advantages and future potential.[6]

Aleck and Julia settled naturally and easily into the dominant planter society of Leon County. Because her father, Alonzo Church, was a Presbyterian minister, as well as president of the University of Georgia, Julia had ingrained in her a steadfast Calvinist loyalty. The result was that she persuaded her husband to join Tallahassee's First Presbyterian

Church, and George Alexander became one of the few Croom family members to abandon his Episcopalian roots. In the decade of the 1850s the couple had four more children, all girls: Julia Church, Elizabeth (died at age two), Ann Eloise, and Louisa Whitfield. The children were raised with the advantages that went with wealth and style. Typical of planters' sons, Hardy and Church lived active, outdoors lives. An uncle remarked of them, "They have a pony apiece and ride into town every day to school. They have a gun apiece and are considerable sportsmen."[7]

Aleck and Julia's role in local society was seen in 1851 when Croom purchased a house and ten acres in fashionable Bel Air from Benjamin F. Whitner Jr. A village located just south of Tallahassee, Bel Air was on high ground studded with pine trees. In a time when the relativity of heat was crucial, the small community, cooler than the capital, became a favorite summer vacation spot for wealthy planters and merchants. In 1853 Aleck and Julia had a painter reside at their home. He remained until some family portraits were completed, and he probably was commissioned by some of their friends. Their guest's artistic skills exceeded those of his horsemanship—on one occasion a pony threw him, and the painter wound up unhurt but humiliated in a puddle of mud.

For all his ties to Florida, George Alexander maintained his interest in Chicot County, and as late as 1858 he visited the region with one of his Whitfield nephews from Demopolis. The Alabamian found his Uncle Aleck "an excellent traveling companion, full of fun and jokes, frolicking of any kind was just playing into his hand." The two men visited their Bellamy and Croom kin in the Delta, and after his Arkansas sojourn, Aleck vowed to return the next year with a steam engine and some slaves and start a settlement. He never did because of his family and the profits from Casa de Lago and because of the sectional crisis confronting the nation.[8] Demonstrating the Croom ability with farming, Aleck soon doubled the cotton crop at Casa de Lago and installed a ten-horsepower steam engine to run his gristmill and cotton gin. In 1860 George Alexander had sixty-four slaves. The value of his plantation, which had 800 improved and 428 unimproved acres, was $15,000. His farm implements were worth $500. He had twenty horses, twenty-two asses and mules, twenty cows, six working oxen, seven other cattle, one hundred sheep, and one hundred hogs, all worth $5,850 (the value of animals slaughtered was $3,000). The two hundred bales of cotton ginned on Casa de Lago made it one of twenty plantations in Leon County to equal or better that total. In addition to three thousand bushels of corn, the plantation produced oats, peas and beans, Irish potatoes, sweet potatoes, hay, and butter.[9]

Although able and prosperous, Aleck never farmed on a scale to match that of his half brothers, Hardy, Bryan, and Richard. Chapter 4 dealt in part with Richard Croom as a cotton planter in Alabama's Sumter County. He and his wife, Winifred, were experiencing the trials and pleasures of raising a large family when, on October 1, 1848, she suddenly died. Richard, who had no choice but to bear his loss and sorrow, was mentally and emotionally strong. Even Bryan had been no more resistant in the legal battle to prevent Henrietta Smith and Susan Armistead from gaining possession of Goodwood. Following Winifred's death, Richard worked to maintain and improve his family's prominent position in the Black Belt, and he would never give up his Alabama citizenship. Yet he was also able to establish a place for himself and some of his children near Goodwood in the Lafayette Grant.

As Croom made adjustments and arrangements, he continued his planting operations. In 1850, Richard's Sumter County plantation had 2,775 acres, 1,575 of them "improved," that is, cultivated land. The cash value of his plantation was $10,000, and his farm equipment was worth $625. His livestock was distributed among seven horses, twenty-nine mules, thirty milk cattle, eight working oxen, fifty other cattle, sixteen sheep, and two-hundred hogs (their total evaluation was $3,000). Croom's labor force consisted of 130 slaves. The major cash crop was cotton, and in 1850 his plantation produced 121 bales. Richard's 3,500 bushels of corn represented the next most important crop. Overall, the planter had a diverse operation that included the cultivation of oats, rice, peas and beans, Irish potatoes, and sweet potatoes, as well as the production of wool and butter.[10] By then Croom was also dealing in the purchase and sale of Leon County land in the Lafayette Grant. Among his holdings was a plantation (discussed below) that was as productive and profitable as his Sumter County property.

When Winifred died, Winifred Bryan, the oldest child, was only seventeen. Richard, availing himself of family ties, looked to Bryan and Eveline to help him with his parental responsibilities. Their home was commodious, and without doubt the childless mistress and master of Goodwood would welcome their young nieces and nephews as temporary or extended guests. Richard's half brothers William and George Alexander were in nearby Gadsden County, and his half sister Ann, her husband, Ned, and their family were not far away at Hickory Hill plantation in Jackson County.

As Richard's various children visited back and forth from Alabama to Goodwood, they were welcomed into Tallahassee society and became active in St. John's Episcopal Church. Croom ties in Leon County were strengthened even more when Aleck and Julia moved from Rocky Comfort plantation to Casa de Lago in 1851. On one visit to Bryan and Eveline's, Winifred Bryan met George W. Sappington, a young lawyer who had come to Tallahassee from Charleston, Virginia. She and Sappington began a courtship that soon ended in their marriage, on April 24, 1851, at Goodwood. The wedding took place when flowers and plants were past their spring peak but before the heat had settled in, and it was a major social event. The Right Reverend Francis Huger Rutledge, bishop of the Diocese of Florida, performed the ceremony. A native of South Carolina, the Episcopal clergyman had been rector of St. John's from 1845 until he became bishop in 1851.[11]

After making a settlement with Bryan concerning his part of Hardy's estate, Richard began acquiring land in Leon County. Some of the property apparently was occupied by Croom or, more probably, by his overseer before the sales were officially recorded. In 1850 Richard had 940 acres in Leon County, 600 of them improved. His land was worth $10,000. His farm machinery was valued at $450 and his livestock at $1,666. Besides producing 200 bales of ginned cotton, Croom's plantation was a diversified operation: 4,500 bushels of corn (used for feeding stock, although much of it was turned into cornbread for his overseer, manager, and eighty-one slaves—all of whom undoubtedly put the 500 pounds of butter made on the plantation to good use), 900 bushels of rice, 500 bushels of peas and beans, 500 bushels of sweet potatoes, and 500 gallons of molasses.[12]

On March 20, 1851, Croom paid the Union Bank $13,860 for Section 34; the 640 acres lay immediately south of Goodwood.[13] In May of the same year, Richard spent $11,200 as payment to Bryan for Section 11 and other land that amounted to 1,120 acres. The property lay north of the Tallahassee–Monticello road and was the northernmost thrust of Goodwood.[14] Seven months later, in a strange transaction, Richard sold Bryan Section 34, which he had acquired from the Union Bank. Goodwood thereby regained 640 of the 1,120 acres Bryan had sold to Richard. The price was $8,200, which meant that Richard sustained a loss of $5,620.[15] Without bothering to explain or regret his uncharacteristic lack of acumen, Richard quickly made another purchase. In January 1852, he paid Muscoe Garnett of Virginia $8,000 for the 640 acres of Section 10 that adjoined Section 11 on the west.[16]

There was no apparent ill will or rivalry between Richard and Bryan. On January 1, 1855, Bryan bought Section 20 and parts of Sections 19 and 30, which adjoined Goodwood on the east and north. The grantor was William Bailey, an important planter and entrepreneur whose major activities were in Jefferson County, Leon's neighbor on the east. The same day Bryan sold the land to Richard for the exact amount he had paid Bailey.[17] In his third transaction on the same New Year's Day, Bryan enriched Richard by $2,150 for parts of the land he had just bought and sold to him: 201 acres in Section 20 and 15 acres in Section 30.[18] Two months later Richard purchased 433 acres in Section 17 (immediately north of Section 20), paying Edward Bradford $4,333.40 for the land.[19] Bradford, a physician and owner of Pine Hill plantation, was one of four brothers who had migrated to Leon County from Enfield, North Carolina, in the 1830s. They all became successful planters and with their families were prominent in the area's social life.

Richard's purpose in acquiring land in Alabama and Florida was based on the inner drive and ambition to succeed that was characteristic of the Croom family, but after Winifred's death he was equally motivated by a desire to leave his children with a large inheritance. To that end, and considering his daughters first, he created a trust in 1855 with his son-in-law, George W. Sappington, as the trustee. Shortly afterward, in 1857, Croom began to break up a large part of his Sumter County holdings, selling first to his son Nicholas P., who, in turn, would sell land to his brother Bryan. For purposes of clarity, the discussion of events in Alabama affecting Richard's sons Nicholas and Bryan will precede an explanation of the trust.

Nicholas, the second oldest child, was born on July 30, 1833. He was an ideal son. Like other Crooms, Nicholas grew up loving the land and farming, but unlike most of his kin, he never married. By the time he was eighteen, young Croom had purchased enough land to establish himself as a planter. The productive earth of Alabama's Black Belt brought high prices, and Nicholas made money on his investments.[20] In 1857, Richard conveyed to Nicholas two plantations, one five miles from Gaston and the other twelve miles from the community. Also included were mules and horses, cattle, hogs, corn fodder, meat, and farming equipment. The price was $32,000, and important to the transaction were ninety-one slaves. The deed did not mention the specific number of acres that were involved.[21]

On occasion, Nicholas sold land (80 acres in 1857 for $100).[22] By 1860 his real estate was worth $25,000, and his personal estate was valued at $70,000.[23] Nicholas's planting operations were more than enough to keep him and S. C. Peyton, his overseer, occupied, and on February 25, 1861, Nicholas sold 1,760 acres to his sister Susan Matilda for $17,600.[24] It would seem likely that Nicholas at least visited his uncle Bryan and aunt Eveline at Goodwood, but he never owned land in Florida and spent his life in Alabama.

Richard's second son, Bryan, was only nine when his mother died. In 1850 the eleven-year-old boy was living, or, more technically, visiting, at Goodwood with Eveline and Bryan (he may have been named for his uncle, although the Croom logic for selecting names could easily have justified any of a large number of Bryans with family connections). Susan, Bryan's nine-year-old sister, was also at Goodwood in 1850. In April the two were baptized at St. John's Church.[25] Neither the regularity nor the duration of Bryan's visits to Goodwood is known, but he returned to Alabama and made his permanent home in Sumter County.

As Bryan reached maturity, Nicholas sold him part of the property he had acquired from their father. Bryan purchased one of the two plantations (1,409 acres), which included twenty-nine slaves, farming equipment, livestock, and corn and fodder. By selling the property to Bryan for $32,000, Nicholas made money, but the slaves and land had increased in value, and Bryan paid a fair price. On February 16, 1861, Bryan married Augusta F. Marshall. The ceremony took place in Sumter County and was performed by the Reverend J. M. Roland.[26] It was not a propitious time to begin a marriage—two days later and only 125 miles away in Montgomery, Jefferson Davis was sworn in as president of the Confederate States of America. By the time Bryan and Augusta's son, Richard Bryan, was born, December 30, 1861, the Civil War had begun.[27] Shortly afterward, Bryan became a private in the Shorter Guards of A. M. Moore's Company of the Sumter County Militia.[28]

Mary Whitfield, Richard and Winifred's third child, was born July 31, 1836, and died June 22, 1867. Her sister Susan was born August 2, 1841, and lived a long life, dying in 1920.[29] It is not clear that Mary ever lived at Goodwood. Yet the young girl, fourteen when her mother died, visited there often. In 1849 she was baptized at St. John's.[30] The younger Susan realized the fact of her mother's death, but she was not old enough to share the grief of her brothers and sisters. She lived at Goodwood for a while in 1850, and by the mid-1850s both she and Mary resided in Leon County with their sister, Winifred, and George W. Sappington.

As mentioned, in 1855 Richard set up a trust for his daughters and placed Sappington in charge. All the trust lands lay in the Lafayette Grant and included Sections 10, 11, and part of 14 lying north of the Tallahassee–Monticello road. The tract contained 480 acres and was known as the Home place or the Garnett place. The Berry place, which included 433 acres in Section 17, was also part of the trust. Richard had obtained the property from Richard Bradford, another of the Bradford brothers from North Carolina. In addition, the Betton place was part of the arrangement. Joseph R. Betton and his son Turbott R. had migrated from Alexandria, Virginia, and Turbott became Tallahassee's leading antebellum merchant. The Betton place had 745 acres, lay mainly in Sections 19 and 20, and had been bought by Richard from his brother Bryan, who purchased it from William Bailey. The plantation lay north and west of the Tallahassee–Thomasville road. Richard had reconveyed to Bryan the Betton lands situated south and east of the road. In all, the trust came to 1,658 acres.

Richard Croom also conveyed to Sappington 139 slaves, as well as farm equipment and livestock. The trust was to last until Susan reached the age of twenty-one, in 1862. Among Sappington's obligations were to pay all Richard's Florida debts and to forward him $600 annually if Croom chose to draw any money. Otherwise, the $600 stipend would be put in the trust fund for its duration. The son-in-law was to handle the three daughters' annual expenses. If Mary or Susan married before the trust expired, they could make annual drafts on their own. Any monetary surplus produced by the plantations was to be invested in the trust. When Susan came of age, the inheritance was to be divided equally among the daughters—their annual advances would be figured in the final settlement. If any of the women died without children, then the remaining daughter or daughters would receive the deceased's share. If children were involved, they would also share in the trust. Since no mention was made of husbands, presumably they would receive nothing.

With responsibilities went benefits: Sappington would receive 5 percent of all net sales (mainly cotton); by obtaining written permission from Richard or Bryan, he could sell such real or personal property that he deemed advisable; while the trust was in effect, he could occupy the residence on either the Betton or the Home place without charge; and he was free to draw needed household expenses and plantation supplies. At no expense to himself, Sappington could maintain an unspecified number of house servants. In addition, so long as Mary and Susan continued to live with George and Winifred Sappington, they were not subject to any charges for room and board. By 1855, the two youngest girls were residing with their sister and brother-in-law, an arrangement that pleased Richard, who wanted them in a household that had a wife and husband.

Sappington managed Richard's Florida lands well. Richard and Bryan had bought or sold land back and forth, and Sappington fit smoothly into the pattern. In October 1855, trustee Sappington (with the concurrence of Richard) sold Bryan parts of Sections 20, 19, and 30 (745 acres) not previously sold by Richard to Bryan and a part of Section 17 (433 acres) for $14,725.[31] George and Winifred's good life was made better by the birth of a son, Richard Bryan. Their happiness was cut short on October 12, 1856, when Winifred, who was in Atlanta, died. Religious, easygoing, and "engaging in manners," she was only twenty-five-years-old. No reason was given for her death, but it must have been unexpected. George Sappington continued to administer the trust.[32]

For the next year or two it seems likely that Mary and Susan divided living arrangements between their father's home in Sumter County and their trust property or Goodwood in Leon County. During that period the sisters met two young brothers who had come to Florida from North Carolina: Richard Allen and James George Whitfield. They were the sons of James Bryan and Sally Wooten Whitfield of Lenoir County. A brother of George, who was close with Hardy and Bryan, James Bryan Whitfield had been a student at Chapel Hill, state senator, and militia general. James and Sally's sons did not look alike. James George had light hair, blue eyes, and a fair complexion, while Richard Allen's hair was black, his eyes hazel, and he had a dark complexion.

As cousins, Mary and Richard, who lived in Wayne County, North Carolina, had mutual and conversational interests. Croom family members did not take their meetings seriously because they assumed that George Sappington, who had lost Winifred two years earlier, would marry Mary. Yet she was not interested, perhaps because, as William Croom said, Sappington had "become as fat as a pig." Whatever the reason, Mary and Richard's relationship soon moved beyond that of kissing kin and became far more personal. They were married on November 2, 1858, in Sumter County (which must have pleased Richard). Stephen U. Smith, the local Episcopal rector, presided over the nuptials.[33]

Richard Croom was only fifty-three when he died on February 20, 1859. The cause of his death is unknown, although the most likely speculation is illness.[34] He left his family well fixed materially and by his example bequeathed them an important legacy: the good name of Croom. Following his death, Richard Allen and Mary Whitfield decided to live permanently in Leon County and began negotiations to alter the trust, which was still in place. In December 1859, Sappington, acting on instructions, asked and received permission from Bryan (who by then had many problems of his own) to sell part of the trust land. Whitfield next secured outright ownership of trusteeship land for Mary and himself: he paid $16,454 for the Home place (Sections 10 and 11 and an additional ninety-three-plus acres in Section 15). Part of the transaction included two notes of $1,829.33 each, obligating Whitfield to Sappington and Susan.[35]

In 1860 Susan, at the age of nineteen, was a woman of means. She was listed in the Sumter County census as a "farmer." Her real estate was worth $15,000, and her personal estate was valued at $40,000.[36] In addition, she owned part of the Leon County trust established by her father. No less than Mary, Susan was attracted to a Whitfield. She and James George, who was eight years younger than her brother-in-law, moved from friendship to courtship and then to marriage, an event that occurred on New Year's Eve, 1861. Like Mary, Susan was married in Sumter County, and once again, the Episcopal minister Stephen U. Smith performed the ceremony.[37] Shortly afterward, and without waiting for the trust to run its course in 1862, Sappington executed its provisions. He undoubtedly did so with the consent of Bryan as well as Mary and Susan. By the final settlement's terms Mary got forty-nine slaves, Susan forty-seven, and they each received the same financial arrangements: two notes, each for $2,344.77, from Joseph John Williams, Leon County's largest slaveholder; two notes, each for $1,829.93, from Richard Whitfield (the deferred payment on the Home place); cash in amounts of $2,344.77 (Sappington's portion of the cash payment made by Williams) and $1,509.36 (Sappington's part of the money paid by Whitfield), and thirteen mules. Each sister signed a document stating, "I do hereby *exonerate* and *release* the said G. W. Sappington from all liability as Trustee."[38]

At first Mary and Richard Allen Whitfield lived in Wayne County, North Carolina, but they returned to Leon County. There Richard enlisted in Leon County in a Confederate cavalry battalion. Mary and Richard had five sons. Their last child, Bryan Croom Whitfield, was baptized at St. John's on April 8, 1867, but two months later Mary, only

thirty-one, became ill with dysentery and died on June 21.[39] Richard
Allen remained in Leon County, married two more times, and had three
more children. He served as a county judge until his death on November 28, 1906. Sappington reputedly moved to Arkansas sometime in
1860. Susan and James George Whitfield made their home in Sumter
County, living in the community that bore the Whitfield name. During
the Civil War James went to Florida, where he served in the same cavalry unit as Richard, but returned to Alabama in 1865. James and Susan
had a daughter, Mary Croom, who was born on September 14, 1868,
but lived for only two months. They later had three more children.[40]

By 1860 Richard and Winifred Croom and some of their children
were dead. Of Bryan's immediate family, George Alexander lived nearby
at Casa de Lago, and William's family seemed settled, at least for the
time being. He and his family had left New York and the Mississippi
Delta, and the latest word had them living in Eutaw, Alabama, the small
seat of government for Greene County in Alabama's Black Belt. Goodwood plantation had undergone its own metamorphosis, and Bryan and
Eveline and her mother had been forced to make radical readjustments.

As has been seen, from the 1840s to the mid-1850s, Bryan, Eveline,
and Ann Hawks lived a busy life at Goodwood presiding over a scene of
frequent visitations and prolonged stays by family members. Bryan had
settled the claims of the other Crooms and the Lafayette heirs to Hardy's
estate of 2,480 acres. Goodwood encompassed Sections 26–29, plus Sections 11, 14, and 23, purchased in 1847 from William P. Craig. The
additional 1,920 acres increased Goodwood to 4,400 acres and caused
Bryan, in effect, to divide it into two plantations.

In 1851 Bryan managed to increase, decrease, and increase Goodwood. In February he paid Joseph Caruthers of Pulaski County, Georgia,
$1,300 for 160 acres that lay in Section 30 on Goodwood's western border.[41] Then in May, as noted, he sold Richard Section 11 and additional
parcels located north of the Tallahassee–Monticello road.[42] Finally, in
December, Bryan purchased Section 34, which Richard had obtained
from the Union Bank. Richard sold it to Bryan for much less than he
paid originally several months earlier.[43]

As Goodwood's limits changed, usually by being enlarged, the plantation remained the centerpiece of a complex operation involving white owners and their chattels whose ultimate purpose was to make money from the sale of cotton. Those who lived there were dependent on each other, and all were dependent on the land and the weather. Yet cotton was not produced in a factory. It was produced by people, and there were always uncertainties. As a caring master, Bryan well knew the value of slaves. He had inherited slaves, profited from their natural increase, bought them, and, under his arrangement with Ann Hawks, worked her slaves at minimal expense to himself. He benefited even more in 1851, when his mother-in-law made him trustee of several of her slaves for as long as she lived. On Ann's death, Bryan would continue as trustee for Eveline. The bequest was valuable because it included twenty-nine blacks, about equally divided between females and males and ranging in age from forty-five to one (most of them were young).[44]

Two years later, in 1853, Bryan paid his kinsman George Whitfield $4,200 for 420 acres in Section 19.[45] Croom continued his purchases in 1855, when he acquired the 640 acres of Section 15 of the Lafayette Grant. The owner, William P. Gould of Greene County, Alabama, asked and got $6,400 for the land.[46]

It has been mentioned that on New Year's Day, 1855, Bryan bought Sections 19, 20, and 30 in the Lafayette Grant from William Bailey for $12,000 and on the same day sold it to his brother Richard for a like amount. Then, making the issue more complicated, the master of Goodwood paid $2,150 to Richard for 201 acres in Section 20 and 15 acres in Section 30.[47] In October 1855, Bryan dealt with George Sappington. The trustee for Richard's daughters sold Bryan parts of Sections 19, 20, and 30 not previously conveyed by Richard to his brother. The acreage was 713 acres, and Sappington sold Bryan an additional 433 acres of Section 17. The total price was $14,725.[48]

Fortunately for Bryan, all the unusual activity in 1855 took place during a good crop year, assuring him greater profits than usual. Charles E. Dyke, a native Canadian who had come to Tallahassee in 1841 and was the editor of the influential *Floridian and Journal,* usually spent his time praising Democrats and excoriating Whigs. Still, in the summer and early fall he ventured out into the county and commented on the agricultural situation. In July, Dyke reported that the "crops of all kinds in Leon were never more promising." "Cotton generally looks beautiful and is loaded with fruit. There is no sign," he added, "as yet of caterpillar that we have heard of. An abundant corn crop is now certain."[49]

In late 1856 and early 1857 Bryan bought land for the last time in Leon County. To do so, he went outside the Lafayette Grant but not far. His purchases were made in Townships 1 and 2, Range 2 North and East, which lay east and slightly north of Goodwood. In December he paid $2,082 to the survivors of Elisha Chauncey for 160.18 acres in Section 9. On January 7, Bryan bought 2,123 acres from David Barrow of West Felicia Parish, Louisiana. Barrow, a wealthy planter and native North Carolinian, had lived in Leon County in the mid-1830s. The price was $15,040 and included parts of Sections 1, 2, 3, 4, 10, 11, 15, 16, and 20. Next, on January 20, Croom acquired 460 acres in Sections 2, 3, 24, and 34, paying William N. Taylor, executor for Jacob Elliot, $15,000. Eighteen slaves were included in the contract, which explained the high price.[50] Bryan had added 2,743 acres to his holdings, and although the land was close to Goodwood, it was not contiguous.

Managing his ever increasing lands and planting operations, looking after his family interests, joining Eveline as host to numerous relatives, and enjoying a social life that included church activities kept Bryan fully occupied. Yet there was one problem that was unresolved: uncontested ownership of Goodwood. Not forgotten was that on December 19, 1837, he had become the legal administrator of Hardy's Florida estate. He also remembered the event, if not the date (February 12, 1838), when Henrietta Smith was made administratrix of his brother's North Carolina holdings. After that the harsh contest over control of Hardy Croom's estate developed.

In the late spring of 1838 Henrietta offered to compromise on division of the estate, both real and personal. She suggested one-half for her and her surviving daughter, Elizabeth Armistead, and one-half for the Crooms as an equitable arrangement. She was also open to any alternative compromise, including arbitration, but wanted a reply by August 1, 1838. After the Crooms counseled among themselves and said no, the Smith-Armistead lawyers filed a bill of complaint claiming possession of all Hardy's personal estate and part of his real estate. At that, Bryan and the Crooms formally answered the bill of complaint, asking the court to dismiss it. Responding, Henrietta and Elizabeth's lawyers moved to file their general replication to the answers, and the case was put at issue.

The trial should have begun, but after the Crooms filed their several replies, Bryan and Richard (in an obviously calculated move) signed the formal agreement, discussed in chapter 5, whereby Bryan agreed to sell Rocky Comfort and all of Hardy's property to Richard. Richard's lawyer then filed Richard's cross-bill of complaint against Smith-Armistead and his own family.

Henrietta's lawyers saw the Bryan-Richard agreement of October 11, 1839, followed shortly by Richard's cross-bill, as illegal and a blatant plot by the Croom family. They were correct in their assessment that it was a plot. That became evident when Bryan and Richard canceled their real estate agreement on October 4, 1842. Bristling with anger, the plaintiffs' lawyers had their clients answer with a deposition on September 9, 1840. In some detail the statement claimed that all of Richard's maneuvers were unconscionable and invalid. Smith-Armistead's lawyers asked the judge to dismiss the cross-bill. The Crooms responded to Richard on January 9, 1841. The defendants' statement expanded on their earlier positions and, in general, agreed with Richard's arguments.

The court records have not been located, but apparently Richard's cross-bill was thrown out, and the case based on the original bill of complaint by Smith-Armistead went forward, albeit slowly. Throughout 1839–40 many depositions were taken, and the trial should have been conducted in 1841. Yet for reasons still unexplained, the litigation went on for a decade, still unsettled. All of that changed dramatically and suddenly in the 1850s, and there was a final reckoning.

9 *"A Most Unrighteous Judgment"*

In the 1850s Henrietta Smith and Elizabeth Armistead reactivated their case against Bryan and the Croom family. After the earlier legal efforts to secure Hardy's estate were deferred, Henrietta remained in New Bern, as did Elizabeth and her daughter, Susan Evelyn. Henrietta lived on the income from her various farming properties and helped support Elizabeth, who also had land and slaves inherited from her father and from her husband, Richard Armistead. On October 29, 1846, twenty-two-year-old Susan married John Still Winthrop Jr., thirty-six, in New York City. His father was also from New York and was related to the distinguished New England family that included John Winthrop, the colonial Puritan who served as the first governor of Massachusetts Bay.[1]

Winthrop and Susan had met during one of her many visits to New York City. Elizabeth approved of her daughter's marriage, but, being a true daughter of Henrietta, she was a good businesswoman and wanted to safeguard Susan's future. To that end, she and Susan signed a wedding agreement with Winthrop in October 1846. Its terms were mutually agreed on and specified that the slaves, land, and other property

Susan inherited from her father would be hers alone. After their marriage, John and Susan moved into a home on Broad Street in New Bern, and he became a planter. Winthrop also served as the unofficial manager of Henrietta's estate and business affairs.[2] In 1848 the couple had a son and, to no one's surprise, named him John III. Although she was wealthy, Henrietta, who was seventy years old in 1850, saw time running out on her effort to obtain Goodwood and other parts of Hardy's estate. At her and Elizabeth's request, Winthrop assumed the responsibility of hiring another set of lawyers and pressing the case to a conclusion.

By that time, the former Territory of Florida had joined the Union as the twenty-seventh state. The constitution, so narrowly ratified in 1839, had gone into effect in 1845 when Florida achieved statehood. Article V of the document established a new system of courts, as superior courts and justices were replaced by circuit courts and justices. These became Florida's basic courts of original jurisdiction in criminal and civil cases. Circuit judges served five-year terms and had an added responsibility: sitting together, they constituted the supreme court, a body that had only appellate jurisdiction.

Yielding to the force of Jacksonian democracy, Florida adopted a constitutional amendment in 1850 requiring the popular election of circuit judges (and thus supreme court justices as well). Still another amendment in 1850, which took effect in 1853, reduced judges' tenure from eight- to six-year terms. Next, the legislature passed a law stipulating that beginning in 1851 Florida would have a separate and independent state supreme court. The appellate tribunal would include a chief justice and two associate justices to be popularly elected for eight-year terms. Although circuit judges were trial judges presiding over inferior courts, the law provided that a circuit judge could fill in if needed for a particular case before the supreme court.[3]

Pretrial activities began as early as 1851, but the Croom case was not heard until the fall of 1856. It proceeded under the reorganized court system. Both parties secured new lawyers, who appeared before a new judge to place depositions in evidence and hear testimony from previous and new witnesses. Southern Circuit judge Thomas F. King, sitting in the Middle Circuit, presided over the trial. A native Georgian, King had moved with his father to Jackson County in 1836, about the same time that Betsy and Sam Bellamy and Ann and Ned Bellamy settled there. King later moved to Tallahassee, where he studied law under Thomas Baltzell and began practice in 1845. He served as secretary of the first Senate and was appointed solicitor for the Southern District of Florida. King engaged in politics and was a delegate to the Democratic national convention of 1852. The next year in the first popular vote for circuit judges, he was elected to serve the Southern Circuit.

The Tallahassee bar in the 1850s was a gifted one. With the ownership of Goodwood and the rest of Hardy Croom's real and personal estate at stake, the defendants and plaintiffs employed its most heralded members. James T. Archer and Mariano D. Papy represented the complainants. Archer was in his forties and at the height of his powers, which both friends and foes acknowledged were considerable. Archer was born in 1819 in South Carolina and moved with his parents (who had suffered financial setbacks) to Tallahassee in 1835, where young James worked in a mercantile store and for a local newspaper. He read law in the office of territorial secretary James D. Westcott Jr. Archer honed his natural talents by participating in a local debating society, and quick recognition came his way: he served as both attorney general and secretary of state under Governor William D. Moseley. He was also United States attorney for the Western District of Florida.

Even greater political advancement seemed certain, but in 1848 Archer resigned as comptroller of public accounts because of ill health. Typically, Archer accepted temporary appointment to aid his successor with the state's account books.

The young counsel's influence continued with his service as confidential adviser to several governors and with his increased prominence as a trial lawyer. The well-known attorney prospered in private practice. Easily recognized—he had a large round head, a broad face, a straight nose with flaring nostrils, and a protruding lower lip that gave him the appearance of having a perpetual smile—Archer was an opponent to be reckoned with.[4]

Mariano D. Papy joined forces with Archer. The thirty-eight-year-old Papy was a native Floridian born in poor circumstances in St. Augustine. Largely self-taught, he worked hard at his profession. With the help of an able overseer, Papy became a successful cotton planter as well. He was less flamboyant than Archer but served steadily and ably as clerk of the Court of Appeals, as attorney general of Florida, and in the state legislature. Private law practice was his forte (a special legislative act admitted him to the bar before he was twenty-one). Known for his perceptiveness and memory, Papy was a good counterpart to Archer.[5]

The Crooms enlisted the services of William George Mackey Davis and Medicus A. Long. Davis, seven years older than Archer, was his rival and friend. Davis was born in Portsmouth, Virginia. His father, who served in the United States Navy, died when Davis was young. Although provided with a good education by his widowed mother, Davis resisted her plan for him to become an Episcopal minister and ran away to sea. He ended up in Savannah and in the next years worked in a printing house in Washington, Georgia, and later published one of the first newspapers in the Chattahoochee River town of Eufaula, Alabama. From there Davis moved to Franklin County, Florida, where he practiced law in Apalachicola and the neighboring boom town of St. Joseph. He lost a race for the Legislative Council but was elected county judge. A strong Whig, Davis moved to Tallahassee in 1848 and became a leading lawyer.[6]

Medicus A. Long was the other member of the defense team. At least part of the native Tennesseean's high place in legal and social circles was due to his wife, Ellen, daughter of territorial governor, planter, and Whig political leader Richard Keith Call. Medicus, who came to Tallahassee in 1843 to practice law, and the future chronicler of local history (*Florida Breezes; or, Florida, New and Old* [1882]) were married in 1844. Long became a member of George Walker's law firm. Walker was a cousin of Call's. Long entered politics as a Democrat and was elected to the state legislature, where he authored the bill in 1850 establishing the seminary that became Florida State University in the twentieth century. Long participated in a public debate with his father-in-law during the campaign of 1856 (the year of the Croom trial) and served as a presidential elector for the successful Democratic candidate James Buchanan. Periodically, Long was subject to severe illnesses, particularly asthma. Seeking to improve his health, he moved to San Antonio, Texas, in 1859 but without his wife. J. B. Galbraith was Long's law partner, but there is no evidence that he participated in the Croom case. A contemporary editor wrote of Long, "He is an able, ingenious, and clear headed lawyer of decided ability," but as one student of Ellen Call Long's writing career put it, Medicus Long was "a shadowy figure."[7]

The principals and townspeople as well looked forward to a final resolution to the long-delayed case that had begun back in 1839. Some additional evidence was introduced in 1856, but the proceeding was basically a repeat of the earlier trial. The same arguments were offered by the opposing lawyers. Davis and Long concentrated on witnesses who had known Hardy in North Carolina and Florida. Mainly, they limited their contact with survivors of the *Home* to interrogatories and cross-examinations.

In the original case the plaintiffs used depositions from citizens in Charleston, and the defense had employed Hugh S. Legare and James L. Petigru, two shining stars in Charleston's constellation of intellectuals, to look after the Croom interests. Charlestonians who had survived the wreck of the *Home* were utilized once again to give depositions. Petigru, besides his status as one of the South's leading lawyers, was by now the conscience of Charleston in his opposition to the secession movement. He operated from his office in St. Michael's Alley next to St. Michael's Episcopal Church and took on an increasingly important role in the litigation. Hardy and Bryan had known Petigru by reputation and probably personally from their visits to Charleston.

As the trial began, Davis and Long laid out the case for the defense. Dr. John M. W. Davidson, a new witness, had been deposed in Tallahassee in 1852. The physician noted that Hardy's health had improved in Florida and that he had spoken of the territory as his home. Hardy wanted Davidson to help him establish a botanical garden at the future Goodwood.[8]

Then in 1852 and again in 1855, Ann Hawks gave depositions. In both instances her remarks were basically the same. Hawks declared that Charleston was never intended as anything but a summer home for the two brothers. Both expected to return to Florida later in the fall of

1837. According to her, at the time of his death Hardy was building a good house, one designed for permanent residence. Frances Croom's illness, described by the witness as epilepsy, was all that prevented her from coming to Florida. The elderly Ann Hawks (in 1855 she was seventy-eight years old and lived at Goodwood with her daughter and Bryan) was mentally alert and blessed with common sense. Her statement that Hardy was disappointed when Henrietta Smith reneged on a promise to come to Florida and help take care of Frances was logical and believable.[9] William L. Blackledge, a new witness, was a Craven County farmer in his sixties who had known Hardy since he was a boy. He was, in fact, his cousin. Deposing in 1855, Blackledge remembered that when he last saw Croom in 1837, he appeared healthier than ever. Hardy had told Blackledge that the Florida climate helped him and that Florida was his residence. Fanny's bad health, Croom added, was the deterrent that kept him from moving his family there.[10]

Three other New Bernians—new witness Mathias E. Manly and former witnesses Robert Primrose and Thomas S. Singleton—gave pro-Croom statements in 1855. Singleton, collector of customs in New Bern, was the brother of Ann Hawks. His straightforward, convincing testimony credited Hardy with being a powerful swimmer.[11] Testimony and depositions from witnesses in the earlier trial were also available to aid Judge King in reaching his decision. Lawyers for Smith-Armistead deposed and examined witnesses from New Bern in an apparent strategy to identify Hardy with the North Carolina city and establish the place as his permanent home. This was done to supply detail and corroboration, even when the witnesses had nothing specific to add, as in the persons of Zachary Slade, a fifty-six-year-old carriage maker who spoke of Hardy and Frances's high social standing and common touch, and Amos Wade, Hardy's tenant in New Bern, who said his employer considered the city his home. Both men were deposed in 1856.[12] In the same year W. C. G. White and Jane Prentiss presented similar statements that gave added credence to the contention that Hardy was a citizen of New Bern.[13]

Susan Armistead Winthrop of New Bern was a new deposer whose personal knowledge of events enhanced her remarks. The articulate granddaughter of Henrietta Smith was twenty years old when she spent the summer and fall of 1837 in New York City with her family. She remembered seeing Hardy and Frances and the children a few days before they sailed. Hardy seemed depressed about going to Charleston. He was sorry to move from North Carolina and regretted having sold his Lenoir County holdings and leaving his mother's grave to be overrun by briars. According to Susan, Hardy chose Charleston because, in sharp contrast to Florida, it offered good educational opportunities. Nor was Florida, beset by Indian wars, a safe place to raise a family. She insisted that Frances was in good health but admitted that having children subjected her to sporadic nervous attacks. As for Hardy, he was so feeble that hearing of his natural death would not have surprised her. Susan was positive that she had never heard Hardy say anything about moving to Florida. In that regard, she said, "I heard him say Florida was a great country to make money [in] and for raising cotton." [14]

Archer and Papy re-called *Home* passengers Henry Vanderzee, the Charleston merchant who had shared a piece of wreckage with William Henry, and Mathilda Schroeder, the fancy dress storekeeper from Charleston who had been impressed by the youth. Both had testified at least twice before, and both strengthened the plaintiffs' case. In the mid-1850s Vanderzee remembered events on board the *Home* and stood by his former statements indicating that William Henry was the last Croom to die.[15] Yet Vanderzee admitted, "There was great fear & noise and confusion aboard the ship. Any cries or bewailing was [*sic*] lost in the roar of the ocean." [16] In 1852 Schroeder's damaging certitude remained unshaken: Hardy died before William Henry.[17]

A number of neutral parties were called to make written statements or recount facts about Hardy and Frances, the other Crooms, and their relatives and acquaintances and to place in context the family's activities in North Carolina and Florida. The trial ended in the second week of October. Waiting for the decision, Bryan and Eveline and other family members took note of various events. As Whigs, the Crooms were disappointed that the Democrats swept Leon County in the races for governor, congressman, state senator, and four house members. More pleasing was Tallahassee's recent connection by steam power with St. Marks over the Tallahassee railroad. Replacing the mule-powered locomotives meant more expeditious transportation of Goodwood's increasing cotton crop. Any lingering political despair vanished quickly on Thursday, October 9, 1856, when Judge King ruled in the Crooms' favor. King's decision held that at the time of his death, Hardy Croom was a citizen of Florida. Accepting the citizenship premise of the defense made it unnecessary for the judge to rule on survivorship. Since Florida law prevailed, King dismissed the plaintiffs' bill of complaint and ordered them to pay the costs of the suit. For the time being, at least, it seemed that Bryan and Eveline had won the long-disputed case.

Bryan and Eveline and all the Croom kin and their friends rejoiced at the verdict. Still, victory was not final, and their possession of Goodwood was not irrevocable. Bryan and Eveline knew that Henrietta and Elizabeth, who had invested so much time and money in the case, would not accept Judge King's decision. The *Tallahassee Floridian and Journal* predicted that although the "important case . . . which ha[d] been pending in Chancery Court for many years" had been decided, an appeal would "probably be filed by the complainants to the [state] Supreme Court." [18]

Some time before that tribunal convened for its January 1857 term, Smith-Armistead's lawyers made clear to the Crooms that they intended to appeal. Before doing so, they offered a compromise. Its specific terms are unknown, but they were generous. The proposal could have been for an even split of Hardy's personal and real estate. No doubt Bryan and Eveline consulted with family members. They also sought advice from their lawyers, particularly from Petigru, who had been engaged earlier as a consultant but apparently had remained in Charleston throughout the circuit court trial. The Charleston lawyer was confident of his own abilities and earlier had won a similar case in South Carolina. Believing further that the Crooms' strong position would prevail in any appeal, the Charleston lawyer advised his clients to reject the compromise. When they accepted his advice, John Winthrop went back to work for the plaintiffs. There was little surprise at Goodwood plantation when word was received that the Crooms' courtroom struggles were not over. With the move to a higher forum, both sides stepped up their legal firepower. Petigru prepared to come to Tallahassee, where he would be a guest at Goodwood during the arguments. When he arrived in late February 1857, the *Tallahassee Floridian and Journal* noted his presence, referring to Petigru as an eminent South Carolina lawyer.[19] He soon conferred with Davis, who was retained by the Crooms. Davis performed well and was coequal with Petigru in making arguments to the high court. Medicus Long fell so ill that his death was expected. Fortunately he recovered, but so slowly that he played only a limited role in the appeal.[20]

The plaintiffs matched Petigru with the fortuitously named William Law of Savannah. Operating from law offices on Bull Street, the sixty-four-year-old Law enjoyed a formidable reputation. He had practiced law since 1819, served as a superior court judge, and been a militia officer. A longtime civic leader in Savannah, Law also owned slaves and plantations. He was a dedicated Whig whose fame was based not on his looks (he had a scrubby beard and a bulbous nose) but on his brilliant oratory and sharp legal mind.[21] Earlier, Law seems to have played an advisory role to Archer and Papy. Now he, too, prepared to come to Tallahassee. Petigru and Law knew and respected each other, although they differed philosophically: unlike Unionist Petigru, Law was a southern rights man and favored secession. On December 22, 1856, Petigru wrote Law about the case, remarking that the Georgian had the advantage and would "renew all [Petigru's] fears by the skillful use of the last word." Further, "You will have the first word too for the case will not be heard till you are on the grounds." Petigru asked Law, "[Let me] know when you are going & let us agree to go together, or at all events not to go against one another except in Court."[22] James Archer and M. D. Papy worked with Law, and although Papy played no major role in making presentations, Archer did. His carefully reasoned arguments matched those of Law and Petigru.

Because Florida did not have a separate supreme court building, the appeal was heard in the capitol. Chief Justice Thomas Baltzell was disqualified because he had been a lawyer for the Crooms in at least one of the cases. He had also been a witness for the defense in the original case. Jesse Johnson Finley, judge of the Western Circuit court, took

Baltzell's place. Finley was born in Tennessee in 1812. His father served under Andrew Jackson, and young Finley himself came to Florida as a volunteer in the Second Seminole War. Later, he studied law in Tennessee, achieving admission to the bar in 1838. Finley moved to Marianna in the 1840s, where without doubt he became acquainted with the Bellamys. He won election to the Florida senate in 1850, and in 1852 he was a presidential elector on the Whig ticket. Selected circuit judge in 1853, Finley was then elected and reelected. He would later become prominent in the Civil War and in postwar Florida politics.[23]

Byrd M. Pearson and Charles H. DuPont were the other two justices. Pearson was a lawyer born and trained in South Carolina. He moved to Alabama, became a planter, and later migrated to Florida. A lawyer-planter, Pearson was living in Jacksonville in 1855 when he was elected to fill a vacancy on the supreme court. Urbane and courteous, Pearson impressed contemporaries with his independence and what was described as his good "legal mind," but his own health was bad. His eyesight failing, Pearson retired from the bench in 1859.[24]

DuPont, who later would be elected chief justice, wrote the court's decision. Born in South Carolina in 1805, he attended college in Georgia and in 1827 moved to Gadsden County, Florida, where he would have known the Crooms. He built a mansion in Quincy and soon became a model example of the male southern aristocrat: successful lawyer, soldier (he served in the Second Seminole War), planter, and politician. A Democrat, DuPont lost a fortune in the Panic of 1837 but made it back. He was elected to the supreme court in 1854 and would be elected chief justice in 1859, defeating his longtime rival Baltzell. The Florida supreme court was known for animosities among its justices. Still, DuPont, dignified in bearing and courteous in actions, was admired for his painstaking hard work and integrity.[25]

The supreme court's busy calendar attracted public attention, as counsel and interested parties gathered. Without question local editor Charles E. Dyke had the Croom case in mind when he reminded readers, "Several cases, involving the adjudication of highly interesting law points are before [the supreme court], the settlement of which will illumine the jurisprudence of our State."[26] At Goodwood, lawyer Petigru was made comfortable. He wrote his daughter in South Carolina, "My

Hostess, Mrs. Croom[,] is so kind that she never thinks I have enough."
He suggested to Eveline that she should get his opponent Law out to
Goodwood and stuff him with food. Petigru told Eveline that it would
not be "good policy" for her to give him "so many good things" before
her case was decided. "I hope there is no danger, but if the decision
should go against them, it would make a sad change. I don't think I
would have the courage to break the news to them." Even so, he continued, "I intend to run the risk of the judgment, by hearing it delivered before I go." Once the decision was handed down, he planned an
excursion to Wakulla Springs, a famed natural attraction fourteen miles
south of Tallahassee.[27]

As revealed in the unpaginated records of the Florida Supreme Court
Minute Book, 1846–68, the state's high tribunal did not move with
speed or efficiency. The opening session was scheduled to begin on
January 6, 1857. Baltzell and DuPont were present, but when Pearson
did not appear, the opening was postponed until January 14. Baltzell
and Pearson showed up on time, but DuPont was absent, and another
postponement was declared until the next day. Finally, on January 15,
the court began its deliberations.

All the delays and a heavy caseload forced the court to hold a special
session in March 1857, and the Croom case was among those continued. On March 3, the three judges took their places on a bench raised
above the level of a table before them, where the opposing lawyers sat.
Interested persons such as Bryan Croom and George Sappington were
present. So were the curious and the idle who simply wanted to listen
to the discourse. With a fireplace at either end of the room, all had a
choice of where to warm themselves. The initial proceeding was brief,
and the case was continued until the next day, when the arguments
finally began.

The tension accompanying the proceedings was felt by all the
Crooms. Bryan's concern was almost matched by that of Richard, as he
revealed in a letter to his daughter Mary: "Before I know the result of
this suit, I wish you to know some of my own private feelings." For
twenty years he had contributed his resources to the case, but he concluded, "That is but a drop in the bucket to the great wear & tear upon
my mind." He admitted mistakes but declared, "My conscience does not

accuse me of any fixed or intentional desire to injure any person['s] character or reputation. . . . Should brother Bryan gain his suit, I have no wish or desire to benefit by it." As for his "own conscientious views on the morality" of the case, "I believe in all the requisites of abstract justice this suit is with the Defendants." [28]

The supreme court's decision proved a complicated one. As written and decided by DuPont, the principal opinion occupied ninety-nine pages in *Florida Reports,* and a belated opinion by Pearson required another nine pages. DuPont's remarks began with a lengthy discussion of the meaning of domicile, and he acknowledged that determination of Hardy's state of domicile—North Carolina or Florida—would govern the distribution of property. Switching subjects, he then noted that under North Carolina law, if any of Hardy's children survived him, then his personal estate would go to that child or children. After that, the property would go to their next of kin, in this case Henrietta Smith. Under Florida law, which controlled the disposition of Hardy's real property in the state, Elizabeth Armistead would be equally entitled with her mother to the part that would go to the maternal side. That fact explained why the two women were both complainants. Bryan's attorneys insisted, of course, that Hardy's domicile was Florida and that Florida law would govern even if it was not.

As a basis for its decision, the court had entertained a broad range of testimony on Hardy's intentions as to his domicile and about the details of the fatal shipwreck. Included were the statements of Dr. John Torrey, Dr. Francis Hawks, Dr. Hugh McLean, B. B. Hussey, Andrew Lovegreen, Mathilda Schroeder, John Bishop, Conrad Quinn, Henry Vanderzee, J. D. Roland, W. L. Blackledge, and Matthias E. Manly. Next, letters and parts of letters written by Hardy to Frances (and some to others) were examined, suggestive that Hardy considered North Carolina his home. Further evidence, buttressing and challenging the letters, came from Dr. Francis Hawks, Dr. Hugh McLean, V. Slade, James Prentiss, Henrietta S. Osgood, John Burgwyn, Thomas Burgwyn, Susan E. Winthrop, Anne Hawks (her testimony in 1852 and 1855 was summarized), William L. Blackledge, Thomas Singleton, Matthias E. Manly, Alexander McConachie, Thomas Baltzell, John M. W. Davidson, Robert H. Berry, Jacob Elliot, Dr. J. T. J. Wilson, and George Whitfield.

Reading the testimony had taken three days, and, as Petigru noted, the chamber's occupants listened while "an apprentice of the Law . . . [read] in monotonous tone page after page of what witnesses [said] about the life and history of Hardy Bryan Croom." On March 5 (the third day), nature intervened. Petigru explained: "It is now ½ after 12, and we have had a real Gulf storm. It was so dark that we had to suspend the sitting for half an hour, while, wind, rain and hail filled the air, and tho' it is now comparatively clear, we have to introduce candles." [29]

Eventually the huge volume of evidence and the challenges of the weather were overcome, permitting the court to reach a decision. Justice DuPont, after explaining the general background of the case, declared that the important issues were whether the father or the children or either was the last survivor and whether Hardy's domicile at the date of his decease was North Carolina or Florida. In accepting survivorship as an issue, DuPont embraced a subject that was not considered by Judge King in the lower court. Even so, in reaching the court's decision, DuPont first considered which family member was the last to die.

The court's problem was that the determination of a fact was dependent upon presumption; that is to say, an inference based on attendant circumstances indicating who was the last to die. Here, DuPont said, "moral conviction" was enough, and it could be based on positive or circumstantial evidence. The justice held further that the precise moment of Hardy's death did not have to be proved. Since there was no question but that Hardy died, the time of his death could be inferred or presumed from circumstantial evidence.

DuPont noted, by way of contrast, that in a common calamity where there were no definable circumstances and no facts other than age, sex, and health, there could be no presumption on which to base a conclusion. On the other hand, when a common calamity consisted of several discernible, separate events that could produce death, then the differences of age, sex, and health became a matter of *evidence*. Thus the court agreed that, in a common calamity, the last person seen or heard while the calamity was occurring had to be adjudged the survivor. Working under those guidelines, the tribunal had labored to reach a decision based on a degree of certainty that would produce a "moral conviction" as to survivorship.

The opinion conceded that Frances and Justina Rosa (and Mrs. Camack) died before Hardy, and so the matter of comparative strength in determining survivorship was between Hardy and William Henry and Henrietta Mary. Justice DuPont mentioned Hardy's general bad health and paraphrased with damning effect the depositions given by Hawks, Torrey, and McLean. After adding observations made by various passengers, the justice concluded, "Mr. Croom's physical condition was such as to utterly incapacitate him for the exertion of any physical effort beyond such as might be compassed by the decrepitude of old age or the feebleness of early childhood."[30] He then contrasted Hardy's bad health with the good health of Henrietta Mary and William Henry. Next, DuPont quoted witnesses who had seen Hardy and family members immediately before waves engulfed them and then immediately afterward when no trace of Hardy remained.

William Henry was seen by several witnesses half an hour or more after that. As for the defendants' contention that Hardy could have saved himself by grasping a piece of wreckage, "That conjecture is within the range of possibility, but it is of too vague a character to combat a rational presumption which has been deduced from known facts."[31] Regarding Henrietta Mary, the court conceded that the evidence was less reliable, but it retraced events and declared that it was "constrained to the conclusion that she also survived her father."[32] Therefore, after reviewing the testimony the court concluded that Hardy "perished before either his daughter Henrietta Mary, or his son William Henry, and that of the sister and brother, the latter was the last survivor."[33]

Once the court established William Henry as the last Croom to die, one crucial question, that of domicile, remained to be decided. All parties agreed that North Carolina was Hardy's original domicile. It remained so until 1830–31, when, acquiring agricultural interests in Florida, he established a divided residence. Various forms of domicile existed in the law, but the court had to determine Hardy's "domicile of succession" because that would govern the succession to his personal property. Admitting the difficulty of defining domicile, DuPont established criteria that would serve the purpose at hand. United States Supreme Court justice Joseph Story's three-part classification of domicile by birth, by choice, and by mere operation of law was noted. DuPont thereafter centered his attention on domicile by choice. The judge declared that a person's residence determined the domicile of succession. Establishing the locality required evidence that included an actual residence and the deliberate intention or purpose to make the place a person's home. The first requirement was easily determined but not so the second. A determination of purpose required an examination of intention. DuPont believed, given relevant texts and decisions, once a domicile was ascertained, it remained a person's domicile until a new one was established. Mere intention to acquire a new domicile without actually moving to it was meaningless.

Hardy Croom's *acts* and *declarations* were used to determine his domicile. Hardy had purchased lands in Florida for agricultural purposes, not for speculation. He settled on them, improved them, and moved his slaves to them. His major agricultural projects and the bulk of his income came from his Florida holdings. Hardy regularly visited his land, spending a large part of each year in Florida, first with Bryan in Gadsden County and later at Goodwood plantation in Leon County, where he built a house and received guests. He thus became a resident or inhabitant of Leon County, an action clearly tending toward establishing a domicile of succession. Importantly, though, he did not actually, or, as DuPont put it, de facto, abandon his domicile in North Carolina. The family house in New Bern was not disposed of and was continued as the residence of his wife and children. The household furniture remained there, and house servants were retained. Florida was the center of Croom's business and where the largest part of his fortune lay, but his wife and children were in North Carolina in the family home and living there by his authority and approval.

The opinion discussed the circumstances in further detail. It admitted the defendants' contention that Frances's health was the reason why she and the children did not move to Florida. That fact was therefore a matter of evidence on the question of intention. Yet DuPont held that no matter how much Hardy may have wished to make money in Florida, or pursue his botanical studies, or restore his own health, the well-being of his wife and family precluded any *present* intent by him to move there. Under local laws he might be a resident or inhabitant of Florida, but it was not his domicile of succession. Intent to acquire a domicile in the future was not an element in proving one's domicile of succession. Hardy had not abandoned his domicile of origin and, with a present intention to acquire a new one, moved to Florida.

DuPont considered the contention that Florida was Hardy's domicile of succession because, after acquiring lands in the state, he voted there and ceased to vote in North Carolina. The argument lacked validity, the justice wrote, because the act of voting did not mean Hardy intended to abandon his domicile of succession or to acquire a domicile of choice. The problem came from confusing other kinds of domicile, such as political or commercial, with domicile of succession. The trouble lay in how various states used the terms *residence, habitation,* and *domicile* in their local and municipal statutes. Such ordinances had validity but could not be compared with the general law governing domicile of succession. DuPont cited several authorities and cases to establish his point that "the act of voting if at all admissible as a criterion of intention, is at best of a very dubious character, and entitled to very little weight."[34]

The judge then moved from the criterion of intention by "acts" to consider intention by oral and written declarations. What about the many witnesses who mentioned Croom's stated intention to move to Florida? DuPont was unimpressed. According to him, evidence from the oral declarations was "so vague in point of date and expression, and so very contradictory in terms, that [the judges were] constrained to reject it entirely from the consideration of the cause."[35] The justice gave intention expressed in "written declarations" more weight. He mentioned Croom's referring to himself as a citizen of Florida in various bills of sale and other documents. Weight accorded to signatures on legal documents depended on the circumstances, according to DuPont. For example, Hardy's act in listing himself as being from Florida in a bill of sale executed in North Carolina did not amount to an abandonment of his domicile of origin. Hardy's nonabandonment continued down to the time of his death, making the legal documents attesting his Florida citizenship subject to each particular circumstance.

Other written declarations proved central to the decision. The large volume of personal correspondence Hardy completed from the time he came to Florida until his death fell into that category. DuPont agreed that, at first, Hardy intended to make Florida his future home. Yet, the justice pointed out, the plan was quickly abandoned, and Hardy's later letters indicated much vacillation. The justice cited snippets of Hardy's letters indicating his intent to consider Georgia, Alabama, and South Carolina as possible residences and his frequent references to North Carolina as home. All of this led DuPont to decide that Hardy's domicile of succession, "at the time of his death, was located in the State of North Carolina, and not in the State of Florida."[36]

The next issue of interpretation involved a clause of Florida's 1829 law regulating descents. This produced the most convoluted, philosophical, "legalistic" (in the arcane sense), and controversial part of the supreme court's decision, and Justice DuPont acknowledged "that the entire argument upon the construction of the statute of descents" was prepared by Judge Finley. The matter had presented itself because of DuPont's conclusion that Henrietta Mary survived Hardy and that William Henry survived her. The law read:

> That whenever an infant shall die without issue, having title to any real estate or inheritance derived by gift, devise, or descent from the father, and there be living at the death of such infant his father, or any brother or sister of such infant on the part of the father, or the paternal grandfather or grandmother of the infant, or any brother or sister of the father, or any descendant of any of them, then such estate shall descend and pass to the paternal kindred, without regard to the mother or other maternal kindred of such infant, in the same manner as if there had been no such mother or other maternal kindred living at the death of the infant, saving *however,* to such mother any right of dower which she may have in such real estate of inheritance.[37]

The complainants argued that the application of the clause was limited and applied only to cases of *immediate* descent from the father, such as descent directly from Hardy to William Henry without first descending to Henrietta Mary. The defendants were equally sure that it meant the estate was derived *mediately,* that is, through an intermediate descent from the father—in this case, through Henrietta Mary. If they were correct, the paternal kindred were let into the inheritance to the exclusion of the maternal kindred.

Judge Finley's reasoning was based on some time-tested principles as to how statutes should be interpreted. Among the rules were: to understand a statute, the intention of the legislature should be discovered; the words of a statute should be taken at face value, and only when the words were not explicit should the matter of legislative intent come into play; and the words of a statute should be taken in their ordinary, commonly accepted meaning and significance. Given that background, what did the crucial phrase "gift, devise or descent from the father" mean? Whatever the court interpreted it to mean, the justices were not "allowed to *presume* the intention of the Legislature, but [were] required to collect such intention from the words of the act."[38]

As seen by the court, the law's particular order of words—"gift, devise, or descent from the father"—was significant. The legislature intended for the paternal kindred to inherit the real estate possessed by an infant who died leaving no children and which the infant inherited from the father. Even so, the legislature did not provide that the real estate should go to the paternal kindred in exclusion of the maternal kindred. Rather, the court held, the legislature, by using "gift," meant *immediate* gift from the father. But a gift from Hardy to Henrietta Mary and, in turn, a gift of the same inheritance from Henrietta Mary to William Henry was not a gift from Hardy to William Henry within the meaning of the statute. Thus, William Henry, a minor, dying without children, did not leave an inheritance that would descend to the paternal blood.

If that reasoning applied to the word "gift," it applied as well to the word "devise." So Hardy lawfully could pass Goodwood to Henrietta Mary. But, if she died and Goodwood passed by operation of the law to William Henry and he then died, the legal effect was not the same as if Hardy had devised Goodwood directly (or immediately) to William Henry. If William Henry died an infant without children, the law would not secure the inheritance of Goodwood through the paternal blood to the exclusion of the maternal blood. The court therefore concluded that the 1829 statute's wording, "gift or devise from the father," did not exclude the Smith-Armistead side of the family from Hardy's real estate inheritance.

Regardless of the words "gift" and "devise," which meant an act of the parties, the defendants claimed that "descent" meant by operation of law. But that view, the court held, was a departure from the plain, explicit words of the act in their natural and obvious meaning. The words "descent from the father" clearly meant an immediate transmission, an inheritance from the father, and excluded the idea of intermediate descents. By surviving Hardy, Henrietta Mary inherited that portion of his estate that descended to her as his daughter. Had she lived, she could have disposed of it by gift or devise or any of several modes of transfer. Henrietta Mary had absolute title to the estate she inherited from her father, and upon her death the estate descended from her to William Henry. The court ruled that the descent was from Henrietta Mary to William Henry rather than from Hardy to William Henry. Beyond that, the court reasoned that the order of the words "gift, devise and descent" and their close connection with each other indicated that the legislature did not intend to include *mediate* descents. The act of 1829 used the words "descent from the father" to mean *immediate* descent from the father just as they meant *immediate* gift and devise from the father.

Henrietta and Elizabeth had claimed that they were entitled to the one-half of the real estate that William Henry inherited from Henrietta Mary and to the entire one-half that *immediately* descended to him from his father. Their lawyer William Law contended that the whole of Hardy's real estate, both that which came *directly* from him and that which descended from Henrietta Mary, was within the meaning and operation of the act of 1829. The Florida Supreme Court agreed. Finally, on March 13, the case ended. Having explained and justified the court's conclusion, DuPont ordered "the bill in this cause to be dismissed, be *reversed,* and that the cause be remanded [to the trial court], with direction to proceed therein in accordance with the rulings contained in this opinion."[39] Justice Pearson's opinion came too late to affect the ruling but made no difference because he agreed with DuPont.

The decision devastated the Crooms. News of the ruling spread quickly to family members. Writing from New York in late March 1857, Julia Croom took time out from the financial difficulties she and William were having to inform son Stephens, "Perhaps you know by this time that your Uncle Bryan has lost his case." She added, "[I consider it] a most unrighteous judgment as anybody in the world would say except perhaps the winning party and even they I should think would have some scruples of conscience about it."[40] Bryan and Eveline did not know what to do. Judge DuPont's obtuse language and esoteric reasoning presented semantic pyrotechnics too difficult for them to follow. Yet it was crystal clear that they had lost. More than ever, the master and mistress of Goodwood had to rely on their lawyers.

Petigru was no less crushed. The decree "was like a blow in the back," filling him "with despair." What did he think of DuPont's decision? "It is marvelous," he wrote Davis from Charleston on April 2, "that the decree should be wrong from beginning to end with perhaps the exception of the survivorship of William Henry and that it should be unanimous."[41] Petigru's anguish was compounded by the news of his brother's death. Petigru had been diminished professionally, and he had the added burden of guilt for having advised the Crooms to reject the Smith-Armistead compromise offer. He wrote, "I would rather have lost my life [than the Croom case]." His failure so tortured Petigru that he doubted if Croom had been out of his thoughts "5 minutes at a time" since he heard the news, "unless when asleep." "Even then, this horrid case continually intrudes upon my dreams."[42]

A student of Petigru's career commented that back in Charleston the disconsolate lawyer passed his time walking in the church garden next to his office muttering to himself. His clerks feared to approach him. At home Petigru spent nights pacing back and forth going over the arguments presented in Tallahassee.[43] Unused to defeat and believing that DuPont's decision was "rendered . . . against evidence," Petigru wrote Davis, "I am in favor of carrying the war into the enemy's country." He wanted to file a bill in North Carolina for Hardy's personal estate (but not his real estate) there. He did not think the North Carolina judges "would hold the doctrine which Dupont [*sic*] ha[d] delivered upon no better authorization than Mr. Law's speech." Nothing came of that idea, but closer to hand, Petigru devised a strategy: "Let us proceed," he instructed Davis, "with caution and render an account of the principal and the profits [of Hardy's estate] as well as we can and file our exceptions and appeal to the Supreme Court of Fla on the final decree and from the Supreme Court of Fla to the Supreme Court of the U.S."[44]

Davis discussed Petigru's plan with Bryan and the others, and on securing their approval, he proceeded on Thursday, April 2, 1857, to file a petition for a rehearing of the case. The court had to track down circuit judge Finley—thinking his work as a supreme court justice substitute complete, Finley probably had left town. Once the judge was located and assumed his place, the court considered the petition and was not long in making a decision.[45] Whether Petigru returned from Charleston is not certain, but most of the argument for the Crooms came from Davis. First, he maintained that the evidence given by witnesses on the *Home* was contradictory, noting that no jury would convict a person on such imprecise evidence. Yet his client was "to be stripped of his estate, and reduced to almost total penury, without having the benefit, so dear to every American citizen, of a trial by jury." Davis declared that to obtain the truth the supreme court should send the case to jury trial to determine the question of survivorship.[46]

The supreme court was a court of appeal, Davis asserted, but had assumed original jurisdiction in considering survivorship. The high court could, he maintained, reverse the lower court's decision, but it could not reverse what that court did not consider. Thus, the supreme court had gone beyond its authority in rendering an original decision.

Davis necessarily wanted the supreme court's conclusion that North Carolina was Hardy's domicile to be reargued. "To my client it involves his all," he said. "He is a man well off, or a beggar in his old age, as it may be decided."[47] To make his point Davis cited Supreme Court justice Joseph Story in *Case v. Clark*, where he ruled that, in order to be a citizen of a state, a person had to have his domicile in the state. To be a citizen of a state, there had to be a bona fide change of domicile, a bona fide intention of removal, and a real change of domicile. To move for business or pleasure did not make a person a citizen, but Story had ruled that moving to another state with the intention of establishing a domicile made the person a citizen of that state. Since citizens of each state were constitutionally entitled to the privileges and immunities of citizens in the several states, the right to sue in a federal court made domicile and citizenship synonymous. Davis quoted various federal judges who had upheld Story's decision.[48]

Counsel for the defendants then cited Story and other judges to the effect that a person could not have two domiciles or citizenships in different states. Contending that moving with the intent of taking up residence automatically made one a citizen of the state where he or she resided, Davis attempted to prove that Hardy was a citizen of Florida in 1833 and 1834. He argued that, given the connection between residence and citizenship, a conclusive test of citizenship was voting. In order to vote a person had to be a citizen. Because some persons declined to vote, casting a ballot did not create domicile, but, even so, citizenship and domicile preceded the right to vote. Documentary evidence existed that Hardy Croom voted in Florida elections. Davis was disdainful of the supreme court's partial reliance on opinions rendered in English courts because the doctrine of domicile was not well understood there and, in any case, English decisions could not prevail over decisions made in the United States. Davis also mentioned the various declarations made by Hardy and documents signed by him that clearly established his Florida citizenship.[49]

Judge DuPont responded for the court to Davis's arguments. As for the assertion that considering the question of survivorship had made the supreme court a court of original jurisdiction, DuPont offered a technical answer. The justice admitted that such logic would apply to an appeal from an interlocutory decree that did not conclude the merits of the case, but, he argued, it did not apply to an appeal from a final decree, as had occurred in the Croom litigation. After the lower court decided against the complainants, the supreme court, by hearing their appeal, had to decide the question of survivorship because Smith-Armistead's claim to Hardy's personal property depended on a ruling.[50] DuPont then used the complainants' earlier actions against them. In the original case, the defendants had permitted Henrietta to style herself as the administratrix of William Henry. That fact, the justice found, meant that the defendants themselves acknowledged her representative character with all the rights attendant. Then DuPont cited cases to show that the court could substantially rehear the case. An appeal in equity constituted a rehearing, and the appeal opened the whole case to the respondent in the appellate court. In effect, survivorship, even if not mentioned in the original case, was important and could be considered by the supreme court.[51]

Davis's insistence that the case be sent to a jury failed to persuade DuPont. He ruled that such a tactic should have been utilized in the original court. Litigation that had gone on for almost twenty years should not be further delayed by a jury trial.[52] The supreme court also had considered the defense's points that too little weight was given to Hardy's exercise of the vote and too much to his family's continued occupancy of their original home in North Carolina. Even with the reconsideration, DuPont decided that the court was correct initially. The original reversal had considered Hardy's votes merely as criteria of intention, more or less important according to circumstances.[53] DuPont reiterated that the defendants had placed too much importance on Croom's voting, letting it override every other indication. Finally, the court was unsympathetic because the defense's application was presented as a written argument. By law it should have been a simple appeal filed within fifteen days. No new brief was needed, so the application for a rehearing of the case was "refused, and the petition ordered to be dismissed."[54]

No less trenchantly, the *Tallahassee Floridian and Journal* announced that the motion "for a rehearing in this case ha[d] been refused by the Supreme Court."[55] Unless there was an appeal to the United States Supreme Court, Bryan and Eveline had lost Goodwood and Bryan's estate. It was early spring, but it is doubtful that they enjoyed the April weather.

10 *"Great Sacrifice" Attended the Loss*

Whether or not Bryan and Eveline appealed the Florida court's devastating decision to the United States Supreme Court, it was important to preserve whatever financial resources they could. Goodwood, like other plantations, functioned on credit. Croom was the typical planter in that his capital was tied up in land and slaves. He had to deal with an intricate economic system that, not even considering the complexities of slavery, was a convoluted chain whose disparate links involved banks, transportation, insurance, merchants, and factors, all underwritten by a myriad of loans, collateral, bank notes, specie, checks, certificates of deposit, bills of exchange, agreements, promissory notes, mortgages, deeds, and indentures. Although cumbersome and often inefficient, the system worked. It was long term and self-perpetuating for the individual planter, provided there was no catastrophic interruption. Unfortunately, such a fate had befallen the master of Goodwood. Bryan's numerous creditors, anxious to collect what they could, would inevitably and sooner than later descend on him. Seeking to have money available for unavoidable contingencies, Bryan (perhaps with advice from his lawyer) conceived a clever plan that required and received the cooperation of Ann Hawks.

In May 1857, Bryan's mother-in-law entered a complaint against him in the Leon County Circuit Court. The complaint, heard by Middle Circuit judge Wayless Baker, accused Bryan of violating a contract concerning payment to Hawks for the use of her slaves. Going back to the early years at Rocky Comfort plantation, Bryan and Ann had made various arrangements for him to use her slaves. The latest contract had been in 1856, when Bryan agreed to pay $1,500 as a satisfactory rate of hire. Bryan never paid because his mother-in-law had not forced the issue. By then the widow's slaves had increased to more than forty, and Bryan, on the advice of his new lawyer, D. P. Hogue (a native of Pennsylvania), admitted his liability to compensate Hawks. He agreed with the allegations brought against him in the case and was willing to make good his obligations. He refused to do so until the court decided the amount owed and when the payment should be made.[1]

In June, Judge Baker appointed D. W. Gwynn as special master to ascertain how many of Hawks's slaves Croom had used since 1837 and the annual value of their hire. That was difficult to do, and Gwynn, a thirty-six-year-old lawyer from Kentucky, was dependent on Bryan's testimony and that of other witnesses. Before 1856 no set amount other than "reasonable" was ever stated. Finally, the special master submitted his estimate to Judge Baker: Bryan owed Ann $23,200 and another $13,155 in interest charges. With some adjustments the total came to $36,456 for the twenty years 1837–57.[2] If Bryan and Eveline decided not to appeal the state supreme court decision, they would lose Goodwood and have numerous outstanding debts to honor. By paying Ann Hawks $36,456 (none of which would actually be disbursed, or, if paid, would be returned to him in private and used for the common good), Bryan guaranteed himself a reserve, a financial cushion. The innovative maneuver by the vanquished but unbowed Croom was entirely within the law.

In another move Bryan forced a court case for a legal evaluation of the estate and was bonded for $20,000 by George Whitfield and Ann Hawks. In the summer of 1857 circuit judge Jesse J. Finley, no stranger to the Croom-Smith litigation, responded by appointing Henry L. Rutgers, a respected commission merchant who was born in New York, as a master in chancery. Rutgers was to examine Bryan's records and report on his administration of Hardy's estate. The master in chancery more than earned his $1,000 fee. He found the files missing for some years, incomplete and irregular for the years that were reported, and Bryan himself uncooperative. Nor was Francis Hyman, one of Bryan's overseers, inclined to aid Rutgers. He could not obtain a reliable inventory on the slaves, and there was evidence of fraud. Bryan and Hyman ignored court subpoenas. Croom had been a conscientious administrator at first, but as time passed he felt less compelled to maintain accurate and detailed records. What he had done was to administer Hardy's estate as if it were his own, and, no doubt, that was what he honestly thought. Despite the handicaps, Rutgers did his best to account for Bryan's stewardship, especially his cotton production—bales ginned, marketed, and with whom, and prices received. In his report Rutgers estimated that as of April 1856, personal property on the estate was worth $167,708.35 (not counting slaves), and the balance for rent was $50,632.87.[3]

In the summer of 1857, Bryan made another attempt to raise money. He placed a running advertisement in the *Tallahassee Floridian* offering the Barrow place (2,500 acres) for sale. His overseer Francis Hyman would show the place to anyone willing to pay one-third in cash and the remainder in two years. Bryan's assumption that the plantation was not part of Hardy's estate was correct, but there were no takers.

Finally, Bryan and Eveline decided not to appeal the state supreme court's decision. To do so would be expensive, and there was the distinct possibility that they would lose. More important, John S. Winthrop, Henrietta Smith's son-in-law, conceived a compromise that was more generous than anything the Crooms could have expected. Their decision was to release all of their property. Petigru would have willingly carried the case to the United States Supreme Court, but Bryan and Eveline, who discussed the alternative with family members, declined. Julia Croom was voicing a consensus view when she wrote to her son Stephens, "I believe brother Bryan is about making a compromise . . . which will clear him from anxiety with the Smiths and at the same time leave him sufficient possessions to be a wealthy man. All sensible people that is all his own family . . . advise him to do it but the lawyers which of course will be benefited if he declines and carries it to another court advise him to refuse. It is to be hoped that having ruin staring him in the face by [losing] he will take warning and sister Ann [Bellamy] thinks he will. You must not mention this as it might be injurious."[4]

With the approval of Henrietta and Elizabeth Armistead, Winthrop contacted lawyers James T. Archer and Mariano D. Papy. Acting as advisers, the attorneys began drafting a document. Archer, who worked out the details, acquainted himself with Bryan's various debts, obtaining data on Croom's slaves, land, cotton crop in 1857, livestock, provisions, and other information pertinent to Goodwood. Papy helped draft what came to be called the "Settlement." Actually, it was a compromise that took the legal form of a deed and a bill of sale from Bryan to Henrietta. The lawyers got their clients to approve the Settlement's specifications, and on December 26, 1857, Archer sent an unofficial letter to Bryan briefly outlining its broad terms.

The most startling aspect of Archer's synopsis, the one mentioned without specifics by Julia to Stephens, was Henrietta's offer to assume all of Bryan's debts falling due after January 1, 1858, up to $100,000. Archer's letter also contained an intriguing provision permitting Croom to retain the "home" at Goodwood and 1,200 acres of land. The price for the dwelling was $8,000 and for the land $15,000 ($12.50 an acre). Interest would be 8 percent annually.[5] The residence-land possibility was a genuine offer, but it was not taken seriously. Bryan and Eveline had decided to move to Montgomery, Alabama, and had already begun preparations. In addition, Croom may well have resented the notion of buying his own home and land from himself. Nor would Bryan be likely to accept such a blow to his pride. Every day would be a painful reminder of his reduced status. The Crooms were not tempted, and the final Settlement made no mention of the proposal.

On December 31, a few days after receiving Archer's letter, Croom met with Archer, Papy, and Winthrop, and all parties discussed the formal document at length. There was some confusion regarding the cotton crop of 1857, but Henrietta Smith's representatives assumed it was included in the bill of sale.[6] In fact, the status of the cotton crop would make for extensive litigation later. At the time goodwill prevailed.

Cooperation between the families was demonstrated by George Alexander Croom's willingness to serve as an administrator of the Settlement so far as it related peripherally to Hardy and Frances's three children. The Settlement awarded the Crooms fifty slaves, and the plaintiffs agreed to pay court costs, including the expenses of the special master and receiver. They also got to keep the furniture in the Goodwood mansion. The $100,000 was an exceptionally large amount of money and was without doubt the reason Bryan and Eveline accepted the arrangement. Why the offer was made remains a mystery. Did Henrietta and Elizabeth feel some sense of guilt, and did the offer represent a final way to end an interminable dispute? No written record has been discovered that offers an explanation.

For their part, Henrietta and Elizabeth received the remaining 187 slaves and were declared free of all debts owed by Bryan to Eveline or Ann Hawks. They obtained the plantations that made up Goodwood and all of the Crooms' other lands, amounting to 8,080 acres. Part of the acreage described did not appear in the deed books because Bryan acquired it in the 1850s, and proper entries had not yet been entered in the official records. Improvements on the lands, all livestock, farming implements, corn and fodder, outbuildings, and personal property were awarded to Henrietta. The new owner of Goodwood was relieved of any responsibility for administrative charges ($530.86) by Aleck Croom. Hardy's personal estate in North Carolina also went to Henrietta.[7]

A much relieved Bryan Croom wrote to John Winthrop on January 2, 1858, providing him with a list of fifteen creditors—individuals and business firms—as well as taxes due the state and costs of the Supreme Court case. Because the expenses of the receiver, Richard L. Saunders (which later came to $1,000), and the circuit court case were still incomplete, they were not itemized. The smallest amount on Croom's list was $140.59 due to two Tallahasseeans, and the largest was $45,559.96 he owed to the New York cotton factorage firm of Smallwood, Anderson, and Company. The initial amount Bryan wanted paid out was $97,169.98. Winthrop replied from Tallahassee (he did not live there by 1858 but was temporarily in residence) on January 4, acknowledging Bryan's letter and stating his willingness to make the payments requested and to honor the full $100,000 on which they had agreed.[8]

As receiver, Saunders, who was also sheriff of Leon County, carried out his considerable task. The forty-year-old North Carolinian accounted for the livestock, agricultural produce, and farm implements. Most difficult of all, Saunders hired six assistants to help him assemble the slaves from Goodwood's divided lands into a single holding area, feed them pork and corn, and guard them for five days at thirty cents per day. The sheriff's operations involved one hundred miles of travel.[9]

In January 1858, Henrietta and Elizabeth made John Winthrop their "true and lawful agent and attorney in fact," a position he had filled unofficially for some time. Throughout that year and into 1859, Winthrop labored long and hard paying off Croom's creditors, including $2,750 to Bryan's attorney Medicus A. Long and another $3,036 to Bryan's lead lawyer in Tallahassee, William George Mackey Davis.[10] The lawyer was owed $5,000, and according to Davis family lore, the remaining $1,964 was remitted in the form of furniture from Goodwood. The items included a mahogany bedstead and wardrobe, mirror and stand, a mahogany sideboard, and a rosewood table with a marble top.[11] Petigru was a man of conscience and confessed his remorse at having lost the case. To have rejected a fee would, however, have been unthinkable, and presumably, Croom paid his Charleston lawyer out of personal funds.

There seemed no end to Bryan's creditors, whether individuals or firms. His several overseers in 1857 were compensated: Francis Hyman $550, D. A. Felkel $116.66⅔, Joseph Dickson $450, and W. I. Akins $1,019. A number of notes to David Barrow, who sold Bryan the Barrow place in 1857, amounting to $3,400 were satisfied. Thanks to payments by Winthrop, Bryan, who had issued a deed of trust (George Whitfield was trustee) for tracts of his property to eight other creditors, was released from its terms.[12] For the first time since he had become an adult, Croom found himself free of major debt.

Correspondence from Smallwood, Earle and Company of New York (successors to Smallwood, Anderson and Company) in January 1860 addressed to John Winthrop at Tallahassee was further evidence that he maintained a part-time residence in Florida.[13] Responding to Winthrop's request, the New York firm sent him records of its business transactions with Bryan. Winthrop was resisting Croom's attempts to claim the proceeds from his 1857 cotton crop. The Settlement had scarcely been signed before Bryan sued Henrietta for failing to live up to its terms. In brief, he claimed that income from the cotton crop was not included in the agreement, and Smith's efforts to claim it were illegal.

By March 1858, Croom was in Montgomery attending to the details of moving. Archer wrote him there expressing disappointment that Croom had intentionally misread the conveyance between himself and Henrietta Smith. Archer had talked with Bryan's attorney Davis in Tallahassee trying to convince him to withdraw from any further litigation. The angry lawyer informed Croom, "It was thro' my intervention the settlement was made & I was fully satisfied there could be no misunderstanding between us concerning the terms . . . of settlement." Yet Archer was forced to admit the bales of cotton were not specifically mentioned in his written proposition. There was definitely a misunderstanding "concerning the terms." The case was to be heard in the spring of 1860 but was delayed. Postponement came because the knowledgeable Archer died unexpectedly of a heart attack on June 1, 1859, because of similar personal problems within the Smith and Winthrop families, and perhaps because of political events and the general confusion that prevailed just before the Civil War. Despite the interruption, the litigation was not over.[14]

Satisfying Croom's various creditors was an involved and expensive task. The longer his debts were outstanding, the higher interest charges drove the total. To meet the debts in January 1858, Winthrop sold five slaves for $3,600 to Peres B. Brokaw, owner of Tallahassee's popular and profitable livery stable operated in conjunction with his carriage and blacksmith shops. Ironically, Winthrop sold two slaves to Bryan for $1,800. Winthrop acquired additional cash by hiring and selling land, hides, and livestock, as well as cotton, corn, and other agricultural produce.[15]

Besides paying Bryan's creditors, the Smith family, with Winthrop as agent, had their own expenses to meet. Archer and Papy received their legal fees, but that left William Law waiting in Savannah for his money. Archer wrote to Law explaining the Settlement's general terms. Then he went personally to Savannah, where he gave the attorney full details.

By April 1858, Winthrop still had not paid his counsel and felt obligated to outline his problems in a candid letter.

After making various sales, Winthrop wrote, there remained "139 Negroes (85 working hands) 6000 acres land, 68 mules, corn and fodder for the plantations and farming implements." He added, "My estimate of their worth if judiciously sold is about $120,000. I hope I may be mistaken in this and that I have placed it entirely too low, but as property is now valued here, I think I am not far from the mark." In carrying out the Settlement he had sought to obtain payment in cash whenever possible. Winthrop was not pleased with the deals he had struck, either by cash or by credit, but rationalized that landed property "could hardly be disposed of at all and the House [Goodwood] particularly, was entirely unsuited to this latitude." His curious reference to Goodwood's shortcomings as a residence went unexplained. Henrietta's conscientious agent began planting crops to take advantage of the remaining property until he could dispose of it. If able to conclude the Settlement's conditions successfully, then "the next season [could] hardly fail to prove more advantageous for selling." Even so, he was willing, if Law wished, to have the property evaluated immediately and used as the basis for further negotiation. Winthrop preferred waiting and clearly hoped to get Law's approval by promising, "If my experiment proves successful my ability to act liberally towards my friends, to whose aid my relatives in North Carolina are indebted for the recovery of their property would be very much increased."[16]

Yet Winthrop's letter did not sugarcoat the situation. "I make these statements with frankness," he declared, "confessing that my pecuniary arrangements have caused me much uneasiness, but [I have] the hope that when I return home I shall be enabled to raise sufficient means in conjunction with my crop to place me in easy circumstances by the close of the year." Winthrop was not pleased with the "encumbrances with which [their] opponents [had] contrived to saddle the Estate," but he added, "I cannot but think that the compromise was an advantageous one."[17] Law replied eight days later. Noting that he understood his debtor's difficulties and consenting to wait, the lawyer added that times were also bad in Savannah. He attached one stipulation: he wanted a statement from Winthrop agreeing to pay him $4,000 by November 1858. Law explained, "[That] you and your friends will be disposed to deal liberally with us we have never doubted, & will cheerfully wait your payment—but the acceptance we ask would be equivalent to so much money to us now, and contribute greatly to our convenience." [18]

In less than a week Winthrop answered that "in order to save the property from ruinous sacrifice," he would have to pay one debt of $20,000 by October 1858 and could do so only "through the aid of [his] friends in North Carolina." Beyond that, he had been forced to postpone another debt of $10,000 but only by pledging his crop. In sum, "My available means will thereby be entirely absorbed." There was nothing he could do. "I would sell Negroes but without them the Plantations would be comparatively valueless (at the moment land is unsalable) and my great reliance for paying debts be cut off." Under the circumstances, Winthrop asked Law not to request payment until after January 1859. He promised to pay "the moment that it [was] in [his] power." [19] It is a safe assumption that William Law received his fee at a later date.

As Eveline and Bryan watched the activity that accompanied the takeover of Goodwood plantation, they worked out the logistics of moving to Montgomery, a city two hundred miles slightly northwest of Tallahassee. Leaving Goodwood plantation was undoubtedly a wrenching act. In general, times were prosperous for the South—since 1855, cotton production had soared, and there was an accompanying rise in the value of bondsmen. As the decade ended, "Colonel" Robert H. Berry, a Tallahassee commission merchant and auctioneer, sold slaves at high prices. At one advertised sale a thirty-five-year-old blacksmith brought $1,500, while Littleton, twenty, sold for $1,250; other figures included Logan, twenty-five, $1,500; Joe, nineteen, $1,400; and Rebecca, sixteen, $1,240. [20]

Economic conditions were particularly good in both Leon County and the state's capital city. Charles Dyke's *Floridian and Journal* and Joseph Clisby's *Sentinel* never tired of touting the region's advantages, and they had the census figures to back them up. The statistics were even more impressive than those previously discussed for 1850. An analysis of the published and unpublished census returns reveals that by

1860 Tallahassee had a total population of 1,932 (997 whites, 889 slaves, and 46 free persons of color). Leon County had 9,089 slaves, 60 free persons of color, and 3,194 whites. The total of 12,343 made Leon the most populous county in Florida.

In 1860 there were 515 slave owners, or slightly less than 17 percent of the population. There were 52 people who owned only 1 slave; the largest single category comprised the 76 people who possessed between 10 and 15 chattels; Ann F. Duval's 28 slaves made her the largest slave-holder among 40 women owning bondsmen. Dorothy Cane, a free black who possessed 10, was included in the list. In 1857 Bryan Croom's slaves placed him in the category of top planters, an echelon that numbered men such as Joseph John Williams, Dr. George W. Parkhill, Edward Bradford, and William Lester.

Constituting two-thirds of Leon's population, slaves were responsible for making it the state's leading agricultural county. Leon led Florida in total acres of farmland, cash value of farmland, and worth of farm machinery. Number one in jacks and mules, sheep, and swine, second in horses, ranked high in milk cows and working oxen, Leon led by a wide margin in total value of livestock. Farmers and planters diversified with oats, rye, rice, Irish potatoes, and tobacco. Leon's 421,654 bushels of corn made it first in Florida, as did its 136,038 bushels of sweet potatoes. Where the county scored most profitably was its premier ranking in bales of ginned cotton: 16,686.

Tallahassee was a town of merchants (forty-three) who supplied a variety of needs and lawyers (twenty) who served a litigious populace. It was by definition a town of politics and was becoming an educational center—the West Florida Seminary opened its doors in 1857, and there were a number of academies. Education helped polish and refine the capital, although Tallahassee's reputation for violence dated from its founding and had not been eliminated. Doctors and dentists attended to physical ills, and a number of ministers in town and country married people, preached to them, baptized them, and buried them. From time to time the capital had a theater and a race track and hosted circuses, lecturers, and entertainers. Parties, balls, and picnics were popular and cut across social and economic lines. Culture was enhanced by a resident "professor" of music and two music teachers. Dirt roads in and out of Tallahassee were nothing to boast about, but by 1856 the Tallahassee Railroad to St. Marks had two steam engines on its line, and the Pensacola and Georgia Railroad was expanding east and west. Railroads vastly improved transportation speed and efficiency and helped explain the surge in agricultural production. A telegraph line was in operation by 1859, connecting the small town with the rest of the nation.

Bryan and Eveline could not have relished leaving. They had been in Florida since the 1820s. First in Gadsden and then in Leon County, the couple had been pioneer settlers. With help from Ann Hawks, they had transformed Goodwood into one of Florida's finest plantations. Now the three were leaving in a time of great promise (if only the mounting issue of slavery and rising political tensions could be quieted) and prosperity. John Winthrop was not insensitive to their feelings on departing from Goodwood. In a letter to William Law, Winthrop said that he realized "the great sacrifice which must have attended" the loss of the plantation.[21] In February 1858, Bryan's Florida affairs were still in flux, but his and Eveline's long-range plans were definite. Bryan journeyed to Montgomery and made his first purchase of property. He may even have made the transaction in late 1857 and its entry in the Montgomery County deed records have been delayed.

While in the capital city, Croom registered at the Exchange Hotel, which had been built in 1847 and was the city's finest, although the Madison Hotel and Montgomery Hall were also favored by visitors. The Exchange was located on Court Square, an area defined by an artesian basin and fountain. As the heart of Montgomery, the basin acted as a hub from which Market and other streets radiated out into the downtown areas. Market Street, the principal artery, inclined gradually but perceptively as it stretched east for three-quarters of a mile to Goat Hill, site of the impressive Greek Revival state capitol. Croom would register frequently at the Exchange, and the 1859–60 edition of Montgomery's city directory listed Bryan's address as the Exchange Hotel and his occupation as that of planter.

Through various contacts Croom discovered that Rosannah C. Taylor, widow of Jesse P. Taylor, needed money to satisfy several debts. She had turned over 708 acres of rich Black Belt land to relatives to sell for her. The land lay six or so miles south of the capital and was accessible by the Norman Bridge road. Situated in Township 15, Range 17, in Sections 23, 25, and 26, it became the main unit of Croom's Alabama holdings. Croom met the asking price of $10,720 by signing three promissory notes (which he paid off by December 1861).[22] Sometime between February and December 1858, the Crooms moved to Alabama. Bryan may have accompanied the slaves and household goods on the laborious and circuitous overland route to Montgomery. Eveline and her mother no doubt went by stage to Chattahoochee, Florida, caught a northbound steamboat to Columbus, Georgia, and traveled from there on the Montgomery & West Point Railroad to the Alabama capital.

On December 8, Bryan made another major investment when he paid William H. Polland $12,500 for 625 acres in Sections 12 and 7 in the same township and range as the land he purchased from Rosannah Taylor. Once again he signed promissory notes requiring him to make fixed payments at specified times.[23] George Alexander and Julia and their large family still lived at Casa de Lago plantation in Leon County. Some of Richard's children remained in Tallahassee or traveled back and forth between there and Sumter County, Alabama. Susan Matilda, Richard's daughter, was still a minor, but she managed her property in Alabama. With the situation so uncertain in Florida, Susan sought to exercise control over her part of the trust that Richard had established for his daughters in 1855. In December 1859, the state legislature passed a special act permitting Susan, despite being a minor in Leon County, to manage her estate there. Richard's trust remained in effect, but Susan had control over her land and slaves and became capable of "suing and being sued and of pleading and being impleaded in any court of law or equity in this State."[24] Bryan and Eveline and Ann Hawks were different. Except for family, they severed all relationships and no longer had legal ties to Goodwood. They would never lose their emotional ties.

Back in Tallahassee, Winthrop continued his efforts to bring order to the Hardy Croom estate by paying off Bryan's debts and by putting Henrietta's property on a profitable or at least break-even basis. The need for money prompted him to sell the Goodwood mansion and its surrounding acreage. In February 1858, two days before Bryan first bought land in Montgomery County, Winthrop, acting as Henrietta Smith's agent, sold the home place. The deal was with Arvah Hopkins, a leading Tallahassee merchant, and included 1,576 acres of land in Sections 20, 28, 29, and 30 and forty-one slaves. The price was $52,862, and the transaction was broken down into three categories: the home (there had been recent improvements on it), $7,712; the land, $19,700; and the slaves, $25,450.[25] It was an ironic turn of events. The Smith-Armistead-Winthrop relatives, who had fought to gain possession of Goodwood for almost twenty years, sold the core section within five weeks after it finally became theirs. They still had other acreage with houses, but the mansion on Section 29 symbolized the plantation and was its heart.

With Arvah Hopkins as owner and much reduced in size, Goodwood plantation entered a new era. Hopkins was born January 18, 1813, on Cayuga Lake, one of upstate New York's scenic Finger Lakes. Hopkins's early life remains obscure, but when he was twenty-three years old, he moved to Tallahassee. Obtaining work as a clerk and bookkeeper in James Gamble's general store, the ambitious Hopkins stayed long enough to accumulate sufficient capital to go into business for himself. He survived in quick order an economic panic, the unrest of the Second Seminole War, a yellow fever epidemic, and a disastrous downtown fire. That he overcame such adversity to become the successful owner of a general store was testimony to Hopkins's business ability. Over time Arvah had various partners, including Daniel B. Meginnis. He and Meginnis operated the store and sometimes bought and sold land together, although Hopkins was usually the dominant partner.

Hopkins's marriage to Susan Branch at St. John's Episcopal Church on December 13, 1849, gave him automatic place among middle Florida's elite. Thirteen years younger than Arvah, Susan was the daughter of John Branch. A native of North Carolina, Branch had served his state in the legislature, as governor, and as United States senator. Andrew Jackson appointed him secretary of the navy. By the mid-1830s Branch had brought his family to Leon County and established himself at Live Oak plantation north of Tallahassee. In 1844, President John Tyler appointed Branch Florida's last territorial governor. After his wife's death in 1851, Branch returned to North Carolina but spent his winters in Tallahassee.

Hopkins was a merchant and only a part-time planter, but by acquiring Goodwood in 1858, he had a place to showcase his and Susan's prominence and gregarious natures. The plantation emerged as a popular social center for planters, merchants, politicians, and their wives. Among his guests was William W. Williams, who had married Susan's sister. On January 6, 1859, Mary Eliza Branch Hopkins became the first white child born at Goodwood.[26] At the same time, far-reaching changes had come into the personal affairs of the Crooms and the various Smith relations as the cycle of their lives began to come full circle.

The move to Montgomery was a logical one for the Crooms. The small city served not only as the seat of government for a county bearing the same name but, more important, as the capital of a leading cotton state. After Mobile, it was Alabama's second-largest city. Founded in 1819 by the merger of rival settlements promoted by land speculators Andrew Dexter and John Scott, Montgomery was located near the headwaters of the Alabama River. Fertile land, convenient water transportation, and the world demand for cotton made Montgomery the natural center of hinterland trade. The town's prominence was given recognition and permanence in 1846 when it was designated as the state capital. On the eve of the Civil War the county had 36,000 people, while Montgomery's population was equally divided between slaves (4,400) and whites (4,341). There were 102 free persons of color. The area was attractive, and one visitor wrote, "The City is picturesque in perch upon bold, high bluffs, which, on the city side cut sheer down to the Alabama river. . . . From the opposite bank spread great flat stretches of marsh and meadow land, while on the other side, behind the town, the formation swells and undulates with gentle rise."[27]

In the 1830s Hardy had talked with Bryan about Alabama as a possible home for their families. Some of Richard and Winifred Croom's children still lived at Whitfield in the Gaston area of Sumter County about 125 miles to the west; Bryan's half brother William and his wife Julia would soon settle in Eutaw, county seat of Greene County, another Black Belt region contiguous to Sumter and no farther than Livingston from Montgomery. Bryan's cousin Isaac Croom, famous for his journal articles advocating scientific agriculture, owned land in Sumter County and was a frequent visitor to Montgomery. Isaac, a great exponent of agricultural associations and fairs, had his major farming operations in Greene County (the part that is present-day Hale County). Instead of living on his plantation, Isaac was an absentee landlord. He and his family lived in Magnolia Grove, their home on the town limits of Greensboro. The six-columned Greek Revival home equaled any planter's mansion in the Black Belt. Whitfield cousins from Demopolis in Marengo County (south and east of Sumter and Greene) were often in Montgomery for business and pleasure.

Stephens, William Croom's son, had graduated from the University of North Carolina in June 1859. His parents were justifiably proud of their twenty-year-old son's excellent record. He was a member of several campus organizations, including the Dialectic Society. Immediately after graduating, Stephens went to New York and worked for three months as a shipping and entry clerk in his father's failing silk and ribbon business. In the fall of 1859 he went to Bolivar County, Mississippi, where he spent four months in the Delta hunting and fishing at Hopoi with members of Edward and Ann Bellamy's family. After enjoying seven months of relative leisure, Stephens moved to Montgomery in the spring of 1860 to study law, a goal he had set for himself with strong parental approval.

He worked under Chancellor Wade Keyes Jr., whose students boarded and studied law at his residence a mile from town. Keyes, a native of Georgia and author of two law books, had lived in Tallahassee during the 1840s and married George Whitfield's daughter Alice on May 16, 1848. During the Civil War he would serve as assistant attorney general of the Confederate States of America. In 1860 Keyes took a special interest in his kinsman Stephens. Earlier, Stephens had visited his Uncle Bryan and Aunt Eveline at Goodwood, and until being admitted to the bar in 1861 and moving to Eutaw to be near his parents, he maintained social contact with them.[28] There were other Croom relatives and friends living in the state, and Montgomery, far from being an alien and strange place to start anew, offered many attractions.

11   *Civil War and the Attrition of Time*

Early on, Bryan's combined purchases in Montgomery County of 1,333 acres in Township 15, Range 17, indicated that he still retained his fondness for real estate deals. If additional proof was needed, in October 1859, he bought 94.5 more acres in Sections 12 and 13, as well as slightly more than 43 acres in Section 14. He obtained the 137.5 acres from William W. Allen for $17,257. The large amount of money involved suggests the presence of a dwelling. Bryan only kept the land until January 1861, when he sold it to Willis R. Callaway for $15,000, taking a loss of more than $2,000.[1] The unprofitable sale was uncharacteristic of him, and there may have been conditions not mentioned in the deed.

It is certain that Bryan, Eveline, and Ann were comfortably settled when the census taker came calling in 1860. Their lifestyle was less grand than at Goodwood, but Bryan owned 650 acres of improved and 70 acres of unimproved land. His census listing included only the property he purchased in 1858 from Rosannah Taylor, a total that Croom would use consistently on his tax returns. The cash value of his plantation was $25,500, and his farm equipment was worth $5,000. The former Floridian had livestock valued at $3,153 (three horses, fifteen mules, two milk cows, nine sheep, and fifty-seven hogs). His forty-nine slaves labored on a typical medium-sized plantation that produced a few bushels of Irish potatoes but concentrated on corn (four thousand bushels) and cotton (one hundred bales weighing four hundred pounds each). The worth of his real estate was $75,000, and his personal estate was valued at $130,000; when combined with Ann Hawks's $28,000 personal estate, these holdings easily established the Crooms as part of the planter class, people of means.[2] No description of the family's home exists, but it was probably smaller than Goodwood. Although the Crooms had given up interior pieces to pay their lawyer Davis in Tallahassee, they were still able to outfit their home handsomely with furniture from Goodwood.

As interested as Bryan might have been in contemporary affairs and their dramatic unfolding, he continued to concentrate on business. On January 9, 1861, two days before Alabama seceded, Croom sold land in several sections and ranges in Township 15 to two prominent Montgomerians. They were James H. Clanton, a leading lawyer and later a Confederate general and postwar politician, and Willis R. Callaway, whom he had dealt with in another real estate matter. The buyers were permitted to put the property up as security, and the note was due January 1, 1863. When the date arrived and there was no payment, Bryan declined to foreclose, and it was finally paid after the war, in November 1866.[3]

Bryan and Eveline had moved at a critical time but with no way of knowing how events in Montgomery would help shape the course of American history. Although Florida was a small state with a total population of 140,424 (77,746 whites, 61,745 slaves, 932 free persons of color), events there moved slightly more rapidly toward secession than in the more densely populated and critical Alabama. Henrietta Smith and her family were caught up in events occurring in Tallahassee. They lived in North Carolina but were closely involved in Florida, mainly through John Winthrop, who spent much of his time there looking after family affairs. On May 9, 1860, he returned to New Bern tired and worn out after spending the winter and spring in Florida's capital. He got off the train (after extended financial and political machinations, the Atlantic and North Carolina Railroad was extended to New Bern in June 1858), walked to the omnibus, and took it to his residence. When he got home, Winthrop became violently ill and was dead within a few hours. The local newspaper speculated that "the fatigue of the trip must have affected him seriously, for soon after his arrival he was attacked and died about 12 o'clock the same night."⁴

Winthrop was buried in New Bern, and Susan and her son, John Winthrop III, continued to live in the town with her mother and grandmother. The Craven County census of 1860 valued Susan's real estate at $22,000 and her personal estate at $14,000. Comparable evaluations for Henrietta were placed at $17,000 and $42,000, but Elizabeth Armistead's name did not appear.⁵ In Florida the remaining property of Hardy Croom's estate was managed by a twenty-seven-year-old overseer named R. S. D. Hays and by Thomas W. Lawrence, also twenty-seven, who was listed as an agent. Hays's personal estate was valued at $32,400 and his real estate at $30,000, and corresponding figures for Lawrence were $10,000 and $30,000. Undoubtedly the totals reflected the estimated worth of the Smith-Armistead estate rather than that of the overseers.⁶

Sometime in late 1860 or early 1861, the three women and John Winthrop III moved to Leon County. Elizabeth Armistead, who had always resisted Hardy's attempts to persuade her to move to Florida, capitulated. What happened to them will be traced before returning to the Crooms in Alabama and elsewhere. The Smith-Armistead-Winthrop family members' decision to leave was prompted by John Winthrop's death, their extensive property holdings in Leon County, the danger that coastal North Carolina would be invaded if war came, and the relative safety offered by Florida. If, after arrival, they had any second thoughts, the expatriate North Carolinians soon dismissed them. In a sense they were "refugeeing," as the term for flight came to be known, before the war began. The potential threat to the New Bern area quickly became reality. Isolated, of limited military importance, and located in the backwaters of the Confederacy, Florida seemed to offer a secure haven.

Abraham Lincoln was elected president in the tumultuous campaign of November 1860, and on December 20, South Carolina became the first southern state to secede. Florida's general assembly set December 22, 1860, as election day for delegates, who were to assemble in Tallahassee on January 3, 1861, and decide what course the state should follow. "Immediate Secessionists" commanded a majority (fifty-one of the sixty-nine delegates were slaveholders), but "Cooperationists" were strong in Leon County. There the white voting population was almost evenly split on whether to wait for action by the other southern states. Large, boisterous crowds attended the debates, and on January 5, a resolution declared both the right of secession and the necessity for it. Then, on January 9, a special committee called for immediate secession. Galvanized by such action, the delegates opted for solidarity and used the next day to pass an ordinance of secession by a vote of sixty-two to seven. It was declared adopted by convention president John C. McGehee, a longtime fire-eater. Florida became the third state to secede (Mississippi was the second), and a huge crowd was present on January 11 to witness the formal signing of the secession ordinance. Governor Madison S. Perry appointed delegates to a regional convention assembling in Montgomery, where Bryan and Eveline and many others would experience an even more significant event: the birth of a nation.[7]

The decision to leave New Bern proved wise. After fighting began in April 1861, Federal officials considered the coastal region of eastern North Carolina strategically important. There would be military activity in the area in 1861, and, later, General Ambrose Burnside, backed by army units and a massive Union fleet, was dispatched to secure the region. New Bern would fall on March 14, 1862, and surrounding towns, such as Washington, were also occupied. New Bern became headquarters for Federal forces, served as a base for raids against Confederate strongholds, and would successfully resist Confederate efforts to recapture it. General John G. Foster succeeded Burnside as commander in July.[8]

John Winthrop III and his mother, grandmother, and great-grandmother settled into the relative comfort of wartime Tallahassee. The only combat in Leon County would be the limited battle of Natural

Bridge on March 6, 1865, and Tallahassee was not occupied by Federal troops until May 10, a month and a day after General Robert E. Lee surrendered at Appomattox, Virginia. The three women attended St. John's Episcopal Church. No longer the owners of Goodwood mansion, they still held considerable land, including the Barrow place, which Bryan had purchased in 1855, and Betton place. They lived on Betton place (the part that Richard had reconveyed to Bryan). On New Year's Day, 1862, Susan bought Lots 106 and 107 in Tallahassee's "North addition" (north Monroe Street). She paid Daniel B. Meginnis, the business associate of Arvah Hopkins, $3,000 for the property.[9] By this time Susan had taken charge of the family's business affairs.

Henrietta was eighty-two when she died of erysipelas (an acute infectious skin disease) on February 10, 1862. The woman buried at what church records called the "Croom place" (more technically, Betton place) was a strong person who had lived much of her life as a widow and had known more than her share of sorrow. Henrietta had survived all her siblings, all her children except Elizabeth, and all her grandchildren except Susan.[10] On March 30, 1865, shortly before the Civil War ended, Elizabeth died of gastritis and chronic diarrhea. The sixty-year-old woman was buried beside her mother in what had come to be called the Winthrop burying ground. In November, Susan appointed Edward R. Stanly, a lawyer in New Bern, to manage and sell her Craven County properties.[11] Susan continued to live in Tallahassee with her son, but in December 1866, she leased the Barrow place for the following year to Cornelius Redding.

The agreement with Redding was notable for its imprecision, except regarding the crucial matter of money, in which Susan demonstrated her mother's and grandmother's talent for business. Times were uncertain. Confederate money was worthless, United States paper money was scarce, and so she got Redding to make two equal payments of $2,000 in gold. He was to pay her for the use of fifteen hundred bushels of corn and five hundred more if she could "spare that amount." In turn she agreed to furnish Redding free of charge with whatever cotton seed he needed, sell him all the hogs on the plantation, and furnish him with fifteen mules and three more if she could procure them.[12]

It is probable that Susan and John III moved to the property on north Monroe Street. John took over family affairs and in April 1873 paid his mother $3,000 for the lots (the amount she purchased them for in 1862).[13] The direct Smith-Armistead-Winthrop relationship with Goodwood plantation ended when Susan died on February 14, 1875. The fifty-two-year-old woman was buried beside her mother and grand-mother. John, who had married Lelia Chouteau of St. Louis, Missouri, about 1874, inherited Susan's estate and continued to make his home in Tallahassee. Later, in the twentieth century, when Guy Winthrop, a descendant, developed the area that had been Goodwood plantation, he removed the women's bodies to St. John's Cemetery in Tallahassee and closed the burying ground.[14]

Goodwood remained the property of Arvah Hopkins throughout the war. The mansion continued its role as a leading social center for Tallahassee and the capital area. In March 1864, a party was held there to honor General Howell Cobb, commander of the military district of middle Florida. Susan Bradford Eppes, whose husband, Francis, was the nephew of Thomas Jefferson and an important civic leader, was among those present. "The party at Goodwood was a grand success," she wrote. "The general and his staff were magnificently attired in new uniforms, just [shipped] from Paris, via Zeigler's Blockade Runner. As many of Colonel [George W.] Scott's Battalion [see below] as could be spared at one time came in from Camp Randolph." She mentioned a large number of strangers in town. One was a wounded captain from a Maryland regiment who was staying at Goodwood. The officer "was the lion of the evening": "He has a lovely baritone voice and accompanies himself on the guitar. He sang 'Maryland, my Maryland,' so feelingly that it brought tears to many eyes." General Cobb's band played for the guests to dance, and according to Susan, "We had a delightful time—as everyone does when at Goodwood."[15]

As the New Bern women and John Winthrop III adjusted to being in Florida, Bryan Croom and his family made the transition to becoming Alabamians. Their entry into life in Montgomery was made easier when they became members of St. John's Episcopal Church, located downtown on Madison Avenue. Attending church brought them in from the country and introduced them to city residents. Circumstances rather than intent placed the family in Montgomery at a critical time in the nation's life, but, all the same, they were close witnesses to monumental historical change.

After Lincoln's victory, the Alabama legislature instructed Governor Albert B. Moore to call for the election of a state convention to decide the state's future. The secession scenario in Alabama was similar to that in Florida. Held on Christmas Eve, 1860, the election revealed a populace closely divided in strength: south Alabama's Immediate Secessionists versus the "wait and see" Cooperationists from the northern counties. When the convention assembled in Montgomery on January 7, 1861, the Secessionists used their slight majority to elect William M. Brooks president. Their ranks were led by William L. Yancey, a fire-eater of national reputation, but the moderates also had powerful leadership, and great excitement prevailed as orators pleaded their causes.

On January 10, Yancey's Committee of Thirteen, appointed to recommend a course of action, reported in favor of secession. A minority report was tabled by a close vote, but defeat broke the Cooperationists' effective opposition, and on January 11, an ordinance of secession passed by a vote of sixty-one to thirty-nine. Spontaneous celebrations followed. The capitol's rooms and corridors and Montgomery's streets swarmed with people shouting their approval. Fourteen years later, Stephens Croom remembered, "I was . . . there on the memorable 11th day of January . . . , when the Alabama ordinance of secession was passed; and although I was in full sympathy with the south, yet I was oppressed with a forboding [*sic*] of ill to come, because I had lived in the North & in the South too, & was thoroughly acquainted with both sections, and I could not help being conscious of the immense odds, in numbers, wealth, ships, & all the means and appliances of war against which we had to contend."[16]

At the suggestion of South Carolina and on the invitation of Alabama, delegates from the seceded states of South Carolina, Mississippi, Florida, Alabama, and Louisiana—all from the lower South—gathered in Montgomery on February 4. The delegates, having little quarrel with the Federal constitution, drafted a provisional document (a permanent one followed shortly thereafter) that was similar to the original constitution of 1787. The convention elected Jefferson Davis of Missis-

sippi as president of the Confederate States of America and Alexander
Stephens of Georgia as vice president. Forced by the lack of direct railroad connections between Mississippi and Alabama, itself a bad portent
for the future, Davis took a roundabout way to Montgomery. From its
start to its termination at the Exchange Hotel, the procession was a
triumphant journey. Even so, the upper South states of Arkansas, Virginia, North Carolina, and Tennessee withdrew from the Union only
after Fort Sumter was reduced on April 12. Montgomery remained the
provisional capital from February 4 to May 21, 1861.

Jefferson Davis was inaugurated on February 18, and Montgomery
was crowded with celebrating people. Cannons boomed endorsement of
the new nation's confidence and spirit. Among the formal events was a
parade that featured prominent politicians, local leaders, military units,
and bands—the stirring notes of a song called "Dixie" drew approving
responses. Surely Bryan and Eveline attended the inauguration, although Ann Hawks probably remained at home. According to authorities of Montgomery's past, as well as members of the Croom family,
Bryan and Eveline furnished the chair that Jefferson Davis sat in on the
front portico of the capitol as he waited to make his inaugural speech.
With its left armrest foreshortened, the handsome piece of furniture
permitted a uniformed person wearing a sword to sit comfortably
(Davis wore a suit). At present, the chair is on permanent display in
Montgomery at the Alabama Department of Archives and History.

Bryan carried on his farming operations and other activities under
the stress of wartime conditions. Yet Montgomery, like Tallahassee, was
not the scene of military activity and was not occupied by Federal forces
until late in the war. The city that would become known to history as
the "cradle of the Confederacy" surrendered to the cavalry units of
Union general James H. Wilson on April 12, 1865. Aside from the Confederates' burning thousands of cotton bales, which created a dramatic
fire, and Federal destruction of military matériel, the city suffered minimum damage.[17]

At first the Crooms fared well. In 1861 Bryan paid state real estate
taxes on 704 acres (he actually owned more but possibly lacked clear
title to the land) of $35.40. His land was appraised at a lower amount in
1862, $14,150 as opposed to $17,700, and he was taxed less: $28.30.[18]

Tax records are missing for 1863, but in 1864 the same 704 acres were raised in value to $20,000, and Croom paid real estate taxes for the year of $50.18. Records on personal property taxes are also available for 1864 and indicate another possible activity of Bryan's. He paid an assessment of seventy-five cents on himself as a white man and modest levies on jewelry, household furniture, a gold watch, a clock, and vehicles that included a $400 carriage assessed at $2. He also paid taxes on ninety-four slaves, most of whom were young—only seven were over fifty. By increasing his slave force by forty-five since 1860, Croom clearly had enough laborers to cultivate his crops and probably was able to hire others out. If that was so, he had an added means of income. Croom's total personal estate taxes for the year amounted to $121.55.[19]

There was further evidence of Bryan's prosperity in 1864. In February he attended a public sale at the Artesian Basin, the usual place for such events, and was high bidder for two city lots of 4.33 acres each. Catherine Baker's heirs came away $1,625 richer, and Bryan and Eveline now had property in Montgomery if they ever decided to sell their plantation and move to town.[20] So far the war had exacted no heavy toll from Bryan, Eveline, and Ann.

As southerners, the other Crooms and their families also had to confront the Civil War. On April 1, 1859, George Alexander and Julia Croom had their eighth and last child, Louisa Whitfield. A son and daughter had died as children. Louisa's sisters in 1860 were Sarah Jane, Julia Church, and Anne Eloise. The three boys were Hardy Bryan Church, seventeen, Alonzo Church, sixteen, and William Church, fourteen.

Hardy Bryan enlisted in Company C, Fifth Battalion, Florida Cavalry, on February 16, 1862, at Pensacola as a private and furnished his own horse. The battalion was closely identified with its commander, Lieutenant Colonel George W. Scott. A native of Pennsylvania, Scott had moved to Florida for his health and become a successful merchant and planter in Leon County. His cavalry command operated in Florida's swamps and backwaters, defending salt-making establishments, opposing landing parties, and controlling local uprisings against the Confederacy. The battalion's activities were limited and sporadic but included Olustee, Florida's most important Civil War engagement, and the battle of Natural Bridge. By the time he was paroled at Tallahassee on May 12, 1865, young Hardy Bryan had been promoted to fourth sergeant and then to second lieutenant.[21]

His younger brother Alonzo Church also served in the Fifth Battalion, Florida Cavalry. He enlisted at Tallahassee on March 5, 1862, and held the rank of corporal before being promoted to sergeant. In the summer of 1864 Alonzo Church was ordered by an army surgeon to the general hospital in Tallahassee and was discharged shortly afterward. Before the war ended, William Church would have been old enough for military duty, but there is no service record for him. He may have remained at home to look after family affairs (between 1862 and 1863 Aleck bought several tracts of land in Leon County) so that his father could enlist. Although he was forty years old when the war began, George Alexander joined Company C, Fifth Battalion, Florida Cavalry, on October 13, 1863, and collected a $50 bounty for enlisting and $80 for furnishing his own horse. His status as one of the oldest privates ended when he was transferred to Lieutenant Colonel Scott's staff as an ordnance sergeant. He suffered a flesh wound in his thigh at the battle of Natural Bridge. Like the other soldiers, Aleck swore not to take up arms against the United States and was discharged at the state capital in May 1865.[22]

Neither Aleck nor his sons suffered any serious injuries during the war, and the family continued to live in Tallahassee after it ended. Aleck soon reactivated his ability to acquire land inexpensively and sell it profitably. In the summer of 1866, his property included the 1,200-acre DeSoto plantation and 1,080-acre Neamathla plantation, both east of Tallahassee. Together with his sons Hardy and Church, Aleck put the property on the market and extended his land buying to Madison County and elsewhere. George Alexander and Julia Croom lived well past the war. She died on April 30, 1888, and Aleck on July 25, 1890.[23]

How Edward Bellamy and William Croom reacted to the sectional crises in the years just before the conflict is unknown. As Whigs and men of established positions before moving to Mississippi's Delta, they probably joined their planter neighbors with similar backgrounds in opposing civil war. But nothing could withstand the fervor of secession.

On January 9, 1861, Mississippi became the second southern state to leave the Union and the setting for some of the war's most bitter and bloody battles.

Edward Bellamy died at Hopoi of unreported causes on November 3, 1860. The fifty-nine-year-old Bellamy must have anticipated death because he drew a will on October 3. The casually phrased document kept all his property together under the management of Bellamy's son Eugene, who became the de facto executor. Eugene received five slaves, and the remaining property was divided equally among him and the rest of the children. Nothing was said about Ann, but it must be assumed that she shared in Edward's personal ($106,000) and real ($70,000) estate. In addition, the wealth that she brought to the marriage had contributed significantly to Edward's success.[24] With the aid of her sons, Ann Bellamy was able to remain at Hopoi after Edward's death.

Unfortunately for Ann and her neighbors, the Delta, whose terrain was a nightmare to attack or defend, was the victim of early military action. Realizing the Mississippi River's strategic importance, Federal commanders moved to take control and divide the South. After New Orleans and Memphis were occupied in 1862, Vicksburg alone remained to prevent free access to the river by Union gunboats. As Vicksburg's hinterland, the Delta counties were exposed to warships by 1862. Yankee soldiers would land, raid, and withdraw, and there was always the threat of stragglers, as plantations, slave cabins, and outbuildings were burned. Confederate troops also destroyed private property to prevent it from falling into northern hands. During the siege of Vicksburg, Union forces stepped up their activity in the Delta to draw Confederate soldiers away from the city, which finally fell on July 4, 1863. Delta women were frequently left to look after their families and slaves and to confront the invaders. Many women such as Ann Bellamy thought about refugeeing, and some did, taking their children and slaves with them.[25]

Ann was forced to call on all her resourcefulness and reserve strength. Her son Hardy Croom, twenty-two in 1860, enlisted at Prentiss, Mississippi, on March 10, 1862, in Company E, Twenty-eighth Regiment,

Mississippi Volunteers. Entering as a lieutenant, he was soon promoted to captain and commander of the company. Hardy Croom was killed leading a charge at the first battle of Franklin, Tennessee, on April 10, 1863. Following his younger brother into Confederate service on August 20, 1862, Eugene, twenty-five and a physician, enlisted as a private in the same Company E, Twenty-eighth Regiment. On the exact day that he joined the army, Eugene was detailed to practice medicine in Bolivar County, where, so far as it is known, he spent the war. Only eighteen in 1860, Harold enlisted soon after the fighting began and served in various commands; among them were the Forty-eighth Mississippi Infantry and the Thirty-fourth Tennessee Infantry. Before the war was over, Harold was promoted to lieutenant. The marriage of Edward, twenty-eight, to his first cousin Elizabeth Croom in 1858 was described in chapter 7, and his career in the Confederate army is discussed below. There is no military record for William Croom, the oldest son, who did not live at home in 1860, or for George Whitfield, the youngest, who was only thirteen in 1860. Ann Elizabeth (sixteen), the sixth child and only daughter, was married, but the wedding date is unknown.[26] Ann's sons, by any criteria, contributed meaningfully to the Confederate war effort.

In 1863, conditions in the Delta had deteriorated to the point that Ann decided to move. She chose Montgomery. The city seemed safe from imminent attack, Bryan and Eveline were doing well there, and there were other relatives in Alabama. Ann got advice from her sons and certainly from Bryan, because she selected eighty acres on the Norman Bridge road, equidistant (3.5 miles) between Montgomery and the Croom plantation. She paid P. H. S. Gayle $500 and two other owners, L. D. Hallonquist and L. B. Hallonquist, $7,500.[27] The price of $8,000 for eighty acres meant that a home was on the property and that land prices were still high. For some reason Ann changed her mind. Perhaps her personal situation became more bearable, or the difficulties of moving proved too difficult. She never occupied her Alabama property and continued to live in Mississippi.

Ann would survive the war, but the cessation of hostilities revealed the costs of the conflict. Only 10 percent of the Delta had been cleared

when the Civil War began, and in 1865 much of it seemed to be revert-
ing to the wilderness. One settler described Bolivar County in 1865 as
"blanketed by cane and briers, where bears play[ed] havoc with the corn
crop and alligators preyed on pigs. . . . Mosquitoes and buffalo gnats
added to the general anxiety and discomfort."[28] The deprivations of Reconstruction were about to begin. In 1866 Ann resided for a time in
nearby Sunflower County. While there she gave her son Harold, by then
a lawyer, power to sell or rent her Alabama land on the best terms
available. In February Eveline Croom bought the tract for $2,700. Why
the purchase was in her name instead of Bryan's was not explained; nor
was it clear whether she acquired the property to aid Ann, or if she and
Bryan, needing less land and wanting to be near the city, intended to
sell their plantation and move to Ann's eighty acres.[29]

Ann soon moved from Sunflower County back to Bolivar County,
where she lived through the years of Reconstruction. Her son George
Whitfield recovered some prosperity and as a lawyer earned enough
income to take advantage of low land prices. He purchased 160 acres
in 1868 and another 161 in 1869, paying only $25 for the latter tract.
George also owned Hopoi, so reduced in size that it was called a place
instead of a plantation, which he rented out in 1870.[30] In 1870 and 1871
George leased Leesland plantation (other property he owned in Bolivar
County) to a sharecropper and sold a city lot in Beulah. In 1871 Eugene,
the son who was a physician, sold 480 acres, which, in those depressed
times, brought only $500, but the sum was considered a good price.
George kept Hopoi going, although he did not farm it himself, and in
1872 he mortgaged the cotton crop there for $500 to a New Orleans
supply house.[31]

Ann also became active. In 1874, she paid George $3,100 for the
160 acres that Hopoi had gradually shrunk to as the result of various
sales. George cosigned a note that enabled her to mortgage her cotton
crop, other agricultural produce, and livestock at Hopoi and receive
credit for supplies.[32] In 1880 George mortgaged his cotton and corn
crops, livestock, and part of his land on three places, including Hopoi,
to Thomas N. Allen Company of Memphis.[33] The authors have not determined when Ann died, but they believe it was between 1879 and

1880. In the latter year Bellamy was listed as managing Hopoi on his own. There is no record of Ann selling the property to him, and it seems probable that she died and George took it over. He then sold it in 1882 to the Thomas Allen Company.[34]

Whatever the exact circumstances and date, Ann's death ended a long life that saw her raised in luxury on her father and mother's North Carolina plantations and continue to prosper with her husband and family on Hickory Hill plantation in Jackson County, Florida. Then the Bellamys acquired Hopoi near Columbus, Georgia, in 1851, and in 1857 they moved to Bolivar County in the Mississippi Delta. Despite the flood of 1858, the family recovered, but prosperity was cut short by Edward's death in 1860 and the Civil War. From then until she died, Ann had a hard life. She was a pioneer woman whose role was that of loyal wife and caring mother. She worked hard but enjoyed much greater luxury in the antebellum period than most of her female contemporaries. The brutal war and postwar years were different, but despite economic setbacks Ann Bellamy was resilient and coped with hard times.

William and Julia Croom's great expectations of wealth they would obtain from Delta cotton were washed away by the great flood of 1858. Attempts to revive their lives there and in New York City proved futile, and sometime in late 1860 or 1861, William secured a home (he probably rented it) and settled in Eutaw, seat of government for Greene County, Alabama. The town attracted him and Julia because family cousin Isaac Croom lived in Greensboro in the same county; some of his brother Richard's family resided in neighboring Sumter County; Bryan and Eveline were in Montgomery; and Eutaw was much closer to Aleck and Julia in Tallahassee than was New York City or the Delta. The biggest reason for moving to Eutaw was that Stephens planned to practice law there after taking the bar examination in 1861. That fact alone made Julia happy. Lizzie was with Edward in Mississippi, where he was attempting to succeed as a planter on his father-in-law's land. The couple's first child, a boy whom they named Bryan, was a year old in 1860.

William was desperately in debt, and perhaps Eutaw, a prosperous town in a Black Belt county containing 7,251 whites, 23,598 slaves, and

10 free persons of color in 1860, might be the place to regain financial stability. The family affiliated with St. Stephen's Episcopal Church, indicative that they planned to stay, and William became a commission merchant on a small scale, marketing cotton for farmers and small planters and purchasing agricultural supplies for them. But in 1860 William owed one man $6,000, another $1,123, another $1,019, and another $1,135. Additional obligations to various individuals and firms were in three-figure amounts, and that included $900 he owed his son-in-law Edward Bellamy.[35] Trying to preserve an inheritance for Stephens, William sold his son 146 acres he still owned in Bolivar County in 1861. Stephens did not have the purchase price of $750, but the land was spared from being foreclosed.[36]

In February 1861, Stephens, recently licensed as a lawyer, moved to Eutaw. He had barely opened his office when the firing on Fort Sumter occurred in April. Croom enlisted as a private in a local company commanded by Captain George Field and went off to war. In time he was promoted to the officer ranks and saw heavy action on several fronts, mainly as General John H. Forney's adjutant general in his various commands. Stephens, who was accompanied by his slave Henry throughout the war, was captured and paroled but emerged from the conflict uninjured.[37]

Life was miserable on the home front for William and Julia. He continued to suffer from rheumatoid arthritis. So long as he kept his slaves, William could hire them out, and the bondsmen represented tangible wealth. But his creditors pressed their cases. He managed to keep two valuable slaves (one of them was a blacksmith) by deeding them to Julia as payment for a $2,000 loan he had received from her estate.[38] Yet in 1863 William had to mortgage his slave Letitia as security for a debt, Simon to secure another loan, and Phillis to obtain another. In 1864 he mortgaged all three to borrow $420.[39] It was only a question of time before he lost all his slaves and his remaining property in the Delta.

Circumstances were almost as bad and much sadder for Elizabeth. Her second child, Elizabeth, who was called Bessie, was born in 1861 but died in 1862, and Bryan died the next year at the age of four. Edward joined the Confederate army in 1862 as an assistant surgeon with the rank of captain and was assigned to Mobile, where Lizzie joined him. Bellamy next was promoted to surgeon and advanced in rank to major. He was transferred to north Georgia with the Thirty-eighth Alabama Regiment, part of the Army of Tennessee, and Elizabeth came home to Eutaw. Heavy fighting was about to begin, and Bellamy was assigned to a hospital at Ringgold, Georgia. Yet he never tended those who would be wounded at Chickamaugua or Missionary Ridge—Major Bellamy contracted typhoid fever and died on July 27, 1863.[40]

After the Atlanta campaign in the summer of 1864, Stephens was given leave and returned to Eutaw to see his parents. Before returning to duty, the young officer got engaged and also paid $1,000 for some town lots in Eutaw.[41] By the time the war ended, he was a major, but his homecoming in 1865 was anything but joyous. "I returned to Eutaw to find my father's family reduced to real poverty, & living in very poor style," he wrote. "My father had no regular occupation, nor I, & we had no strong friends to stand by us." Further disappointment came when his fiancée broke their engagement because of, as Stephens recorded, his "fallen fortunes" and because of "her mother's ambition for a rich & influential alliance." He added, "I do not think I have ever been more unhappy than at this period."[42]

The situation became worse when Julia, fifty-three, died in Eutaw on December 18, 1867. "It was the greatest affliction I have ever had to endure," Stephens remembered in 1875. "It seems to me that I owe all that is good in me to her. She was the best companion and friend I have ever had—not even excepting my dear wife."[43] Julia was buried in Eutaw, and her death broke up the family. In May 1868, William was declared bankrupt, and his personal estate and real estate were sold at public auction (no land was involved). Elizabeth could have felt nothing but despair at seeing Edward's medical library of forty or fifty volumes among the "household goods" up for bid. At the same time and place Stephens's property was also offered for sale.[44] Stephens moved to Mobile in 1869, and that same year William, whose bad health continued, gave him power of attorney. Stephens then sold two lots in Eutaw that William had acquired over the years. The property contained seven or eight acres and brought $1,000—a most welcome windfall.[45]

In Mobile Stephens opened his practice, married Mary Marshall, and became a respected lawyer with a large practice. Elizabeth moved to nearby Gainesville in Sumter County, where she taught at a school for boys—all courses, plus music—and began a successful writing career. Her short stories and local-color novels reached a national market. Never remarrying, she moved to Mobile in 1876 or 1877 and lived with Stephens and Mary. She continued to teach and enjoy fame with such novels as *Four Oaks* and *Old Man Gilbert*. The latter was set near Tallahassee on a fictional plantation named Thorne Hill (possibly modeled on Goodwood).

After suffering setback after setback, William saw his fortunes improve. His command of French, long unused but not forgotten, enabled him to obtain a job teaching at a small private college in Rome, Georgia. His cousin Charles Graves, who was a graduate of the naval academy at Annapolis and a prominent citizen of Rome, may have helped him obtain the position. Situated in the northeastern hills and mountains, Rome had a climate that improved William's health. Free from penury, he spent the early 1870s teaching French, operating a small-scale farm, pursuing an interest in bee culture, writing nostalgic letters, and enjoying visits from his children. On May 19, 1876, William died of apoplexy. Stephens returned his body to Eutaw, where, with family members and friends in attendance, he was mourned. Stephen Uriah Smith, the elderly Episcopal minister who had performed the marriage ceremonies for several of Richard Croom's children and had buried Julia Croom, was present when William was interred in a grave next to hers.[46]

Of the various Crooms, William and Julia had the saddest, most tragic existence. Suffering from painful health problems and chronically in debt, William struggled against odds that proved too much for him. For all his difficulties, William had the unwavering support of Julia, and Stephens and Elizabeth based their lives and successful careers on the principles their parents instilled in them.

As has already been seen, Richard and Winifred Croom and their daughter Winifred, who had married George Sappington, were all dead when the Civil War began. Sappington had moved to Arkansas, where he died in Little Rock in 1906. Bryan, second oldest of the five children, had married Augusta F. Marshall in Livingston in February 1861. A month later he enlisted as a private in the Shorter Guards of A. M.

Moore's Company of the Sumter County Militia. Originally a ninety-day man, Bryan stayed in the army and was listed on a muster roll in March 1862. He was promoted to fourth sergeant and two months later was serving with Company K, Fortieth Alabama Infantry Regiment.[47] Bryan died on November 12, 1863. It is not known where or whether his death was the result of illness, an accident, or combat. Within a month Augusta was appointed administratrix of his estate. From then until the war's end and through the years of Reconstruction, she managed her Sumter County plantation as a widow and demonstrated skill in buying and selling land.[48]

The oldest son, Nicholas, was only twenty-eight in 1861 and was already a successful planter. There is no record of his military service, and he may have received an exemption as a planter or sent a substitute. Nicholas never married. In February 1861, he sold his sister Susan 1,760 acres of land for $17,000.[49] Nicholas became ill in 1866 and prepared for death by drafting a will that bequeathed part of his estate to "old and faithful servants" and the remainder, $28,000 in cash, to his sister Susan. When Nicholas died on March 11, James George Whitfield, Susan's husband, was named executor.[50] They were known to their kin as Susie and Jimmie and were married in 1861 (according to family stories, Susan took on the responsibilities of a wife armed with uncommon good sense, an affectionate nature, and a cake knife that her sister Mary gave her as a wedding present).

Mary Croom and her husband, Richard Allen Whitfield (James George's older brother), had been married since 1858. They resided at first in Wayne County, North Carolina, but when the Civil War began, the couple was living in Leon County. Both owned property there, but they lived on the Home place, which Mary had inherited as her share of her father's trust. Richard and his friends were in the martial tradition of young planters and were attracted to the cavalry. Richard furnished his own mount and enlisted as a private in the Fifth Florida Cavalry on August 1, 1863.[51] He remained under Colonel Scott's command until his discharge at Tallahassee on May 12, 1865. After Mary died on June 21, 1867, Richard Allen remained in Leon County, married twice more, had three more children, and before his death on November 28, 1906, had a distinguished career as a county judge.[52]

James George Whitfield did not want to serve in an Alabama unit so long as he had the opportunity to be with his brother and friends from Leon County. On October 21, 1863, he enlisted at Tallahassee as a private in the Fifth Florida Cavalry Battalion. In April 1864, he was promoted to sergeant major and transferred to Colonel Scott's staff and remained in that position and rank until he was paroled at Tallahassee on May 10, 1865.[53] After the war Jimmie and Susie remained in Sumter County and lived well into the twentieth century. She died on June 30, 1920, and was followed three years later by James George on May 5, 1923.

William Croom, his wives, Mary Bryan and Elizabeth Whitfield, their children and their husbands and wives, and their children's children lived out their lives in the ways described in this book. Many other people affected these generations of Crooms and were, in turn, affected themselves. The story, as recounted here, is incomplete. Despite the availability of many records and the authors' efforts to provide an accurate accounting, it can never be told in its entirety. Noting the last years of Bryan and Eveline and Ann Hawks and taking a forward and backward look at Goodwood plantation will close the circle.

12 *"Well Known and Highly Respected"*

Like many southerners, Bryan, Eveline, and Ann saw their world collapse with the end of the Civil War. From the relative prosperity and optimism of 1864, the Crooms plunged into hard times and despair. They abandoned the Norman Bridge road plantation but still lived in the country. In 1866 they were reduced to living on twelve acres of land and paying real estate taxes of $8.40 and personal estate taxes of $19.40. It was a far cry from having a $400 vehicle taxed at $2.00 in 1864 to paying a tax of twenty-five cents on its replacement in 1866.[1]

There was no improvement in 1867. Croom now had thirteen instead of twelve acres of land valued at $1,000 and paid $4.00 in taxes. He also acted as agent for the eighty acres Eveline had bought from Ann Bellamy, which was taxed $6.40 for its assessed value of $1,600.[2] In that bleak year Bryan and Eveline needed any kind of financial support they could get. Earlier Bryan had sold 137.95 acres to Willis R. Callaway, but Callaway was unable to meet the annual notes, and Bryan extended them for a year. William C. Bibb, another citizen of Montgomery, bought the deed from Willis, although the debt to Bryan was still unpaid. Unable to pay cash, Bibb mortgaged to Bryan property on the place valued at $6,000: eighteen mules, farm implements, wagons, a cotton gin and press, corn, and other produce. In addition Bibb mortgaged half of his cotton crop.[3] As matters turned out, Bibb failed to satisfy his obligation, but Bryan did not repossess the property.

The Crooms managed as best they could, but Bryan's physical well-being limited his activities. In May 1867, Eveline wrote her niece Mary Croom Whitfield, who with her husband, Richard, lived on the Home place in Leon County, "Your Uncle [Bryan] says he is afraid that Richard & Mary are vexed because we did not get to see them in the winter. I don't think you are—& if you were I think your vexation would soon be at an end if you could see how feeble & thin your Uncle is. Dr. Baldwin says he must go away this summer, that he will not get well without a change of climate." Eveline had to limit her social visits to friends and on one occasion turned down an invitation: "I was afraid to be so long from him [Bryan] fearing he might have a chill in my absence."[4]

Mary's letter was full of family information, church news, gossip, and inquiries about old friends in Tallahassee. She had written to Ann Bellamy, who, with some of her sons, was still in Bolivar County, Mississippi, and was hoping to hear from Mary's sister Susan Croom Whitfield in Sumter County. Eveline sent love to "Brother Aleck [Croom] & all his family" and hoped his wife, Julia, had recovered her health. She also extended greetings in Tallahassee to the Long, Betton, Randolph, and Gamble families but did not mention the Hopkins or affairs at Goodwood.[5]

Eveline took solace in going to church, but even that was difficult. As she wrote Mary, "I did not get to church but once during lent. Uncle Bryan was sometimes well enough, but one of my horses was dead, & the other lame so I was obliged to stay at home—last Sunday Mr. Carraway [a neighbor] lent me one of his & Aleck put him in the carriage with the lame one & we got to church in good time." Eveline found it "unpleasant to be in the country without any way of getting about when one wishes." She continued, "I do hope Mr. Croom will be able to get a house in town next year—there was none for rent when we broke up housekeeping in the country." She hoped Bryan would get well enough for them to visit Tallahassee. Declining to "appoint any particular time again for visiting," she simply promised, "When we [are] ready to start I [will] telegraph to you." In closing she added, "Mr. C. sends much love to you all & says to write to him—do find time my dear child to write."[6] Unfortunately, Mary would not find time to write. She died a month later.

If 1867 was a year of economic adversity, 1868 was more of the same. In addition, the family suffered an emotional loss: Ann Hawks died in the summer. She was buried in Oakwood Cemetery, the large city burying ground located on the hills of northeast Montgomery. The inscription on her tomb read, "Sacred To Ann Singleton Widow Of Samuel Hawks Died July 15, 1868." Ann was buried in a plot across from that of William Burr Howell, who had died in 1863. The father of President Davis's wife, Varina, had remained in Montgomery after the family moved to Richmond, Virginia. Eveline, who had been extremely close to her mother, began making weekly visits to the grave, taking flowers whenever possible.

Bryan's last contact with Goodwood was a suit he filed on December 6, 1869, in the Federal Circuit Court in the Northern District of Florida against Susan Winthrop, executrix of Henrietta Smith. She was accused of breach of contract and sued for $25,000. The case revived the previous attempt by Croom to obtain damages involving his cotton crop of 1857. The original suit had been interrupted by the Civil War. Apparently the litigation never got beyond its preliminary stages, and although the outcome is unknown, it is certain that Bryan never collected.[7]

As debilitated as Bryan was, Eveline preceded him in death. On February 8, 1870, she died and was buried the next day beside her mother in Oakwood Cemetery. Her simple tombstone was inscribed with the word "Peace." Eveline's brief will, probated June 14, stated, "I give to my dear husband, Bryan Croom my entire property of every description, real personal and mixed, of every name, nature and description."[8]

Later in 1870, Bryan's confused conflict with Bibb over land was resolved. Bibb may have made good on one or more of the promissory notes and been able to string the business out, but, finally, the property was sold at public auction. Croom himself was high bidder at $12,000, an amount of money he did not have, but he probably paid part of it and made arrangements for future payments. In any event, he acquired title to land (137.95 acres) that could be farmed and help him survive.[9]

Apparently Croom moved onto the property because the census taker in 1870 listed him as a sixty-nine-year-old farmer who owned real estate worth $10,000 and whose personal estate was $3,000. Because of his age and declining health, Bryan was unable to do much work, but Jesse R. Jones, a twenty-one-year-old white man, was living in Croom's household and was described as the farm "agent." Even younger, John Wright, a white youth of fourteen, lived there also and was old enough to help with the crop. Living nearby as farm laborers (and probably as Bryan's tenant farmers) were three black families. The largest was a household of eight, and the smallest consisted of an elderly black woman of eighty-five named Sarah. All the blacks, except for two children born after the war, were former slaves. Without exception the blacks had taken Croom as their surname.[10]

With Eveline and her mother dead, no children to look after him, and, at best, infrequent contacts with family members, Croom lived the next few years in loneliness and sorrow and with limited means. The seventy-five-year-old man died on Christmas Eve, 1875. Funeral services were held at St. John's, and he was buried beside Ann and Eveline. The *Montgomery Advertiser* printed a brief obituary noting that Croom, "a well known and highly respected citizen of Montgomery county, died at his residence a few miles from the city, Thursday."[11] Bryan left no will, and the inventory of his estate revealed little of value: ninety-three ounces of silverware worth eighty-five cents an ounce; one pair of plated candlesticks, sixteen nut crackers, two knife rests, two salt stands, one toast rack, one egg stand, two decanter waiters on wheels, four additional single decanter waiters, one strainer, one American watch, one mahogany chest, and one sole leather trunk.[12]

Bryan and Eveline were married for forty-four years. Other than the

years of Reconstruction, they had enjoyed the privileged existence of a
planter family. It was not a life of ease, and their twenty-year lawsuit
was unique. As it turned out, the decision was of landmark proportions,
so significant that it would be frequently cited in subsequent cases involving the question of survivorship in a common calamity. By any
yardstick Bryan, Eveline, and her mother were admirable people: hardworking, devoted to each other and to their kin, religious, respectful of
others' rights, and considerate of their slaves.

The Goodwood that Arvah Hopkins bought in 1858 had the mansion
and 1,576 acres of land. He and Susan retained possession and by 1870
had enlarged it to 3,300 acres and cultivated it with black tenant farmers, making payments both in cash and as shares of the crops. The story
of Goodwood under the Hopkins's management and that of subsequent
owners, and its present status as the Margaret E. Wilson Foundation,
a private nonprofit organization established in 1989 to restore it to the
public as a museum, awaits its future chronicler.

Briefly, the crippling economic depression that struck the nation in
the 1870s was especially devastating in the South, already struggling to
recover from the effects of the Civil War and the dislocations of Reconstruction. In 1874 Hopkins was forced to give up most of his land but
kept Goodwood and 160 acres from forced sale by claiming a state constitutional provision that protected homesteads. From that time forward, Goodwood ceased to be a viable, working plantation. When Arvah
died in 1883, he left Susan with a Goodwood threatened by a sheriff's
sale. Susan was forced to move to town and care for her family there. At
a public auction in late 1883 Susan was high bidder for the Goodwood
homestead and reclaimed its possession. Then in the summer of 1885
(August 31), Susan sold Goodwood for $6,000. The new owners expected
to use it as a country estate.[13]

In the summer of 1872, Dr. John Torrey finally made his often promised but never fulfilled visit to Florida. It was a nostalgic journey for
the botanist, who was past his mid-seventies. Torrey spent several days
in Tallahassee, where his fame was known, and was pleased to see a
Torreya tree that was supposed to have been planted by his colleague
Hardy Croom. The scientist visited St. John's Church for a specific rea-

son: "The monument to this endeared friend [Hardy Croom] was visited by me with a sad interest," he wrote. For Torrey 1872 was the present, and he was even then contemplating a time long past when he added, "I copied the inscription—& my thoughts went back to the pleasant days that we had spent together."[14] Torrey died the next year. Then he, like the Crooms, became a part of history.

Appendix: Croom Family Genealogical Chart

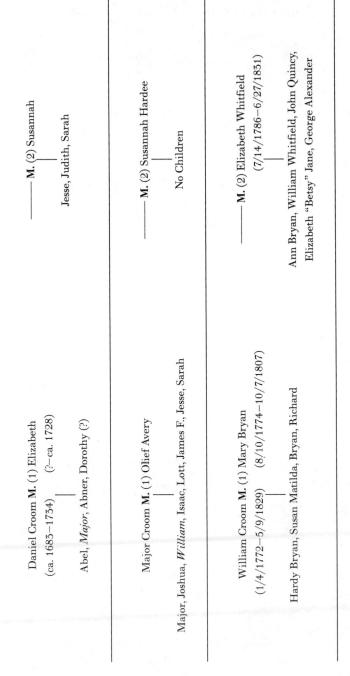

Daniel Croom **M.** (1) Elizabeth   **M.** (2) Susannah
(ca. 1683–1734)   (?–ca. 1728)

Abel, *Major*, Abner, Dorothy (?)   Jesse, Judith, Sarah

Major Croom **M.** (1) Olief Avery   **M.** (2) Susannah Hardee

Major, Joshua, *William*, Isaac, Lott, James F., Jesse, Sarah   No Children

William Croom **M.** (1) Mary Bryan   **M.** (2) Elizabeth Whitfield
(1/4/1772–5/9/1829)   (8/10/1774–10/7/1807)   (7/14/1786–6/27/1831)

Hardy Bryan, Susan Matilda, Bryan, Richard   Ann Bryan, William Whitfield, John Quincy,
                                            Elizabeth "Betsy" Jane, George Alexander

Children of William Croom and Mary Bryan

A. Hardy Bryan Croom **M.** (6/19/1821) Frances Smith
(10/8/1797–10/9/1837)   (?–10/9/1837)

Henrietta Mary, Eugene Lafayette, Frances Elizabeth,
William Henry, Justina Rosa

B. Susan Matilda Croom **M.** Edmund Whitfield
(ca. 1799–ca. 1821)

No Children

C. Bryan Croom **M.** (7/27/1826) Eveline Singleton Hawks
(10/8/1801–12/24/1875)   (1800–2/8/1870)

No Children

D. Richard Whitfield Croom **M.** (4/9/1829) Winifred Bryan Whitfield
(9/20/1805–2/20/1859)   (10/17/1802–10/1/1848)

Winifred Bryan, Nicholas Pavolich, Mary Whitfield,
Bryan, Susan Matilda, James

Children of William Croom and Elizabeth Whitfield

E. Ann Bryan Croom **M.** (12/8/1929) Edward Croom Bellamy
(ca. 1812–ca. 1879)   (ca. 1801–11/3/1860)

William Croom, Charles Edward, Eugene, Hardy, Harold,
Ann Elizabeth, George Whitfield

F. William Whitfield Croom **M.** Julia Stephens
(1814–5/19/1876)   (1814–12/18/1867)

Elizabeth Whitfield, Cicero Stephens

G. John Quincy Croom
(died in infancy)

H. Elizabeth "Betsy" Croom **M.** Samuel Crowell Bellamy
(3/28/1819–5/11/1857)   (?–12/1853)

Male, name unknown, died in infancy

I. George Alexander Croom **M.** (2/13/1843) Julia Church
(10/7/1821–7/25/1890)   (5/8/1824–4/30/1888)

Hardy, Alonzo Church, William Church, Sarah Jane, Julia Church,
Elizabeth, Ann Eloise, Louisa Whitfield

Notes

1. "Fertile Country . . . Never Failing Streams and Fine Springs"

1. Knauss, "William Pope DuVal," 117–18. See also Censer, "Southwestern Migration," 407–26.

2. Powell, *North Carolina Biography*, 1:463–64. Daniel Croom had six children. See Outlaw, "Croom Family," 7–8, 12–13. This bound 342-page typescript was compiled in 1955–57; a second version was issued in 1962. It is an important family record. There is also an unsigned Croom Family typescript in the North Carolina Collection, University of North Carolina Library, Chapel Hill. See also Wood, "Daniel Croom of Virginia," a 20-page typescript on file at the Library of Congress, Washington, D.C.

3. Powell, *North Carolina Biography*, 1:463–64; Outlaw, "Croom Family," 7–8, 12–13; see also Watson, *History of New Bern and Craven County*.

4. See notice of surveyor general Robert Butler in Carter, Territory of Florida, 1824–28, in *Territorial Papers of the United States*, 23:124.

5. Powell, *North Carolina Biography*, 1:464; Outlaw, "Croom Family," 268. Apparently the will was contested in 1833. See also Censer, *Planters and Their Children*, 152; Powell, *Annals of Progress*, 20–21; and Johnson and Holloman, *Kinston and Lenoir County*. See Moore, "Records of Craven County," 1:170, quoting an unsigned letter in *New Bern North Carolina Sentinel*, July 26, 1828, containing anecdotal material on William Croom. For William Croom's death, see Hardy Croom to Bryan Croom, May 12, 1829, and June [?], 1829, Croom Family Letters. Court cases concerning the Crooms in Florida produced a vast and unorganized mass of evidence, including a number of Croom family letters, mainly those written by Hardy Croom. Several thousand pages of unpublished material relevant to the lower-court cases have been sorted out and placed in the archives at Goodwood plantation, Tallahassee, Florida. The correspondence is hereafter cited as Croom Letters, and letters concerning family members are cited by first names only. Other letters are documented to the sources in which they occur.

6. Outlaw, "Croom Family," 273. For more information on Edmund, see Monroe County Book Committee, *History of Monroe County*, 904–5.

7. Hawks tutored one of his brothers, Cicero Stephens Hawks, a graduate of the University of North Carolina (1830). The younger brother also had a distinguished career in the Episcopal Church. See Powell, *North Carolina Dic-*

tionary, 3:76–77. Information on the Crooms and their relatives in college may be found in Battle, *University of North Carolina,* vol. 1. For the school's early years, see Henderson, *First State University,* chaps. 1 and 5. The university's impact on the state is detailed in Snider, *Light on the Hill.* For Gaston, see J[oseph] Herman Schauinger, *William Gaston: Carolinian* (Milwaukee: Bruce Publishing Co., 1949), 35–36.

8. For Hawks's remarks, see Croom, *Catalogue of Plants,* 7–8; see also *Henrietta Smith . . . and Elizabeth M. Armistead v. Bryan Croom . . . and Others, Florida Reports* 7 (1857), 84–85, 96, testimony of Matthias E. Manly, 127. This major litigation contains numerous references to Croom family letters and is hereafter cited as *Case.*

9. Bryan and Stanly, *Orations,* 11. Hardy's remarks had been made earlier at Kinston to Captain J. H. Bryan's Company of Volunteers.

10. The authors are indebted to Professor J. Patrick Lee of Barry University for bringing to their attention Hardy's 1823 translation and inscription to Lafayette. French scholar Lee discovered the book in the Bibliothèque Nationale in Paris. See also MacIntire, *Lafayette,* 142–45.

11. After reaching Virginia in September 1710, the settlers traveled by wagon to North Carolina. See Watson, *History of New Bern and Craven County,* 4:7–8. See also Dill, *Governor Tryon.*

12. For Nathan Smith's death, see *Newbern Carolina Sentinel,* March 1, 1823. *Case,* 121, 135. The lower courts' civil cases regarding the Croom estate are all in manuscript form. They are cited by the number assigned them with appropriate pages and are on file at the Leon County Courthouse, Tallahassee, Florida. Copies are at the Goodwood Archives. For Smith's will and the division of his estate, see Case 1203, 88–93, 122–26. See also Case 1214A, 84–96. In addition, Hardy received a pair of wheels, thirty-two bales of cotton, and the hire of five slaves. This last cited case is so extensive and bulky that it has been divided by the authors and referred to as Case 1214 and Case 1214A with appropriate pages. Citations to them refer to the same case. For Hardy and Frances's wedding, see Craven County Marriage Book 1. For Hardy's infrequent collection of his mail, see *New Bern North Carolina Sentinel,* July 26, 1828, as quoted in Moore, "Records of Craven County" 1:147–48.

13. North Carolina *Senate Journal,* 1828–29, 9, 22–23, 91, 108–9. For his votes on slavery, see 55–56, 91.

14. Hardy to Frances, September 13, 1928, Croom Letters; William Croom, will, June 2, 1829.

15. Hardy to Bryan, March 1, 1830, Croom Letters; Hardy to Frances, No-

vember 23, 1830, *Case*, 97. Hardy, of course, relied heavily on Bryan to look out for their father's holdings in Florida in the period immediately following his death. See Hardy to Bryan, November 15, 1829 [?], Croom Letters.

16. Henrietta Smith to Hardy, January 20, 1933, *Case*, 100; deposition of Ann Hawks in ibid., 122–23; Hardy to Frances, December 4, 1831, Croom Letters. For Nathan B. Whitfield, see Whitfield and Whitfield, *Whitfield, Bryan, Smith, and Related Families*, 99–101, and Barrett, "Whitfields Move to Alabama."

17. Deposition of William B. Blackledge, Case 1214, 254–53. For Hardy's rent payment, see Case 1214, 909.

18. Deposition of Zachary Slade, Case 1214A, 509. For the baptisms, see Parish Register Entries, 1:13, 17, on file at Christ Episcopal Church, New Bern. See also Carraway, *Crown of Life*. For Nathan Smith's land troubles, see Moore, "Records of Craven County," 1:172.

19. Hardy to Bryan, October 21, 1831, Croom Letters.

20. For the sale of Hardy's slaves, see bill of sale, October 31, 1831, in Parrott Collection. Hardy to Bryan, October 10, 1831; October 27, 1831; April 27, 1832; and May 13, 1832, Croom Letters.

21. Hardy to Bryan, May 13, 1834; May 14, 1834, Croom Letters.

22. Ibid., July 1, 1832; July 8, 1832.

23. Hardy to Frances, November 23, 1830; November 26, 1830, Croom Letters. See *Florida Legislative Council Laws*, 1832, 11, for the academy's incorporation (hereafter cited as *LC* with appropriate year and pages). See also Hardy to Frances, March 24, [1833?], Croom Letters. The year is not included in this letter, but it was written from Gadsden County, and Hardy discusses his health and that of his son.

24. Justina B., the fifth child, died at the age of sixteen. See another copy of Nathan Smith's will in Case 1214A, 464–68, and for the earliest will (made in 1821), see Craven County Record of Wills. For the Armistead-Smith wedding, see Craven County Marriage Book, 1:8. Hardy and Nathaniel corresponded with each other in Florida, but Nathaniel never came to Gadsden or Leon Counties. See Hardy to Frances, March 24, [1831?]; and May 5, 1831, Croom Letters. For Armistead's death. see *Raleigh Register*, March 27, 1824.

25. Hardy to Bryan, July 22, 1832, Croom Letters.

26. Ibid., August 17, 1832.

27. Ibid., October 6, 1832.

28. Redfearn, *"Steamboat Home"* (May 1935), 407. A lawyer in Miami, Redfearn was primarily interested in the legal trials involving the Croom family.

Even so, his valuable research included various aspects of the family's history, and he used some family letters since lost. The article cited above was reprinted as "Presumption as to Order of Death in a Common Disaster: *The Steamboat Home*" (February, 1963). See also Redfearn, "Croom Case." For an overview, see Dodd, "Steamboats *Home* and *Pulaski*."

29. See typescript of the *Harbinger* article in North Carolina Collection, University of North Carolina Library, Chapel Hill; for comments on Hardy's scholarship, see remarks of Dr. John Torrey in Croom, *Catalogue of Plants*, vol. 4. See also Croom, "Botanical Observations."

30. Deposition of George Wilson, Case 1214A, 553–55.

31. Rogers, *John Torrey*, 4, 118–19, 229–30; see also Gray, "John Torrey"; Redfearn, *Steamboat Home*, 422.

32. A courthouse fire destroyed the early deed records, but data in neighboring Gadsden County show that the Crooms had property in Jackson County. Trial testimony and depositions confirm the fact.

33. Watson, *History of New Bern and Craven County*, 267.

34. Hardy to Frances, December 14, 1831, *Case*. Sometime before July 29, 1828, William Croom bought the Gadsden County plantation of Colonel Henry Yonge. See Case 1214A, 636–39. See also Craven County Marriage Book, 1:77.

35. Hardy to Frances, December 14, 1831, *Case*. Hardy to Bryan, June 20, 1833, Croom Letters; Battle, *University of North Carolina* 1:790; see Moore, "Records of Craven County," 1:67–70.

36. For Ann's property lots, see Case 1214, 204; see also deposition of Ann Hawks, ibid., 90–101. She realized $750 from the sale of four lots in New Bern. See Case 1214A, 345–48.

37. See Coker and Watson, *Indian Traders*; Upchurch, "Development and Exploration of the Forbes Purchase." See also Womack, *Gadsden*, 10, 51.

38. Womack, *Gadsden*, 19.

39. William Croom, will; Hardy to Frances, November 23, 1830, Croom Letters; unpublished Florida census of 1830, Population, Gadsden County, 152.

40. See complaint of Ann Hawks against Bryan Croom, Case 1214, 392–99; see also ibid., 797–800, for Bryan's explanation of the arrangement.

41. Gadsden County Deed Book A, 97, 529–30 (hereafter cited as GCDB with appropriate book, letter, and pages). For the joint sale of Fayette County land, see copy of unnumbered pages from Gadsden County Deed Book used as an exhibit in the case.

42. Castelnau, "Essay On Middle Florida," 206; Hardy to Frances, December 4, 1831, Croom Letters.

43. See Avant's illustrated index in Stanley, *Gadsden County.* See also Womack, *Gadsden*, 20–21.

44. Hardy to Bryan, July 12, 1831, Croom Letters. In 1828 William Croom, who had purchased Gadsden County land from Henry Yonge, promised to deliver the grantor a certain number of packages of seed cotton. See Case 1214A, 636–39.

45. For their business dealings, see Hardy to Bryan, September 2, 1833; October 9, 1833, Croom Letters.

46. Bryan to Hardy, June 4, 1832, Croom Letters. Hardy and Richard got along less well. See Richard to Hardy, October 6, 1832, ibid. For Hardy's purchase in Section 25, see Case 1214, 909–11, and Davidson, *Florida Land.* For a discussion of Mexican cotton, see Moore, *Agriculture,* 33.

47. Hardy to Bryan, June 20, 1833, Croom Letters.

48. Ibid., October 6, 1832.

49. Ibid.

50. Frances to Hardy, June 11, 1833, *Case,* 100.

51. Hardy to Bryan, July 20, 1833, *Case,* 136–37. Hardy spoke of Dr. Edward C. Bellamy, Samuel's brother, as sharing his enthusiasm.

52. See indenture signed August 15, 1832, in Case 1214A, 470–76.

53. Hardy to Bryan, June 20, July 20, 1833, Croom Letters.

54. For discussion of travel, prices, and mail deliveries affecting Tallahassee, see Carter, Territory of Florida, 1834–39, in *Territorial Papers of the United States,* 25:543, 559, quoting *Tallahassee Floridian,* November 17, and January 5, 1839.

55. Hardy to Bryan, June 28, 1833, Croom Letters.

56. Ibid.

57. Ibid., July 20, 1833; Redfearn, "*Steamboat Home,*" 408. The neoclassic capitol was completed in 1840. Also present was Hardy's brother, Richard, and all three men represented Lenoir County at the convention. See Johnson and Holloman, *Kinston and Lenoir County,* 93. Isaac Croom moved to Alabama in 1837 and settled in Greensboro, where he built his town house mansion, Magnolia Grove. After the Civil War, Greensboro became the county seat of newly created Hale County. Croom was an intellectual, Whig, state legislator, Episcopalian, and large planter and slaveholder. See Nicholas H. Cobbs Jr., "Col. Isaac Croom, Builder of Magnolia Grove," *Greensboro (Ala.) Watchman,* June 2, 1983.

58. Hardy to Bryan, October 9, 1833, Croom Letters.

59. Ibid. For an example of minor litigation involving the Crooms, see *Tallahassee Floridian,* May 2, 1835.

60. Rivers, "Slavery In Microcosm," 242.

61. *Case,* 138; Case 1214A, 633–35, 310–14.

2. Planting and Planning

1. For developments in Tallahassee and Leon County, the work of Clifton Paisley is indispensable. See his *From Cotton to Quail* and *Red Hills of Florida;* Groene, *Ante-Bellum Tallahassee;* Smith, *Slavery and Plantation Growth;* and Appleyard, "Plantation Life in Middle Florida." For population statistics, see Dodd, "Florida Census of 1825," 34, 39.

2. Frances to Hardy, February 9, 1834, *Case,* 101, 137.

3. Depositions of Susan Winthrop and Prudence Rice, Case 1214, 405–11, 412–14. Pansy and Tempe, who had two children, were other house servants. See inventory of Hardy's New Bern estate in Case 1214A, 430.

4. Carter, Territory of Florida, 1824–38, in *Territorial Papers of the United States,* quoting John McKee to George Graham, commissioner of the General Land Office, April 21, 1825, 238.

5. For Murat, see Hanna, *Prince in Their Midst.*

6. See Abbey, "LaFayette and the LaFayette Land Grants" and "Story of the LaFayette Lands in Florida"; Bishko, "French Would-Be Settler."

7. Leon County Deed Book, I:180 (hereafter cited as LCDB with appropriate book and pages).

8. See Shofner, *Jefferson County,* 21, 31, 85, 88, 98, 113.

9. Paisley, *Red Hills,* 88–89; Groene, *Ante-Bellum Tallahassee,* 49; Smith, *Slavery and Plantation Growth,* 57, 101–31.

10. Hardy to Frances, March 21, 1834, *Case.* See also Frances to Hardy, March 24, April 15, 1834, *Case,* 103–4. Hardy's negotiations with Nuttall, Braden, and Craig and with Laporte are frequently cited in Cases 1214 and 1214A. See also Doherty, *Richard Keith Call,* 45, and esp. chap. 6, "A Florida Entrepreneur," 84–92.

11. Frances to Hardy, April 15, 1834, *Case,* 137.

12. Hardy to Frances, March 21, 1834, Croom Letters. For the bill of sale, see Case 1214, 271–72.

13. Hardy to Bryan, July 28, 1834, Croom Letters.

14. Ibid.

15. See signed statement in Case 1214A, 603. The relative was George Whitfield.

16. Hardy to Seth P. Lewis, August 12, 1834, Croom Letters.

17. *Farmers' Register* 2 (June 1834): 1–3.

18. Ibid. (February 1835): 590–91; (April 1835): 710. See also ibid. (May 1835), 769–70. The magazine contained at least eight other articles by Croom. For more on Spalding and long-staple cotton, see Coulter, *Thomas Spalding of Sapelo,* 63–75.

19. Hardy to Seth P. Lewis, August 12, 1834, Croom Letters.

20. See Case 1214, 536–39, and 657–52 for deposition of Dr. Wilson.

21. Deposition of Robert W. Williams, ibid., 722.

22. Hardy to Frances, November 26, 1834, Croom Letters. The previous summer Hardy had visited Philadelphia, New York, and Boston. He enjoyed Philadelphia because a doctor there examined him and told him his lungs were "not *seriously* affected but only weak." He also met Dr. Charles Pickering, a doctor, botanist, and literary man in charge of plants at the Philadelphia Academy of Natural Science, who gave him unlimited access to the institution. See Hardy to Frances, September 5, 1834, ibid. He returned to New Bern in late September. See Hardy to Mrs. Smith, November 24, 1834, ibid. For Pickering, see Ruschenberger, *Origin, Progress, and Present Condition of the Academy,* 28, 30, 64, 77.

23. Hardy to Frances, May 1, 1835, Croom Letters; Hardy to Frances [?], July 29, 1835; Bryan to Hardy, July 26, 1835, ibid; deposition of Ann Hawks, Case 1214, 93.

24. Hardy to Thomas Baltzell, August 16, 1835, Croom Letters; testimony of Thomas Baltzell, *Case,* 127–29, and Case 1214, 417. For their sale of town lots, see LCDB E, 345.

25. See Pendleton, "Henrietta Mary Croom," 4. This typescript article was written when Ms. Pendleton was an undergraduate at Florida State College for Women (Florida State University). She located several letters in the Leon County Courthouse and Florida Supreme Court Library at Tallahassee. On the larger scene, Censer, *Planters and Their Children,* 152, noted that on the frontier, planter parents "wished to be friends and confederates as well as figures of authority to their children."

26. Hardy to Frances, July 29, 1835, Croom Letters. Hardy also took the children to Saratoga for a week's vacation as he recovered from a cold.

27. Pendleton, "Henrietta Mary Croom," 10, quoting Henrietta Mary to Hardy, March 9, 1836; for a description of the school, see ibid., quoting Marian Gouveneur, *As I Remember* (New York: D. Appleton & Co., 1911), 50, 52.

28. Henrietta Mary to Hardy, March 9, 1836; see also Hardy to Frances, January 12, 1836, and Hardy to Bryan, July 28, 1836, Croom Letters.

29. Henrietta Mary to Hardy, March 9, 1836, Croom Letters.

30. Hardy to Dr. John Torrey, October 6, 1835, Croom Letters.

31. Frances to Hardy, November 4, December 29, 1835, *Case,* 103–4.

32. Hardy to Frances, November 8, 1835, Croom Letters.

33. Ibid.

34. Frances to Hardy, December 29, 1835, *Case,* 103–4; see also Hardy to Frances, January 30, 1836; Hardy to Bryan, July 20, 1836, Croom Letters. For the inheritance, see Records of Craven County, book 51, 366–69, quoted in Case 1203, 75–78. The dowry had been given to Henrietta by her mother in 1835.

35. Hardy to Frances, undated letter, in Redfearn, "*Steamboat Home,*" 406–7. See also Hardy to Frances, January 12, 30, 1836, Croom Letters.

36. LCDB D, 623.

37. For Hardy's attempts to encourage people to move to Florida, see deposition of Thomas Baltzell, Case 1214, 415–16. Noah Thompson recalled that in 1837 he traveled by stage with Hardy from Quincy to Augusta and that during the trip the latter convinced him to migrate to Florida. See deposition of Noah Thompson, ibid.

38. Hardy to Frances, January 12, 1836, Croom Letters. For the bill of sale, see Case 1214, 273–74.

39. For the bills of sale, see Case 1214, 277–78.

40. Henrietta Mary to Hardy, March 9, 1836, Croom Letters.

41. Hardy to Frances, January 30, 1836, Croom Letters.

42. Ibid.

43. LCDB D, 623.

44. Ibid., E, 172–73. See also Case 1214, 275; Case 1214A, 234–36.

45. Hardy to Bryan, July 28, 1836, Croom Letters.

46. Testimony of George Whitfield, *Case,* 312. See also 133.

47. Bryan to Hardy, July 8, 1836, Croom Letters. For the destruction of the *Ohioan,* see *Apalachicola Gazette,* April 27, 1836; *Savannah Daily Georgian,* May 4, 1836, quoting *Columbus (Ga.) Sentinel,* April 29, 1836; and Mueller, *Perilous Journeys,* 36.

48. Hardy to Bryan, July 28, 1836, Croom Letters.

49. Bryan to Hardy, July 8, 1836, *Case,* 105; deposition of Ann Hawks, ibid, 126.

50. Bryan to Hardy, July 28, 1836, August 15, 1836, Croom Letters.

51. Ibid.

52. For overviews of Florida's economic situation in this period, see Dovell,

History of Banking in Florida; Thomas, "History of Banking in Florida"; Martin, *Florida during the Territorial Days;* Doherty, *Whigs of Florida* and *Richard Keith Call;* and Thompson, *Jacksonian Democracy.* For Hardy's evaluation, see Hardy to John B. Carroll, February 4, 1837, Croom Letters.

53. Bryan to Hardy, September 29, 1836, *Case,* 106.

54. Hardy to Bryan, October 13, 1836, Croom Letters.

55. Hardy to John Torrey, October 17, 1836, Croom Letters. For an overview of Charleston in this period, see Fraser, *Charleston! Charleston!,* esp. chap. 4, "The Antebellum City," 169–246.

56. Hardy to John B. Carroll, October 14, 1836; Hardy to Brothers Peugnet, October 14, 1836, Croom Letters.

57. Hardy to John B. Carroll, October 14, 1836, Croom Letters.

58. Ibid., October 18, 1836.

59. Ibid.

60. Hardy to Frances, November 18, 1836, *Case,* 108; testimony of George Whitfield, ibid., 130–31.

61. Elizabeth Armistead to Hardy, December 3, 1836, *Case,* 109–10.

62. Hardy to Frances, December 6, 1836; Hardy to Bryan, September 2, 1833, Croom Letters.

63. Hardy to Frances, December 6, 1836, Croom Letters.

64. Ibid., January 23, 1837.

3. A Passage to Charleston

1. Hardy to Frances, January 29, 1837, Croom Letters.

2. Hardy to Dr. John Torrey, February 7, 1837; Hardy to John Carroll, February 4, 1837, Croom Letters. See Rippy, *Joel R. Poinsett,* 205. For more on Bachman, see Jay Schuler, *Had I the Wings: The Friendship of Bachman and Audubon* (Athens: University of Georgia Press, 1995). See also O'Brien and Moltke-Hansen, *Intellectual Life in Antebellum Charleston.* The authors are indebted to Ms. Martha Zeirden of the Charleston Museum for arranging interviews, providing maps, and locating the various properties owned by Poinsett in Charleston.

3. Hardy to Bryan, February 3, 1837, Croom Letters.

4. Hardy to Dr. John Torrey, February 7, 1837, Croom Letters.

5. Hardy to Bryan, February 3, 1837; Hardy to John B. Carroll, February 4, 1837, *Case,* 112.

6. Hardy to Elizabeth Armistead, March 13, 1837, Croom Letters.

7. Ibid.

8. Hardy to Dr. John Torrey, March 15, 1837, Croom Letters.

9. Hardy to Frances, March 23, 1837, Croom Letters. For Dr. Wray and Augusta, see Jones, *Memorial History*, and Salem Dutcher . . . . *From the Close of the Eighteenth Century to the Present Times*. This is a reprint of the 1890 edition. For the best study on the Indian conflict, see Mahon, *Second Seminole War*.

10. Deposition of Ann Hawks, Case 1214, 90—91.

11. Bryan to Hardy, March 7, 1837, Croom Letters; deposition of Henrietta S. Osgood, Case 1214A, 336.

12. Hardy to Frances, April 3, 1837, Croom Letters.

13. Chapman, "Torreya taxifolia, Arnott," 251. See also Winifred Chapman, "Life of Dr. Chapman," *Journal of the New York Botanical Garden* 22 (January 1921): 1—11 (reprint of a typescript). Chapman's wife was Mary Ann Simmons Hancock of New Bern, North Carolina.

14. For Chapman's quote, see Rogers, *John Torrey*, 172; see also Hardy to Dr. John Torrey, April 4, 1837, Croom Letters.

15. Hardy to Henry Gaskins, April 17, 1837, Croom Letters. Unpublished Florida census of 1840, Population, Leon County, 63, notes that Gaskins was married and owned no slaves.

16. Deposition of Ann Hawks, Case 1214, 90.

17. Both quotes are Hardy to Henry Gaskins, April 28, May 2, 1837, Croom Letters.

18. Hardy to Bryan, June 9, 1837, Croom Letters.

19. Hardy to Dr. Samuel C. Bellamy, June 9, 1837, Croom Letters.

20. Ibid., July 25, 1837.

21. Hardy to Henry Gaskins, June 26, 1837, Croom Letters.

22. Hardy to Dr. Samuel C. Bellamy, June 27, 1837, Croom Letters. See also *New Bern Spectator*, June 23, 1837.

23. Hardy to Dr. Samuel C. Bellamy, July 25, 1837, Croom Letters. William A. Grant of Marianna, Florida, kindly furnished the authors with a photograph of Elizabeth Jane Bellamy's gravestone that he took in 1958 and a copy of her burial inscription.

24. Hardy to Henry Gaskins, July 30, 1837, Croom Letters. See ibid., June 26, September 21, 1837.

25. Hardy to Bryan, September 21, 1837, Croom Letters.

26. "Notes Concerning Two Itineraries," 319.

27. Deposition of Ann Hawks, Case 1214, 99.

28. Hardy to Bryan, March 11, 183[?], Croom Letters.

29. Long, *Florida Breezes*, 123.

30. Deposition of George Whitfield, *Case*, 133.

31. Sales account of Hardy Croom's Lake Lafayette Estate, Case 1214, 889, 894. See Croom's letter quoted in Conrad, "Notices of the Geology."

32. Deposition of George Whitfield, *Case*, 131. See also statement of Richard Hayward in Case 1214, 9–17.

33. Deposition of Henry J. Gaskins, Case 1214, 1032–34.

34. See inventory in ibid., 569–70. The authors thank Ms. Marcy L. Koontz, a graduate student (Ph.D. 1995) in the College of Human Sciences, Department of Historic Costume, at Florida State University, for her interpretation of the manuscript material describing Frances's clothing.

35. Hardy to Bryan, September 18, 1837, Croom Letters.

36. Ibid., September 28, 1837.

37. *Tallahassee Floridian*, October 21, 1837.

38. See list of shipments by James Donaldson to Hardy, Case 1214, 963–65.

39. Depositions of Thomas Baltzell and John M. W. Davison, *Case*, 128–29. See additional remarks by Baltzell in Case 1214, 415–27.

40. Deposition of Ann Hawks, Case 1203, 541; Hardy to Bryan, June 20, 1833, Croom Letters.

41. Hardy to Bryan, October 5, 1837, Croom Letters.

42. *New York Herald*, October 20, 1837; Heyl, *Early American Steamers*, 211.

43. *New York Herald*, October 19, 1837. The journal's morning and evening editions borrowed freely from each other, and the newspaper is referred to here simply as the *Herald*.

44. Ibid.

45. Quoted in *Tallahassee Floridian*, October 21, 1837; Heyl, *Early American Steamers*, 211.

46. Deposition of Francis Hawks, 80–86; John Torrey, 87–89; Alexander McConochie, 703; Susan Winthrop, 406–7, all in Case 1214.

47. *Charleston Courier*, October 20, 1837; deposition of B. B. Hussey, Case 1214A, 385–86, 589–90.

48. Deposition of Henry Vanderzee, 1046–53; deposition of Mathilda Schroeder, 1065–73, both in Case 1214.

49. *New York Herald*, October 19–20, 1837.

50. *Charleston Mercury*, October 13, 1837. For more concern, see *Charleston Courier*, October 14, 1837. See *New York Herald*, October 19, 1837, for disarm-

ing statements that other packets also at sea would report any problems the *Home* was encountering.

51. See letter of Captain White published in *New York Herald,* October 18, 1837; see also *Charleston Mercury,* October 19, 1837; *Charleston Courier,* October 19, 1837. Numerous contemporary accounts, as well as depositions and trial testimony later, provided vivid descriptions. Captain Hill engaged in a letter-writing controversy with David B. Milne, the steward, who accused him of interfering with Captain White's authority. See *Charleston Mercury,* November 2, 1837. Good general secondary studies are Snow, *Secrets of the North Atlantic Islands,* 22–30, and Ballance, *Ocracokers,* 30–35; see also Redfearn, "Common Disaster," 83.

52. Some accounts claimed that three life preservers were on board, but most concluded there was only one. All survivors and observers agreed that there were too few lifeboats.

53. Depositions of B. B. Hussey, Mathilda Schroeder, John Bishop, Conrad Quinn, and Henry Vanderzee, *Case,* 78–88; 89; 89–90; 94–95; 91; 92.

54. *Charleston Mercury,* October 17, 1837.

55. Quoted in *Mobile (Ala.) Daily Commercial Register and Patriot,* October 27, 1837.

56. *Charleston Courier,* October 19, 1837.

57. Ibid., October 30, 1837; Redfearn, "*Steamboat Home,*" 417. Conrad Quinn, a young passenger, was one of those who found William Henry's body. He recounted that the body was located on Portsmouth shore. See deposition, March 19, 1840, Case 1214, 48–59.

58. *New Bern Spectator,* October 20, 1837.

59. See ibid., October 27, November 24, December 1, 1837.

60. *Wilmington Advertiser,* October 20, 1837; *Mobile Daily Commercial Register and Patriot,* October 20, 1837; *New York Herald,* October 19, 1837.

61. *Charleston Courier,* October 19–20, 1837.

62. Quoted in *Charleston Mercury,* October 19, 1837.

63. *Tallahassee Floridian,* November 1, 1837; see also October 25, 1837; *New Orleans Picayune,* October 23, 1837.

64. *Charleston Courier,* October 20, 1837. A few stories claimed that dead bodies were robbed, trunks broken into and looted, and some survivors rudely treated and refused aid by certain residents of Ocracoke Island. The allegations were not widely circulated, and their truth was never established. See *Mobile Daily Commercial Register and Patriot,* November 3, 1837, quoting *Baltimore (Md.) Chronicle;* and Snow, *Secrets of the North Atlantic Islands,* 30. The *New Bern Spectator,* November 3, 1837, denounced the *New York Journal of Com-*

merce for printing the rumors. Based on its own interviews, the *Spectator* claimed that looting was at a minimum and was done exclusively by members of the *Home*'s crew. See *New Bern Spectator,* December 1, 1837, quoting *New York Express* for letter of John Pike of Ocracoke describing how the residents tended to the survivors and took care of the dead. And see *New Bern Spectator,* January 5, 1838, for more on the controversy.

65. *Charleston Courier,* October 20, 1837. See October 18, 1837, for similar letter by "Traveller." For a good description of structural deficiencies, see "A Subscriber," writing to *New York Herald,* October 19, 1837. See also *Charleston Courier,* October 21, 1837; Dunn and Miller, *Atlantic Hurricanes,* 311.

66. *Charleston Courier,* October 23, 1837; *Charleston Mercury,* October 23, 1837.

67. Deposition of Ann Hawks, Case 1214, 91.

68. *Charleston Courier,* October 30, 1837; see also "A Subscriber," in *New York Herald,* October 19, 1837.

69. *New Bern Spectator,* October 20, 1837.

70. Quoted in ibid., December 1, 1837.

71. *Tallahassee Floridian,* November 18, 1837, quoting *New York Commercial.*

72. Quoted in *Tallahassee Floridian,* November 11, 1837.

73. Quoted in *Charleston Mercury,* October 25, 1837.

74. White's "Protest" was quoted in *New Bern Spectator,* December 1, 1837. See also *Narrative of the Loss of the Steam-Packet Home.*

75. Heyl, *Early American Steamers,* 211.

76. *Pensacola Gazette,* October 21, 1837.

77. *United States Statutes at Large,* 5:304. The act passed July 7, 1838, and among other things required all steamboats to take out new licenses, have regular inspections by experts appointed by district judges, and have an adequate number of lifeboats and signal lights. Misconduct by a ship's captain or other officers that resulted in the death of any passengers carried with it a manslaughter charge and upon conviction ten years in prison. See ibid., 626–27, for an even stronger and more detailed safety act passed March 3, 1843.

78. *New Bern Spectator,* November 3, 1837.

4. *"The Issue Joined" and the Croom Network*

1. Deposition of Ann Hawks, Case 1203, 51.

2. Bryan to Hardy, September 18, 1837, Croom Letters.

3. James Donaldson to Bryan, October 26, 1837, Croom Letters.

4. Case 237, 1, on file at the Leon County Courthouse. The case is 107 manuscript pages in length, and a copy is filed at the Goodwood Archives.

5. Case 1214A, 282–84.

6. Case 237, 38–40.

7. Case 1214A, 468–69.

8. See inventory filed September 3, 1852, in ibid., 424–31.

9. Case 1214, 162; Bryan's meticulous expense account for his North Carolina trip totaled $189.45. See ibid., 562–63.

10. Ibid., 889–94.

11. John B. Carroll to Bryan Croom, June 5, 1838, Case 1214A, 511–12.

12. Case 1214A, 521–26.

13. Ibid., 671.

14. Ibid., 568–76.

15. LCDB I, 412. For the 1847 settlement, see ibid., I, 245.

16. William Croom, will.

17. Hardy to Frances, [December 1829?], Croom Letters.

18. Outlaw, "Croom Family," 269; Broughton, *Marriage and Death Notices,* 52, 117; Battle, *University of North Carolina* 1:790–91. For a description of Betsy's wedding, see Hardy to Bryan, July 28, 1834, Croom Letters.

19. Hardy to Frances, November 26, 18[?], Croom Letters.

20. See unpaginated Jackson County Land Grants Book A.

21. See Jackson County Deed Book A, 63, 198, 199, 200, 310, 426, 427; B, 128 (hereafter cited as JCDB with appropriate book and pages).

22. Hardy to Frances, December 6, 1836, Croom Letters.

23. Caroline Lee Whiting to Dr. Thaddeus William Hentz, no day, no month, 1855, Hentz Family Papers.

24. Shofner, *Jackson County,* 51, 74, 102; Stanley, *History of Jackson County,* 90.

25. Edward C. Bellamy to Hardy, March 25, 1836, Croom Letters.

26. Hardy to Samuel C. Bellamy, June 27, 1837, Croom Letters. Hardy offered to help secure an artist in New York City to make copies of a portrait of Betsy.

27. Jackson County Land Grants Book A; for Bellamy as grantor, see JCDB A, 26; B, 149, 153, 291, 292, 442, 601.

28. Whitfield and Whitfield, *Whitfield, Bryan, Smith, and Related Families,* 1:143; Battle, *University of North Carolina,* 1:503–8.

29. Shofner, *Jackson County,* 179; Stanley, *History of Jackson County,* 77; see *Journal of the Second Annual Convention of the Protestant Episcopal Church,* 4.

30. Paisley, *Red Hills,* 122; Stanley, *History of Jackson County,* 144–45.

31. Hentz, *Marcus Warland*, 7, 58.

32. Case 1214A, 142–52.

33. Battle, *University of North Carolina*, 1:315, 792.

34. Broughton, *Marriage and Death Notices*, 56.

35. General Bryan Whitfield was a militia captain in the Revolutionary War, member of the North Carolina House of Commons, 1783, and a trustee of the University of North Carolina, 1805–8. See Whitfield and Whitfield, *Whitfield, Bryan, Smith, and Related Families*, 1:72; Battle, *University of North Carolina*, 1:822.

36. William Croom, will.

37. The grantee was Jesse Kennedy. See deed in Parrott Collection.

38. Historical notes in the private possession of Elizabeth Bell Stegall of Livingston, Alabama.

39. Baldwin, *Flush Times*, 84. See also 82, 88–89.

40. Sumter County Tract Book, 188. The authors thank Judson Arrington of York, Alabama, who provided them with geographical information and a list of the Crooms interred in the family burying ground located five miles east of Gaston.

41. For his purchases, see Sumter County Deed Book C, 160; D, 193; E, 533; F, 242; M, 494, 695; O, 608 (hereafter cited as SCDB with appropriate book and pages).

42. Ibid., G, 252–53.

43. Ibid., B, 166; C, 44; D, 319; E, 105; I, 480; L, 247–48, 782; M, 526; N, 596.

44. Whitfield and Whitfield, *Whitfield, Bryan, Smith, and Related Families*, 1:72.

45. LCDB H, 206, 208.

46. William W. Croom to Stephens Croom, December 30, 1857. This letter is part of an important collection of Croom family material in the private possession of Velma Lassiter Croom, the William W. Croom Papers (hereafter cited as W. W. Croom Papers).

47. William Croom, will. For the letter, see William W. Croom to Stephens Croom, February 22, 1857, W. W. Croom Papers.

48. See Hardy to Bryan, September 2, 1833; July 30, 1834, Croom Letters. One sibling, Samuel Barron Stephens, was an attorney, leading mason, legislator, and colonel in the Confederate army. See Stanley, *Gadsden County*, 138, 40, 48–49, 85, 100, 126, and Womack, *Gadsden*, 29–30, 52, 56, 65, 72, 78.

49. William W. Croom to Stephens Croom, December 30, 1857, W. W. Croom Papers.

50. Unpublished Florida census of 1840, Population, Gadsden County, 106. He bought Lots 143, 144, and 146, as well as portions of 139, 140, and 141 from John W. Malone.

51. The price was $1,000 and was paid to Arthur I. Forman and Hudson Muse. See GCDB A, 59. Croom paid $1,127.68 to Baker. See ibid., 183.

52. Ibid., 114–15.

53. Unpublished Florida census of 1850, Slaves, 181; Population, 177, Gadsden County.

54. See Hadley, Horton, and Strowd, *Chatham County,* 262–66. There were other schools in Pittsboro, but Pittsboro Academy was undoubtedly the institution that George Alexander attended.

55. William Croom, will.

56. Hull, *Historical Sketch,* contains unpaginated "Catalogue of the Trustees, Officers and Alumni of the University of Georgia from 1785 to 1894." Croom was among thirty-six in school in 1841 who did not graduate.

57. See Dyer, *University of Georgia,* 32–37; see also Mitchell, "Memoir." See also Boney, *Pictorial History,* 16–40.

58. Clarke County Marriage Records, Book C, 61; *Athens (Ga.) Southern Banner,* February 24, 1843. For Bowman, see Scott, *Ministerial Directory.*

59. GCDB A, 97.

60. Ibid.

61. Joseph M. White to Bryan, September 28, 183[8], Case 1214A, 531–34.

62. In ibid., 761–75, there is a partial but lengthy reply to the bill of complaint by all the Crooms. The moderate, well-reasoned document ends abruptly with the Crooms about to depart from New York on the *Home.* The answer bears no date.

63. Ibid., 595–605.

64. Ibid., 606–32.

65. Ibid., 142–52. For Croom's self-analysis, see Richard Croom to Mary Croom, March 20, 1857, in Richard Croom, Family Papers.

5. *"Too Feeble to Concede the Artifice"*

1. LCDB F, 265–69.

2. Case 1214A, 668–97.

3. Case 237.

4. Ibid.

5. Case 1214A, 250–52.

6. Deposition of George Whitfield, 102–7; deposition of Benjamin Hawks, 135–38, 152–56, both in Case 1214. For a brief account of Hawks's death, see *Tallahassee Floridian,* December 12, 1840.

7. Deposition of Thomas S. Singleton, Case 1214A, 557–58.

8. For the depositions of Lamotte, Wilson, Primrose, Harvey, Eustis, and Sente, see Case 1214A, 549–50, 550–52, 553–55, 555–56, 558–62, 562–67.

9. For the depositions of Miller, Gaskins, S. Miller, Thompson, and Berry, see Case 1214, 1030–32; Case 1214A, 161–67; Case 1214, 1027–29; Case 1214A, 157–60.

10. Deposition of Dr. Hugh McLean, Case 1214, 42–47.

11. Deposition of Dr. Francis Hawks, Case 1214, 80–86.

12. Deposition of Dr. John Torrey, Case 1214, 87–89.

13. Deposition of Conrad Quinn, Case 1214, 48–49.

14. Deposition of John Bishop, Case 1214, 60–78; John B. Carroll to John Bishop, March 3, 1840, Case 1214, 78–79.

15. Deposition of Andrew A. Lovegreen, Case 1214, 1054–58; Case 1214A, 398–404. Lovegreen was deposed twice.

16. Deposition of Benjamin B. Hussey, Case 1214, 1059–64; Case 1214A, 373–386, 589–90. Like Lovegreen, Hussey and several other passengers were deposed more than once.

17. Deposition of Mathilda Schroeder, Case 1214A, 387–97, 591–94; Case 1214, 1065–73.

18. Unpublished Florida census of 1840, Population, Leon County, 77. For Bryan's activities, see Carter, Territory of Florida, 1839–45, in *Territorial Papers of the United States,* 26:205–6, 254.

19. LCDB H, 252.

20. Ibid., 254.

6. Brick and Mortar and "Very Likely Slaves"

1. Much of the information for the Goodwood complex, including the description of the mansion, is taken from Shepard, "Goodwood Historic Structures Report." The project involved a number of professors and graduate students in various fields and was under the direction of Professor Herschel E. Shepard, F.A.I.A., College of Architecture, University of Florida.

2. See Paisley, *Red Hills,* 150–59; Groene, *Ante-Bellum Tallahassee,* 50, 124, 133; and Groene, "Lizzie Brown's Tallahassee," 157; Rhodes, "Mission Bells," 74.

3. Phelps, *People of Lawmaking,* 87; unpublished Florida census of 1860, Population, Leon County, 9; unpublished Florida census of 1860, Slaves, Leon County, 247. For Shine's efforts in behalf of public education, see *Tallahassee Floridian and Journal,* December 29, 1849. Shine died December 28, 1862; his wife died in March 1874. See also Rosalie Rodriguez, "Richard A. Shine, 1810–1862, Tallahassee's Premier Ante-bellum Builder," unpublished article, 1995, in Goodwood Archives.

4. Deposition of R. A. Shine, July 31, 1857, Case 1203, 139–41.

5. Shepard, "Goodwood Historic Structures Report."

6. LCDB I:180, 182.

7. Ibid., K, 163–64. The agreement was transferred in the spring of 1850 to Robert W. Williams, and Bryan received the title.

8. Deposition of George T. Ward, Case 1214A, 482. Ward's statements were made in 1857, and he was speaking about the earlier sections bought by Hardy and Bryan.

9. Deposition of Richard Saunders, Case 1214A, 168–70.

10. Case 1214, 563.

11. LCDB 1:147.

12. Case 1214, 797–800, 1015–20.

13. Deposition of Hinton J. Saunders, Case 1214, 214–15.

14. Olmsted, *Cotton Kingdom,* 193. For a good study of the workings of ante-bellum plantations, see Scarborough, *The Overseer.* For drivers, see 16–18, and esp. chap. 4, "Managerial Duties and Responsibilities."

15. Deposition of Richard Saunders, Case 1214A, 168–70.

16. Olmsted, *Cotton Kingdom,* 194, 106.

17. Deposition of Richard Saunders, Case 1214A, 168–70.

18. Case 1214, 594.

19. Ibid., 547.

20. Deposition of Hinton J. Saunders, Case 1214, 206–15. It should be noted that Job. T. Ackins swore in 1857 that he had been an overseer for a "Mr. Croom." He may have been W. I. Akins, who was an overseer at Goodwood in the late 1850s. He described Croom slaves as having some of the same names remembered by Saunders, including Fortune. The ages Ackins provided were not consistent with those of Saunders. Ackins also mentioned a number of slaves not named by Saunders. See ibid., 192–95.

21. Unpublished Florida census of 1850, Slaves, Leon County, 87–89. For an overview, see Williams, "Negro Slavery in Florida."

22. Unpublished Florida census of 1850, Agriculture, Leon County, 171.

23. Ibid.

24. Ibid. For Saunders's remarks, see Case 1214, 206–14. Scholars differ about the degree of self-sufficiency southern plantations achieved. Schmidt, "Internal Commerce," argues that planters were heavily dependent on imported food. Gallman, "Self-Sufficiency in the Cotton Economy," 5–24, takes the opposite viewpoint.

25. Unpublished Florida census of 1850, Agriculture, Leon County, 171; *Seventh United States Census,* 1850, 408. For the quotes on the cotton crop, see *Tallahassee Floridian and Journal,* August 11, 1849. See also the journal's issues of August 4, November 3, 17, 1849; August 3, 5, 1850.

26. *Seventh United States Census,* 1850, 400–401, 407–8. In 1850 Leon County had 3,183 whites, 56 free persons of color, and 8,203 slaves, for a total population of 11,442.

7. Some Crooms, the Bellamys, and Their Ventures

1. Julia Croom to Stephens Croom, December 10, 1853, W. W. Croom Papers. A few days later Julia asked her son to give her love to "Aunt Julia & Aunt Eveline & Mrs. Hawks." Ibid., December 18, 1853.

2. Ibid., December 18, 1853.

3. Stephens Croom to Julia Croom, December 29, 1853, W. W. Croom Papers.

4. JCDB A, 63.

5. Shofner, *Jackson County,* 188.

6. Jackson County Estate Books.

7. Estate of Samuel C. Bellamy, Jackson County Estate Books.

8. See advertisement in *Tallahassee Florida Sentinel,* December 2, 1851.

9. Quoted in *Tallahassee Floridian and Journal,* January 21, 1854; Paisley, *Red Hills,* 122.

10. Estate of Samuel C. Bellamy, Jackson County Courthouse; Shofner, *Jackson County,* 188; Paisley, *Red Hills,* 122.

11. JCDB A, 94–95.

12. Shofner, *Jackson County,* 118.

13. For an early study, see Martin, *Columbus, Geo.,* and Lupold, *Columbus, Georgia;* for Apalachicola, see Willoughby, *Fair to Middlin',* and Owens, "Apalachicola before 1861."

14. Muscogee County Deed Book F, 19, 20 (hereafter cited as MCDB with appropriate book, volume, and pages).

15. See Whitfield and Whitfield, *Whitfield, Bryan, Smith, and Related Families*, 1:143; Muscogee County Marriage Record E, 160.

16. For an anticipated visit in 1856 by Bryan and Eveline to Hopoi, see Julia Croom to Stephens Croom, August 6, 1856, W. W. Croom Papers. For a similar visit in 1857, see Harold Bellamy to Stephens Croom, September 22, 1857, W. W. Croom Papers.

17. Julia Croom to Stephens Croom, October 12, 1856, W. W. Croom Papers; see also Battle, *University of North Carolina*, 1:803. For the sale, see Bolivar County Deed Book F, 226 (hereafter cited as BCDB with appropriate book, and pages). Many Bolivar County records are available on microfilm at the Mississippi State Archives, Jackson.

18. Julia Croom to Stephens Croom, June 5, 1857; William Croom to Stephens Croom, June 27, 1857, W. W. Croom Papers.

19. BCDB G, 154–55.

20. Ibid., F, 229–31.

21. Kamper, "Social and Economic History." The authors benefited from an interview with Professor John Hebron Moore of Florida State University, a leading authority on agriculture in antebellum Mississippi, on July 17, 1993. See also William Croom to Stephens Croom, September 3, 1857, W. W. Croom Papers. Bellamy's land purchases in Tennessee have not been located or confirmed, but see Julia Croom to Stephens Croom, November [?], 1857, W. W. Croom Papers.

22. Cobb, *Most Southern Place On Earth*, 7, 8, 30; Gonzales, "Flush Times," 284; William Croom to Stephens Croom, September 3, 1857, W. W. Croom Papers.

23. MCDB I, 1:273–74; William Croom to Stephens Croom, September 3, 1857, W. W. Croom Papers.

24. Croom Bellamy to Stephens Croom, November 8, 1857, W. W. Croom Papers. See also BCDB F, 227–28.

25. GCDB A, 159.

26. Ibid., 48, 208, 283, 476, 544.

27. Ibid., 105, 208–9.

28. See files of the County Judge's Court, Estate of George A. Croom, Gadsden County Courthouse.

29. Ibid. The release from guardianship came May 26, 1856.

30. GCDB A, 543, 544, 547.

31. Ibid., 550.

32. William Croom to Stephens Croom, September 27, 1857, W. W. Croom Papers.

33. Ibid., September 27, 1857.

34. Ibid., April 14, 1857.

35. "Autobiography of Stephens Croom," 6–7. This 88-page manuscript was begun in 1875; it continued until 1876 but was never finished.

36. Ibid., 7–9.

37. Ibid., 8–10; see also Julia Croom to Stephens Croom, October 9, 1856, W. W. Croom Papers.

38. "Autobiography of Stephens Croom," 8.

39. William Croom to Stephens Croom, September 3, 1857, W. W. Croom Papers.

40. BCDB G, 590–91. In a separate deal Croom paid $898.80 for a federal patent to 149.80 acres. See ibid., 319–20.

41. William Croom to Stephens Croom, August 5, 1857; see also ibid., September 3, 1857; Elizabeth Croom to Stephens Croom, July 31, 1857; Julia Croom to Stephens Croom, August 6, 1857; Harold Bellamy to Stephens Croom, August 11, 1857, W. W. Croom Papers.

42. BCDB G, 339–40. In 1857 they paid $250 for Lot 5, Block 10, and exchanged it the next year for a bay horse. See ibid., 340–41.

43. Harold Bellamy to Stephens Croom, August 11, 1857, W. W. Croom Papers.

44. Julia Croom to Stephens Croom, August 16, 1857, W. W. Croom Papers.

45. Elizabeth Croom to Stephens Croom, September 5, 1857, W. W. Croom Papers.

46. Julia Croom to Stephens Croom, November 2, 1857, W. W. Croom Papers.

47. Ibid., September or October [?], 1857; William Croom to Stephens Croom, September 3, 1857, W. W. Croom Papers.

48. Julia Croom to Stephens Croom, February 2, 1858, W. W. Croom Papers.

49. William Croom to Stephens Croom, September 27, 1857, W. W. Croom Papers.

50. Ibid., October 30, 1857.

51. Julia Croom to Stephens Croom, November [?], 1857, W. W. Croom Papers.

52. See William Croom to Stephens Croom, November 2, 1857, and November 10, 1857; see also Julia Croom to Stephens Croom, February 2, 1858, W. W. Croom Papers.

53. Elizabeth Croom to Stephens Croom, September 30, 1857, W. W. Croom Papers.

54. Edward Bellamy to Stephens Croom, November 3, 1857, W. W. Croom Papers.

55. Julia Croom to Stephens Croom, November 15, 1857, W. W. Croom Papers.

56. Ibid., November 17 [?], 1857.

57. Julia Croom to Stephens Croom, December 13, 1857; Elizabeth Croom to Stephens Croom, December 20, 1857, W. W. Croom Papers.

58. Julia Croom to Stephens Croom, January 9, 1858, W. W. Croom Papers.

59. William Croom to Stephens Croom, January 13, 1858, W. W. Croom Papers.

60. Ibid., December 3, 1857.

61. Harold Bellamy to Stephens Croom, December 21, 1857, W. W. Croom Papers.

62. William Croom to Stephens Croom, January 17, 1858, W. W. Croom Papers.

63. Elizabeth Croom to Stephens Croom, February 26, 1858, W. W. Croom Papers. An examination by the authors of the deed record books at the Chicot County Courthouse, Lake Village, Arkansas, did not reveal any land purchases by George Alexander Croom.

64. Julia Croom to Stephens Croom, March 9, 1858, W. W. Croom Papers.

65. N. B. Whitfield Jr. to Stephens Croom, March 19, 1858, W. W. Croom Papers.

66. Julia Croom and Elizabeth Croom to Stephens Croom, April 4, 1858, W. W. Croom Papers. See Cashin, *Family Venture*, 120–21.

67. Julia Croom to Stephens Croom, April 25, May 9, 17, 1858; Edward Bellamy to Stephens Croom, May 10, 1858; William Croom to Stephens Croom, May 12, 1858, W. W. Croom Papers.

68. Julia Croom to Stephens Croom, August 5, 1858. See also Elizabeth Croom Bellamy to Stephens Croom, July 18, 1858; William Croom to Stephens Croom, August 10, 1858; Harold Bellamy to Stephens Croom, August 2, 1858, W. W. Croom Papers.

69. Julia Croom to Stephens Croom, July 25, 1858, W. W. Croom Papers.

70. See *New Orleans Daily Picayune,* June 20, 1858, quoting *Memphis Avalanche.* For other reports of bad weather and flooding see, *New Orleans Daily Picayune,* April 30; May 2, 4, 10, 15, 22; June 12, 17, 1858.

71. *Memphis Daily Appeal,* July 7, 1858. See also issues of July 8–9, 20, 1858, and *New Orleans Daily Picayune,* July 15, 1858, quoting *Memphis Eagle and Enquirer.*

72. "Jennie" in *Memphis Daily Appeal,* July 18, 1858.

73. William Croom to Stephens Croom, July 28, 1858, W. W. Croom Papers.

74. Julia Croom to Stephens Croom, August 5, 1858; Elizabeth Croom Bellamy to Stephens Croom, August 26, September 17, 1858, W. W. Croom Papers.

75. Edward Bellamy to Stephens Croom, October 5, 1858, W. W. Croom Papers.

76. Julia Croom to Stephens Croom, September 25, 1858, W. W. Croom Papers.

77. William Croom to Stephens Croom, September 4, 1858, W. W. Croom Papers.

78. Julia Croom to Stephens Croom, October 20, December 17, 26, 1858, W. W. Croom Papers.

79. BCDB H, 1, 381.

80. Ibid., 20–22, 575.

81. Unpublished Mississippi census of 1860, Bolivar County, 511–12.

8. The Inner Circle

1. GCDB A, 116–17.

2. Unpublished Florida census of 1850, Slave, Gadsden County, 236–37; ibid., Agriculture, 79.

3. Whitfield and Whitfield, *Whitfield, Bryan, Smith, and Related Families,* 1:143.

4. LCDB K, 189. The acreage was bounded north and east by Lake Jackson and south and west by the lands of Robert Butler and others. See also Paisley, *Red Hills,* 132–33. The authors are grateful to Ms. Martha Brown Whitner of Jacksonville, Florida, who provided them with biographical information about the Whitners and an unsigned contemporary description of Casa de Lago and activities there.

5. GCDB A, 143.

6. In 1854, Whitner and his son were chosen to survey the disputed boundary line between Florida and Georgia. Representatives from Georgia were also appointed. Although the survey was made, its results were not accepted. Young Whitner participated in an 1859 survey that was later adopted by both states. See Rogers, *Foshalee,* 36–37.

7. Register of Communicants, First Presbyterian Church, 1832–34, Tallahassee, 26; Whitfield and Whitfield, *Whitfield, Bryan, Smith, and Related Families,* 1:143; W. W. Croom to Stephens Croom, January 24, 1857, W. W. Croom Papers.

8. For the trip to Mississippi and Arkansas, see N. B. Whitfield Jr. to Ste-

phens Croom, March 19, 1858, W. W. Croom Papers. See LCDB K, 188–89. In 1856, Croom bought another house and a five-acre parcel in Bel Air for $1,000. See LCDB L, 699. For the painter "in residence," see Stephens Croom to Julia Croom, December 29, 1853, W. W. Croom Papers.

9. Unpublished Florida census of 1860, Slave, Leon County, 26; ibid., Agriculture, 4–5. See also Paisley, *Red Hills*, 133; *Tallahassee Floridian*, October 10, 1857.

10. Unpublished Alabama census of 1850, Agriculture, Sumter County, 717–18; ibid., Slave, 313–15. In 1855, Richard had reduced his slave force to eighty-eight. See Population Index to the 1855 Sumter County Census, Alabama Department of Archives and History, Montgomery (hereafter cited as ADAH).

11. Leon County Marriage Records, Book 10:158. See also Cushman, *Goodly Heritage*, 27–28; Stauffer, *God Willing*, 73–90; Tallahassee *Floridian and Journal*, April 26, 1851; Parochial Records Of St. John's Episcopal Church, Tallahassee, Florida, 1832–80, 49 (hereafter cited as St. John's Parochial Records).

12. Unpublished Florida census of 1850, Slave, Leon County, 55; ibid., Agriculture, 169–70.

13. LCDB K, 178. The Union Bank held the mortgages of John G. Gamble. John G. and his brother Robert Gamble came to Leon County from Virginia. John owned Waukeenah plantation in Jefferson County, while Robert owned Welaunee there. John was the largest stockholder in the Union Bank. He later moved to Neamathla plantation in Leon County near Tallahassee. Both brothers were strong Whigs in their politics.

14. LCDB K, 206–7.

15. Ibid., 308–9.

16. Ibid., 294–95.

17. Ibid., L, 95. The partial acreage was in the southeastern quarter of Section 19 and the northeastern quarter of Section 30.

18. Ibid., 137.

19. Ibid., 35.

20. In 1852, he paid $1,624 for 55 acres and in 1857 $3,200 for 320 acres. See SCDB O, 241, 186.

21. Ibid., 224–26.

22. Ibid., B, 609.

23. Unpublished Alabama census of 1860, Population, Sumter County, 467.

24. SCDB Q, 45.

25. St. John's Parochial Records, 18.

26. SCDB P, 511–12; Sumter County Marriage Records, 2:461.

27. Historical notes of Ms. Joy Paisley of Tallahassee.

28. Alabama Confederate Service Records, 1861, Service Card.

29. Stegall historical notes.

30. St. John's Parochial Records, 17.

31. LCDB L, 137.

32. St. John's Parochial Records, 19; *Tallahassee Floridian and Journal,* November 1, 1856.

33. Sumter County Marriage Records, 2:389; Whitfield and Whitfield, *Whitfield, Bryan, Smith, and Related Families,* 1:102–3; Julia Croom to Stephens Croom, September 25, 1858, W. W. Croom Papers.

34. Stegall historical notes.

35. LCDB M, 373.

36. Unpublished Alabama census of 1860, Population, Sumter County, 467.

37. Sumter County Marriage Records, 2:389.

38. LCDB M, 370–71. Richard Whitfield cosigned with Mary.

39. St. John's Parochial Records, 39; Whitfield and Whitfield, *Whitfield, Bryan, Smith, and Related Families,* 1:148.

40. See St. John's Parochial Records, 51, 30, 44, 52. Richard married Ella Talbot in 1872. She died the next year, and in 1875 he married her sister, Anna Marie Talbot.

41. LCDB K, 147–48.

42. Ibid., 206–7.

43. Ibid., 308–9.

44. Ibid., 269–70.

45. Ibid., 462–63. Whitfield had sold part of Section 19 to former territorial governor John Branch.

46. LCDB L, 79.

47. Ibid., 137.

48. Ibid.

49. *Tallahassee Floridian and Journal,* July 21, 1855.

50. LCDB L, 433; 425–26; 419–20. Floyd, *Barrow Family,* 28–33.

9. "A Most Unrighteous Judgment"

1. Winthrop family genealogical records; see copy on file at Goodwood plantation archives (hereafter cited as Winthrop Papers). These records and other family materials were donated by Mrs. Guy Winthrop-King of Tallahassee.

2. Ibid. See also Marsh, "Winthrop Family."

3. See Florida State Constitution, 1838, Article 5 and amendments.

4. James T. Archer file. The file contains contemporary newspaper clippings and eulogies written following his unexpected death in 1859.

5. See obituary notices in *Tallahassee Sentinel,* July 10, 1875. For Papy's admission to the bar, see *LC* 1844, 1–2.

6. See Davis, "General William G. M. Davis"; for Papy, see unpublished Florida census of 1860, Population, Leon County, 4.

7. *Tallahassee Floridian and Journal,* July 2, 1859. See Margaret Chapman's introduction to Long, *Florida Breezes,* 10. See *Florida Acts* 1850, 28, for Long's higher-education statute. His wife was a wealthy woman in 1860 and had two children, but she ran a single-parent household. See unpublished Florida census of 1860, Population, Leon County, 52.

8. Deposition of John M. W. Davidson, Case 1214, 388–91.

9. See deposition of Ann Hawks, August 25, 1855, Case 1214, 33–39, 90–101. For her deposition of December 13, 1852, see Case 1203, 49–59.

10. Deposition of William L. Blackledge, Case 1214, 251–54.

11. For Singleton, see Case 1214A, 353. For Singleton, Manly, and Primrose, see Case 1214, 295–99.

12. Deposition of Zachary Slade, Case 1214A, 499–509; deposition of Amos Wade, Case 1214, 361–66.

13. Deposition of W. C. G. White, Case 1214A, 320–25; Deposition of Jane Prentiss, ibid., 326–34.

14. Deposition of Susan Winthrop, Case 1214, 405–11.

15. Deposition of Henry Vanderzee, Case 1214, 262–67, 288–94.

16. Case 1203, 46. Vanderzee was deposed between April 27 and May 1, 1855.

17. Deposition of Mathilda Schroder, Case 1214, 2–23. New witness, Captain John D. Roland of Columbus, Georgia, deposed in 1853 supporting the conduct of Captain Charles White on the *Home,* but he said nothing that supported or harmed the Crooms' defense.

18. *Tallahassee Floridian and Journal,* October 11, 1856.

19. Ibid., February 28, 1857.

20. Ibid., April 11, 18, 1857.

21. Terrell, "William Law."

22. James L. Petigru to William Law, December 22, 1856, James L. Petigru Papers (hereafter cited as Petigru Papers).

23. *Jacksonville Florida Times-Union*, November 7–8, 1904; October 10, 1906.

24. *Tallahassee Floridian and Journal*, April 16, 1859.

25. For a sketch of DuPont, see Memoriam in *Florida Reports*, 1876–78, 16:5–12. For a good discussion of the court in this period, see Manley, Brown, and Wise, *Supreme Court of Florida*, 154–83.

26. *Tallahassee Floridian and Journal*, April 16, 1859.

27. James L. Petigru to Susan Petigru King, March 5, 1857, quoted in Carson, *Life, Letters, and Speeches*, 322.

28. Richard Croom to Mary Croom, March 20, 1857, letter in private possession of William and Susan Cowles.

29. James L. Petigru to Susan Petigru King, March 5, 1857, quoted in Carson, *Life, Letters, and Speeches*, 321.

30. *Case*, 146.

31. Ibid., 148.

32. Ibid.

33. Ibid., 149.

34. Ibid., 160.

35. Ibid., 161.

36. Ibid., 166–67.

37. *LC* 1829, 80–81.

38. *Case*, 169.

39. Ibid., 178–79.

40. Julia Croom to Stephens Croom, March 29, 1857, W. W. Croom Papers.

41. James L. Petigru to W. G. M. Davis, April 2, 1857, Petigru Papers.

42. James L. Petigru to Adele Allston, April 4, 1857, R. F. W. Allston Papers.

43. Carson, *Life, Letters, and Speeches*, 322. See also Pease and Pease, *James Louis Petigru*, 121.

44. James L. Petigru to W. G. M. Davis, April 2, 1857, Petigru Papers.

45. *Tallahassee Floridian and Journal*, April 4, 1857.

46. *Case*, 182. See also 180–81.

47. Ibid., 183.

48. Ibid., 186–87.

49. Ibid., 189, 192–93.

50. Ibid., 194–95.

51. Ibid., 196.

52. Ibid., 197.

53. Ibid.

54. Ibid., 199.

55. *Tallahassee Floridian and Journal,* April 11, 1857.

10. *"Great Sacrifice" Attended the Loss*

1. Case 1214, 797–800.

2. Ibid., 1015–20.

3. Report of master in chancery in Case 1203, 99–111. See ibid., 156–59, for Bryan's bonding. Rutgers's report contained additional information on other aspects of the estate.

4. Julia Croom to Stephens Croom, September or October [?], 1857, W. W. Croom Papers.

5. James T. Archer to Bryan Croom, December 26, 1857, Winthrop Papers, folder 1.

6. See deposition of Mariano D. Papy, June 15, 1872, Case 1203, 142–45.

7. LCDB L, 623–25.

8. Bryan Croom to John S. Winthrop, January 2, 1858; John S. Winthrop to Bryan Croom, January 4, 1858, Winthrop Papers, folder 1.

9. See bill of costs, September 28, 1859, Winthrop Papers, folder 3.

10. Craven County Deed Book L, 656 (hereafter cited as CCDB). For Davis, see receipt of payment by Davis, June 30, 1858, Winthrop Papers, folder 1.

11. For the payment to Davis in furniture, see Davis, "General William G. M. Davis," 37 n. 7. In 1862 Davis sold the Crooms' furniture to Marie Louise DeMilly of Tallahassee for $1,178. See bill of sale dated November 13, 1862, in Goodwood Archives. This document was kindly made available through Clifton Paisley and Mrs. R. A. "Angel" Brooks of Tallahassee. A close examination of Petigru's accounts and his other records has failed to reveal the amount he charged Croom, or when he was paid.

12. Winthrop Papers, folder 1.

13. Smallwood, Earle and Company to John S. Winthrop, January 25, 1858, Winthrop Papers, folder 2. See additional correspondence, ibid., March 23, 1860, for confirmation that Winthrop was residing in Tallahassee.

14. James T. Archer to Bryan Croom, March 30, 1858, Winthrop Papers, folder 2. Commenting on Archer's death, the *Tallahassee Floridian and Journal,* June 4, 1859, remarked, "We supposed him to have been by much the most popular man in the Middle District, not to say in the whole of Florida."

15. See account of payments received from Bryan Croom to June 30, 1859, Winthrop Papers, folder 3.

16. John S. Winthrop to William Law, April 4, 1858, Winthrop Papers, folder 3.

17. Ibid.

18. William Law to John S. Winthrop, April 8, 1858, Winthrop Papers, folder 3.

19. John S. Winthrop to William Law, April 14, 1854, Winthrop Papers, folder 3.

20. *Tallahassee Floridian and Journal,* February 19, 1859.

21. John S. Winthrop to William Law, April 4, 1858, Winthrop Papers, folder 3.

22. Montgomery County Deed Book 9, 718–19 (hereafter cited as MCDB with appropriate book and pages). See ibid., 624–25.

23. Ibid., 10, 523–24; 11, 736–37.

24. *Florida Acts,* 1859, 87–88.

25. LCDB L, 657–58; resources obtained from Hardy estate, Winthrop Papers, folder 3.

26. Clark, "Goodwood." For a thorough look at the Branch family in Leon County, see Baptist, "Migration of Planters."

27. For the description, see DeLeon, *Four Years In Rebel Capitals,* 23. See also Williams, "Early Ante-Bellum Montgomery" and "Conservatism in Old Montgomery"; McMillan, "Selection of Montgomery."

28. "Autobiography of Stephens Croom," 8–11; Owen, *History of Alabama,* 3:430; for Keyes, see Owen, *History of Alabama,* 3:974, and Daughters of the American Revolution, "Book of Records of Leon County," 5.

11. Civil War and the Attrition of Time

1. MCDB 11, 613; 13, 153–55.

2. Unpublished Alabama census of 1860, Population, Montgomery County, 305; ibid., Slave, 154; ibid., Agriculture, 3–4.

3. MCDB 13, 89; 14, 93.

4. *Newbern Weekly Progress,* May 15, 1860.

5. Unpublished North Carolina census of 1860, Population, Craven County, Carolina, 110.

6. Unpublished Florida census of 1869, Leon County, 356.

7. There is no monograph on Tallahassee and Leon County during the Civil War. The best state study is Johns, *Florida during the Civil War.*

8. Watson, *History of New Bern and Craven County,* esp. chap. 4, 369–468, which covers the Civil War. See also *Newbern Weekly Progress,* March 8, 13, 1862. The issue of March 8 was also concerned about the activities of "tories" intent on sabotage and betrayal: "the sooner a few traitors are hung or shot in such communities where they exist the better it will be for the cause of freedom in the south."

9. See Graetz, "Triumph amid Defeat," and Jones and Rogers, "Surrender of Tallahassee." For Susan's purchase from Meginnis, see LCDB N, 17.

10. St. John's Parochial Records, 41.

11. Ibid., 42; Marsh, "Winthrop Family," 8, quoting CCDB 67, 242.

12. LCDB N, 404–5.

13. Ibid., S, 129.

14. St. John's Parochial Records, 44; Marsh, "Winthrop Family," 10. See Susan and John Winthrop III, Planting Records. The authors thank U. Bowdoin Marsh, a genealogist and researcher on the Winthrops and other Leon County families, for taking them on May 17, 1995, to the Winthrop burying ground on Hickory Avenue.

15. Eppes, *Through Some Eventful Years,* 236. See 35 for Eppes's confusing Howell Cobb with his brother T. R. R. Cobb, who was killed at the Battle of Fredericksburg on December 13, 1862.

16. "Autobiography of Stephens Croom," 11–12.

17. See Fleming, *Civil War and Reconstruction,* and also Atkins, "At War with the Union."

18. Montgomery County Tax Book, Real Estate, 1861, n.p.; 1862, n.p.; 1864, n.p., ADAH.

19. Montgomery County Tax Book, Personal Estate, 1864, n.p., ADAH.

20. MCDB 14, 751.

21. See Military Service Record of Hardy Bryan Croom, Florida Department of Archives and History (hereafter cited as FDAH). See also Lucas, "Civil War Career."

22. Military Service Record of Alonzo Church Croom and of George Alexander Croom, FDAH; Graetz, "Triumph amid Defeat," 80. For Aleck's land transactions, see LCDB N, 114–15, 130–31, 149, 151.

23. LCDB N, 475; Whitfield and Whitfield, *Whitfield, Bryan, Smith, and Related Families,* 1 : 143; *Tallahassee Weekly Floridian,* July 30, 1890.

24. Branton and Wade, "Early Mississippi Records," 41. See also unpublished Mississippi census of 1860, Population, Bolivar County, 511–12.

25. Cobb, *Most Southern Place On Earth*, 29–46.

26. See Military Service Record of Hardy Croom Bellamy, Eugene Bellamy, and Harold Bellamy, Mississippi Department of Archives and History.

27. MCDB 14, 434, 506.

28. Quoted in Cobb, *Most Southern Place On Earth*, 42. How the conflict affected the Delta is largely taken from Cobb's chapter "The Stern Realities of War" in ibid., 29–46.

29. MCDB 15, 460–61, 461–62; Mississippi Delta Chapter, Daughters of the American Revolution, *History of Bolivar County*, 57.

30. BCDB L, 253; N, 219, 498. A search of deed records in the Sunflower County Courthouse at Indianola and of the adjoining Le Flore County Courthouse at Greenwood did not indicate that she purchased property there.

31. Ibid., O, 8, 31, 310, 405; R, 307–8. George continued to buy land but not in large amounts. See a purchase of 161 acres in ibid., M, 219.

32. Ibid., V: 242–43; X: 265–66.

33. Ibid., CC, 53–57.

34. Ibid., EE, 349.

35. Branton and Wade, "Early Mississippi Records," 3: 129.

36. BCDB H, 689–90.

37. "Autobiography of Stephens Croom," 35.

38. Greene County Deed Book 5: 901 (hereafter cited as GCDB with appropriate volume and pages).

39. Ibid., 902–3, 903, 903–4, 958.

40. "Autobiography of Stephens Croom," 35. See also MacInerney, "Elizabeth Whitfield Bellamy," esp. chaps. 5–8. This literary biography provides important information, including personal letters, on William Croom and his family.

41. "Autobiography of Stephens Croom," 12–25; GCDB V, 957.

42. "Autobiography of Stephens Croom," 33–34.

43. Ibid., 34–35.

44. Undated and unnamed newspaper clipping discovered at the Greene County Courthouse; Branton and Wade, "Early Mississippi Records," vol. 3, quoting BCDB R, 315.

45. GCDB 10: 255–56.

46. The school was probably Shorter College, which was private with strong

Baptist ties, but it could have been Rome Female College, a Presbyterian institution. See Gardner, *On The Hill,* 11–44. For Croom's death, see Jones and Gandrud, "Alabama Records," vol. 70, n.p., quoting *Livingston Journal,* June 2, 1876.

47. Confederate Service Records, 1861–65, ADAH. Croom's name appeared on muster rolls.

48. Orphans Minutes, Sumter County, 749. For examples of Augusta's business ability and real estate transactions, see SCDB R, 269–70, 270, 284, 357; S, 97; T, 285, 780, 780–81.

49. Ibid., Q, 45.

50. Sumter County Will Book 2, 1851–72, 339; Sumter County Probate Minutes 11 and 11.5 combined volumes, 489; Stegall historical notes.

51. See Military Service Record of Richard Allen Whitfield, FDAH.

52. Whitfield and Whitfield, *Whitfield, Bryan, Smith, and Related Families,* 1:148. Richard Allen married Ella Talbot on July 2, 1872. They had one child, George Talbot, before Ella died in 1873. Then Whitfield married his deceased wife's sister, Anna Maria Talbot, September 14, 1875. They had two children, Mary Talbot and Louis Talbot. His third wife died in 1904.

53. See Military Service Record of James George Whitfield, FDAH.

12. *"Well Known and Highly Respected"*

1. Montgomery County Tax Assessment on Real Estate and Personal Property for 1866, n.p., ADAH.

2. Montgomery County Tax Assessment on Real Estate for 1867, n.p.

3. MCDB 17, 299–301.

4. Eveline Croom to Mary Whitfield, May 17, 1867, Goodwood Archives.

5. Ibid.

6. Ibid.

7. See various legal documents in Winthrop Papers, folder 3.

8. See St. John's Episcopal Church Register, 2:380.

9. MCDB 9, 624–25.

10. Unpublished Alabama census of 1870, Population, Montgomery County, 102.

11. *Montgomery Advertiser,* December 25, 1875.

12. Inventory Records, Montgomery County, 1870–1901, 100–101, ADAH.

13. Clark, "Goodwood," 14–18.

14. Rogers, *John Torrey,* 296.

Bibliography

Primary Sources

UNITED STATES DOCUMENTS

Carter, Clarence Edwin, ed. The Territory of Florida, vols. 23, 25, 29, in *Territorial Papers of the United States* (Washington, D.C.: Government Printing Office, 1937–38).

Davidson, Alvie L., comp. *Florida Land: Records of the Tallahassee and Newnansville General Land Office, 1825–1892*. N.p.: Heritage Books, n.d.

Florida Acts, 1847–48, 1850.

Florida Legislative Council Laws, 1829, 1832, 1844.

Florida Reports, 1876–78.

Florida State Constitution, 1838.

Phelps, John B., comp. *The People of Lawmaking in Florida, 1822–1991*. Tallahassee: Florida House of Representatives, Office of the Clerk, 1991.

Seventh United States Census, 1850.

United States Statutes at Large, 5, State and County Documents.

UNPUBLISHED STATE AND COUNTY RECORDS

Alabama Confederate Service Records, Alabama Department of Archives and History, Montgomery.

Bolivar County Deed Book F, G, H, L, N, 0, R, V, X, CC, EE, Bolivar County Courthouse, Rosedale, Miss.

Clarke County Marriage Records, Book C, 1838–67, Clarke County Courthouse, Athens, Ga.

Craven County Deed Book L, Craven County Courthouse, New Bern, N.C.

Craven County Marriage Book 1, Craven County Courthouse, New Bern, N.C.

Craven County Record of Wills, C, Pt. 2, 1810–39, Craven County Courthouse, New Bern, N.C.

Florida Confederate Service Records, Florida Department of Archives and History, Tallahassee.

Gadsden County Deed Book A, Gadsden County Courthouse, Quincy, Fla.

Greene County Deed Book 5, 10, Greene County Courthouse, Eutaw, Ala.

Jackson County Deed Book A, B, Jackson County Courthouse, Marianna, Fla.

Jackson County Estate Books, Jackson County Courthouse, Marianna, Fla.

Jackson County Land Grants Book A, Jackson County Courthouse, Marianna, Fla.

Leon County Deed Book D, E, F, H, I, K, L, N, S, Leon County Courthouse, Tallahassee, Fla.

Leon County Marriage Records, Book 10, Leon County Courthouse, Tallahassee, Fla.

Mississippi Confederate Service Records, Mississippi Department of Archives and History, Jackson.

Montgomery County Deed Book 9, 10, 11, 13, 14, 15, Montgomery County Courthouse, Montgomery, Ala.

Montgomery County Tax Book, Personal Estate, 1864, Alabama Department of Archives and History, Montgomery.

Montgomery County Tax Book, Real Estate, 1861, 1862, 1864, 1867, Alabama Department of Archives and History, Montgomery.

Muscogee County Deed Book F, I, Muscogee County Courthouse, Columbus, Ga.

Muscogee County Marriage Record E, Muscogee County Courthouse, Columbus, Ga.

Sumter County Deed Book B, D, E, F, G, I, L, M, N, O, P, Q, R, S, T, Sumter County Courthouse, Livingston, Ala.

Sumter County Marriage Records, 2, Sumter County Courthouse, Livingston, Ala.

Sumter County Orphans Minutes, Sumter County Courthouse, Livingston, Ala.

Sumter County Probate Minutes 11 and 11.5 combined volumes, Sumter County Courthouse, Livingston, Ala.

Sumter County Tract Book, 188, Sumter County Courthouse, Livingston, Ala.

Sumter County Will Book 2, 1851–72, Sumter County Courthouse, Livingston, Ala.

FAMILY HISTORIES AND SPECIAL STUDIES, PRINTED AND BOUND
TYPESCRIPTS, AND MANUSCRIPTS

Allston, R. F. W. Papers. South Carolina Historical Museum, Charleston.

Archer, James T. File. Florida Department of Archives and History.

"Autobiography of Stephens Croom." Private possession of Velma Lassiter Croom of Mobile, Ala. A copy is located in the Goodwood Archives, Goodwood plantation, Tallahassee.

Branton, Katherine Clements, and Alice Clements Wade, eds. "Early Mississippi Records, Bolivar County, 1836–1861." Vol. 8 (1988). Bolivar County Library, Cleveland, Miss.

Broughton, Carrie L., comp. *Marriage and Death Notices from Raleigh Register and North Carolina State Gazette, 1826–1845*. Baltimore: Genealogical Publishing Co., 1966.

Clark, Erica. "Goodwood: Gift from the Past." Goodwood Archives, Goodwood plantation, Tallahassee, 1996.

Croom, Richard. Family Papers. Private possession of William and Susan Cowles of Tallahassee.

Croom, William. Will. North Carolina Department of Archives and History, Raleigh.

Croom, William W. Papers. Private possession of Velma Lassiter Croom of Mobile, Ala.

Croom Family Letters. Goodwood Archives, Goodwood plantation, Tallahassee.

Daughters of the American Revolution. "Book of Records of Leon County [Florida]." Florida Department of Archives and History.

Hentz Family Papers. Southern Historical Collection, University of North Carolina at Chapel Hill.

Jones, Kathleen Paul, and Pauline Jones Gandrud. "Alabama Records." Vol. 70. Sumter County, ADAH.

Mitchell, William. "Memoir: Of Rev. Alonzo Church, D.D." Written September 20, 1865. Biographical File, University of Georgia Library, Athens.

Moore, Elizabeth. "Records of Craven County, North Carolina." Vol. 1. Blandensburg, Md.: n.p., 1960.

Outlaw, Doris C. "The Croom Family." Compiled 1955–57 and reissued 1962. Kinston, N.C.

Parrott, Mrs. Mattie Kennedy. Collection 1744–1875. North Carolina Department of Archives and History, Raleigh.

Pendleton, Annie. "Henrietta Mary Croom." Undergraduate paper, Florida State College for Women, Tallahassee, 1937.

Petigru, James L. Papers. South Caroliniana Library, University of South Carolina, Columbia.

Shepard, Herschel E., director. "Goodwood Historic Structures Report and Master Plan for the Margaret E. Wilson Foundation." September 30, 1992. Goodwood Archives, Goodwood plantation, Tallahassee.

Terrell, James E. "William Law." Georgia Historical Society, Savannah.

Thomas, David Y. "A History of Banking in Florida." Typescript. 1906. Special Collections, Florida State University Library, Tallahassee.

Unsigned Croom Family typescript. North Carolina Collection, University of North Carolina Library, Chapel Hill.

Whitfield, Emma Morehead, comp., and Theodore Marshall Whitfield, ed. *Whitfield, Bryan, Smith, and Related Families.* Privately published, n.d.

Winthrop, Susan and John, III. Planting Records. Special Collections, Florida State University Library.

Winthrop Family Papers. Goodwood Archives, Goodwood plantation, Tallahassee. This extensive collection was the gift of Mrs. Guy Winthrop-King of Tallahassee.

Wood, Lillian F. "Daniel Croom of Virginia: His Descendants in North Carolina." Library of Congress, Washington, D.C.

HONORS THESES, MASTER'S THESES, AND DOCTORAL DISSERTATIONS

Appleyard, Lula Dee Keith. "Plantation Life in Middle Florida, 1821–1845." Master's thesis, Florida State College for Women, 1940.

Graetz, Robert Bruce. "Triumph amid Defeat: The Confederate Victory at Natural Bridge, Florida[,] March 1865." Honors thesis, Florida State University, 1986.

Kamper, Anna Alice. "A Social and Economic History of AnteBellum Bolivar County, Mississippi." Master's thesis, University of Alabama, 1942.

MacInerney, Dorothy McLeod. "Elizabeth Whitfield Bellamy: The Life and Works of a Southern Belle." Ph.D. diss., University of Texas, 1996.

Owens, Harry P. "Apalachicola before 1861." Ph.D. diss., Florida State University, 1966.

Upchurch, John Calhoun. "Aspects of the Development and Exploration of the Forbes Purchase." Master's thesis, Florida State University, 1965.

CHURCH RECORDS

Journal of the Second Annual Convention of the Protestant Episcopal Church in the Diocese of Florida. . . . Tallahassee: Knowles and Hutchins, 1839.

Parish Register, Christ Episcopal Church. New Bern, N.C.

Parochial Records of St. John's Episcopal Church. Tallahassee, Fla., 1832–80. On file at Florida State Library, Tallahassee.

Register of Communicants, First Presbyterian Church, 1832–34. First Presbyterian Church, Tallahassee, Fla.

St. John's Episcopal Church Register. Vol. 2. Montgomery, Ala.

Scott, Rev. E. C., comp. *Ministerial Directory of the Presbyterian Church: U.S., 1861–1941.* Austin: Von Bolckmann-Jones, 1942.

NEWSPAPERS AND PERIODICALS

Apalachicola Gazette, 1836.

Athens (Ga.) Southern Banner, 1843.

Charleston (S.C.) Courier, 1837.

Charleston (S.C.) Mercury, 1837.

Farmers' Register (Petersburg, Va.), 1834, 1835.

Greensboro (Ala.) Watchman, 1983.

Jacksonville Florida Times-Union, 1904, 1906.

Memphis Daily Appeal, 1858.

Mobile Daily Commercial Register and Patriot, 1837.

New Bern (N.C.) Spectator, 1837.

Newbern (N.C.) Weekly Progress, 1860.

New Orleans Picayune, 1837, 1858.

New York Herald, 1837.

Pensacola Gazette, 1837.

Savannah Daily Georgia, 1836.

Tallahassee Florida Sentinel, 1851.

Tallahassee Floridian (variously *Floridian and Journal*), 1835, 1837, 1849, 1851, 1855, 1856, 1857–58.

Tallahassee Weekly Floridian, 1890.

Wilmington (N.C.) Advertiser, 1837.

Secondary Sources

Abbey, Kathryn T. "LaFayette and the LaFayette Land Grants." *Tallahassee Historical Society Annual* 1 (1934): 1–9.

———. "The Story of the LaFayette Lands in Florida." *Florida Historical Quarterly* 10 (January 1932): 115–33.

Atkins, Leah Rawls. "At War with the Union." In William Warren Rogers, Robert David Ward, Leah Rawls Atkins, and Wayne Flynt, *Alabama: The History of a Deep South State,* 186–202. Tuscaloosa: University of Alabama Press, 1994.

Baldwin, Joseph G. *The Flush Times of Alabama and Mississippi: A Series of Sketches.* New York: D. Appleton & Co., 1853.

Ballance, Alton. *Ocracokers.* Chapel Hill: University of North Carolina Press, 1989.

Baptist, Edward E. "The Migration of Planters to Antebellum Florida: Kinship and Power." *Journal of Southern History* 62 (August 1996): 527–54.

Barrett, Kayla. "The Whitfields Move to Alabama: A Case Study in Westward Migration, 1825–1835." *Alabama Review* 48 (April 1995): 96–113.

Battle, Kemp P. *History of the University of North Carolina.* Vol. 1. Raleigh: Edwards & Broughton, 1907.

Bishko, Lucretia Ramsey. "A French Would-Be Settler on LaFayette's Florida Township." *Florida Historical Quarterly* 62 (July 1983): 44–61.

Boney, F. N. *A Pictorial History of the University of Georgia.* Athens: University of Georgia Press, 1984.

Bryan, John H., and John Stanley. *Orations on the Death of Thomas Jefferson and John Adams, Delivered at the Request of the Citizens of Newbern, on the 17th July, 1826.* New Bern, N.C.: *Carolina Sentinel,* 1826.

Carraway, Gertrude S. *Crown of Life History of Christ Church, New Bern, N.C.* New Bern, N.C.: Owen G. Dunn, 1940.

Carson, James P., ed. *Life, Letters, and Speeches of James Louis Petigru: The Union Man of South Carolina.* Washington, D.C.: W. H. Lowdermilk & Co., 1920.

Cashin, Joan E. *A Family Venture: Men and Women on the Southern Frontier.* New York: Oxford University Press, 1991.

Castelnau, Comte de. "Essay on Middle Florida, 1837–1838." Translated by Arthur R. Seymour, foreword by Mark F. Boyd. *Florida Historical Quarterly* 26 (January 1948): 199–255.

Censer, Jane Turner. *North Carolina Planters and Their Children, 1800–1860.* Baton Rouge: Louisiana State University Press, 1984.

———. "Southwestern Migration among North Carolina Planter Families: 'The Disposition to Emigrate.'" *Journal of Southern History* 57 (August 1991): 407–26.

Chapman, A. W. "Torreya Taxifolia, Arnott." *Botanical Gazette* 10 (April 1885): 251–54.

Cobb, James C. *The Most Southern Place on Earth.* New York: Oxford University Press, 1992.

Coker, William S., and Thomas D. Watson. *Indian Traders of the Southeastern Spanish Borderlands: Panton, Leslie, and Company and John Forbes and Company, 1783–1847.* Pensacola: University of West Florida Press, 1986.

Conrad, Timothy Allen. "Notice of the Geology of West Florida." *Advocate of Science and Annals of Natural History* 1 (March 1835): 351–52.

Coulter, E. Merton. *Thomas Spalding of Sapelo.* Baton Rouge: Louisiana State University Press, 1940.

Croom, Hardy Bryan. "Botanical Observations." *American Journal of Science and Arts* 25 (January 1833): 69–78; 26 (July 1834): 313–20; and 27 (April 1835): 165–68.

Croom, H[ardy] B[ryan]. *Catalogue of Plants, Native or Naturalized, in the Vicinity of New Bern, North Carolina, with Remarks and Synonyms*. New York: G. P. Scott, 1837.

Cushman, Joseph D. *A Goodly Heritage: The Episcopal Church in Florida, 1821–1892*. Gainesville: University of Florida Press, 1965.

Davis, Mary Lamar. "Brigadier General William G. M. Davis, C.S.A." *Florida Law Journal* 23 (1949): 36–40.

Davis, William C. "A Government of Our Own." In *The Making of the Confederacy*. New York: Free Press, 1994.

DeLeon, T[homas] C. *Four Years in Rebel Capitals: An Inside View of Life in the Southern Confederacy, from Birth To Death*. Mobile: Gossip Printing Co., 1890.

Dill, Alonzo Thomas. *Governor Tryon and His Palace*. Chapel Hill: University of North Carolina Press, 1955.

Dodd, Dorothy. "The Florida Census of 1825." *Florida Historical Quarterly* 22 (July 1943): 34–40.

———. "The Steamboats *Home* and *Pulaski*." *Apalachee* 4 (1950–56): 66–75.

Doherty, Herbert J., Jr. *Richard Keith Call: Southern Unionist*. Gainesville: University of Florida Press, 1961.

———. *The Whigs of Florida, 1845–1854*. Gainesville: University of Florida Press, 1959.

Dovell, J. E. *History of Banking in Florida, 1828–1945*. Orlando: Florida Bankers Association, 1955.

Dunn, Gordon E., and Banner I. Miller. *Atlantic Hurricanes*. Baton Rouge: Louisiana State University Press, 1960.

Dyer, Thomas G. *The University of Georgia: A Bicentennial History, 1785–1985*. Athens: University of Georgia Press, 1985.

Eppes, Susan Bradford (Mrs. Nicholas Ware Eppes). *Through Some Eventful Years*. Gainesville: University of Florida Press, 1968. Facsimile reprint of 1926 edition.

Fleming, Walter L. *Civil War and Reconstruction in Alabama*. New York: Columbia University Press, 1905.

Floyd, William Barrow. *The Barrow Family of Old Louisiana*. Lexington, Ky.: Published by the author, 1963.

Frazer, Walter J., Jr. *Charleston! Charleston!: The History of a Southern City.* Columbia: University of South Carolina Press, 1989.

Gallman, Robert E. "Self-Sufficiency in the Cotton Economy of the Ante-bellum South." In *The Structure of the Cotton Economy of the Ante-Bellum South,* edited by William N. Parker, 5–24. Washington, D.C.: Agricultural History Society, 1970.

Gardner, Robert G. *On the Hill: The Story of Shorter College.* Kingsport, Tenn.: Kingsport Press, 1972.

Gouveneur, Marian. *As I Remember.* New York: D. Appleton & Co., 1911.

Gonzales, John Edward. "Flush Times, Depression, War, and Compromise." In *A History of Mississippi,* edited by Richard Aubrey McLemore, 1:284–309. Hattiesburg, Miss.: University and College Press of Mississippi, 1973.

Gray, Asa. "John Torrey: A Biographical Notice." *American Journal of Science and Arts* 5 (June 1873): 1–11.

Groene, Bertram H. *Ante-Bellum Tallahassee.* Tallahassee: Florida Heritage Foundation, 1971.

———. "Lizzie Brown's Tallahassee." *Florida Historical Quarterly* 48 (October 1969): 155–75.

Hadley, Wade Hampton, Doris Goerch Horton, and Nell Craig Strowd. *Chatham County [North Carolina], 1771–1971.* Durham, N.C.: Moore Publishing Co., 1976.

Hale, James W., comp. *Authentic Account of the Loss of Steam Packet Home, from New York Bound to Charleston. Compiled from Various Sources: Together with Many Facts, Incidents, and Anecdotes Never Published Before.* New York: J. F. Trow, 1837.

Hanna, A. J. *A Prince in Their Midst: The Adventurous Life of Achille Murat on the American Frontier.* Norman: University of Oklahoma Press, 1946.

Henderson, Archibald. *The Campus of the First State University.* Chapel Hill: University of North Carolina Press, 1949.

Hentz, Mrs. Caroline Lee. *Marcus Warland: Or, The Long Moss Spring. A Tale of the South.* Philadelphia: T. B. Peterson and Brothers, 1852.

Heyl, Erik. *Early American Steamers.* Buffalo: Erik Heyl, 1963.

Hull, A. L. *A Historical Sketch of the University of Georgia.* Atlanta: Foote & Davies, 1894.

Johns, John E. *Florida during the Civil War.* Gainesville: University of Florida Press, 1963.

Johnson, Talmadge C., and Charles R. Holloman. *The Story of Kinston and Lenoir County.* Raleigh: Edwards & Broughton, 1954.

Jones, Charles. *Memorial History of Augusta, Georgia from Its Settlement in 1735 to the Close of the Eighteenth Century.* And Salem Dutcher. *From the Close of the Eighteenth Century to the Present Times.* 1890. Spartanburg, S.C.: Reprint Co., 1980.

Jones, James Pickett. *Yankee Blitzkrieg Wilson's Raid through Alabama and Georgia.* Athens: University of Georgia Press, 1976.

Jones, James Pickett, and William Warren Rogers. "The Surrender of Tallahassee." *Apalachee* 6 (1967): 103–10.

Knauss, James Owen. "William Pope DuVal: Pioneer and State Builder." *Florida Historical Quarterly* 11 (January 1933): 95–139.

Long, Ellen Call. *Florida Breezes; or, Florida, New and Old.* Gainesville: University of Florida Press, 1962. Facsimile reprint of 1883 edition.

Lucas, Marion B. "Civil War Career of Colonel George Washington Scott." *Florida Historical Quarterly* 58 (October 1979): 129–49.

Lupold, John. *Columbus, Georgia, 1828–1978.* Columbus, Ga.: Columbus Sesquicentennial, 1978.

MacIntire, Jane Bacon. *Lafayette, the Guest of the Nation: The Tracing of the Route of Lafayette's Tour of the United States in 1824–25.* Newton, Mass.: A. J. Simone Press, 1967.

Mahon, John K. *History of the Second Seminole War, 1835–1842.* Gainesville: University of Florida Press, 1967.

Manley, Walter W., II, E. Canter Brown Jr., and Eric W. Wise. *The Supreme Court of Florida and Its Predecessor Courts.* Gainesville: University of Florida Press, 1997.

Marsh, U. Bowdoin. "The Winthrop Family of New York, North Carolina, and Leon County, Florida." *Tallahassee Genealogist* 11 (November 1991): 6–21.

Martin, John H., comp. *Columbus, Geo., from Its Selection as a "Trading Town" in 1827, to Its Partial Destruction by Wilson's Raid, in 1865. History—Incident—Personality.* 2 parts. Columbus: Thomas Gilbert, 1874.

Martin, Sidney Walter. *Florida during the Territorial Days.* Athens: University of Georgia Press, 1944.

McMillan, Malcolm Cook. "The Selection of Montgomery as Alabama's Capital." *Alabama Review* 1 (April 1948): 79–90.

Mississippi Delta Chapter, Daughters of the American Revolution, comps. *History of Bolivar County, Mississippi.* Jackson, Miss.: Hederman Brothers, 1948.

Monroe County Book Committee. *A History of Monroe County, Mississippi.* Dallas: Curtis Media Corporation, 1988.

Moore, John Hebron. *Agriculture in Ante-Bellum Mississippi.* New York: Book-
man Associates, 1958.

Mueller, Edward A. *Perilous Journeys: A History of Steamboating on the Chattahoochee, Apalachicola, and Flint Rivers, 1828–1928.* Eufaula, Ala.: Historic
Chattahoochee Commission, 1990.

*Narrative of the Loss of the Steam-Packet Home. Carleton White, Master, on a
Voyage from New-York to Charleston, with Affidavits Disproving the Charges
of Misconduct against the Master.* New York: James Ormond, 1837.

"Notes Concerning Two Itineraries from Charleston To Tallahassee by Count
Francis De Castelnau." *Florida Historical Quarterly* 26 (April 1948): 300–
324.

O'Brien, Michael, and David Moltke-Hansen, eds. *Intellectual Life in Ante-
bellum Charleston.* Knoxville: University of Tennessee Press, 1986.

Olmsted, Frederick Law. *The Cotton Kingdom: A Traveller's Observations on
Cotton and Slavery in the American Slave States.* Edited with an introduction
by Arthur M. Schlesinger. New York: Alfred A. Knopf, 1953.

Owen, Thomas McAdory. *History of Alabama and Dictionary of Alabama Biography.* Vol. 3. Chicago: S. J. Clarke Publishing Co., 1921.

Paisley, Clifton. *From Cotton to Quail: An Agricultural Chronicle of Leon
County, Florida, 1860–1967.* Gainesville: University of Florida Press,
1968.

———. *The Red Hills of Florida, 1528–1865.* Tuscaloosa: University of Alabama Press, 1989.

Pease, William H., and Jane H. Pease. *James Louis Petigru: Southern Conser-
vative, and Southern Dissenter.* Athens: University of Georgia Press, 1995.

Powell, William S. *Annals of Progress: The Story of Lenoir County and Kinston,
North Carolina.* Raleigh: State Department of Archives and History, 1962.

———, ed. *Dictionary of North Carolina Biography.* Vols. 1, 3. Chapel Hill:
University of North Carolina Press, 1979.

Redfearn, D. H. "The Croom Case, 7 Fla. 81–205." *Florida Law Journal* 23
(November 1949): 298–301.

———. "Presumption as to Order of Death in a Common Disaster: *The
Steamboat Home.*" *Florida Bar Journal* 27 (February 1963): 78–99.

———. "*The Steamboat Home:* Presumption as to Order of Death in a Common Calamity." *Florida Law Journal* 9 (May 1935): 405–24.

Rhodes, Mary Margaret Pichard. "From Mission Bells to Cathedral Chimes."
Apalachee 9 (1980–83): 67–88.

Rippy, J. Fred. *Joel R. Poinsett, Versatile American.* Durham, N.C.: Duke University Press, 1935.

Rivers, Larry. "Slavery in Microcosm: Leon County, Florida, 1824–1860." *Journal of Negro History* 66 (Fall 1981): 235–45.

Rogers, Andrew Denny. *John Torrey: A Story of North American Botany.* Princeton: Princeton University Press, 1942.

Rogers, William Warren. *Foshalee: Quail Country Plantation.* Tallahassee: Sentry Press, 1989.

Ruschenberger, W. S. W. *A Notice of the Origin, Progress, and Present Condition of the Academy of Natural Sciences of Philadelphia.* Philadelphia: T. K. and P. G. Collins, 1852.

Scarborough, William Kaufman. *The Overseer: Plantation Management in the Old South.* Baton Rouge: Louisiana State University Press, 1966.

Schauinger, [Joseph] Herman. *William Gaston: Carolinian.* Milwaukee: Bruce Publishing Co., 1949.

Schmidt, Louis Bernard. "Internal Commerce and the Development of the National Economy." *Journal of Political Economy* 47 (December 1939): 798–822.

Shofner, Jerrell H. *History of Jefferson County [Florida].* Tallahassee: Sentry Press, 1976.

———. *Jackson County, Florida: A History.* Marianna, Fla.: Jackson County Heritage Association, 1985.

Smith, Julia Floyd. *Slavery and Plantation Growth in Antebellum Florida, 1821–1860.* Gainesville: University of Florida Press, 1973.

Snider, William D. *Light on the Hill: A History of the University of North Carolina at Chapel Hill.* Chapel Hill: University of North Carolina Press, 1992.

Snow, Edward Rowe. *Secrets of the North Atlantic Islands.* New York: Dodd, Mead and Co., 1950.

Stanley, J. Randall. *History of Gadsden County.* Illustrated index by David A. Avant Jr. Tallahassee: L'Avant Studios, 1985.

———. *History of Jackson County, Florida.* Marianna, Fla.: Jackson County Historical Society, 1950.

Staufer, Carl. *God Willing: A History of St. John's Episcopal Church, 1829–1879.* Tallahassee: St. John's Episcopal Church, 1984.

Thompson, Arthur W. *Jacksonian Democracy on the Florida Frontier.* Gainesville: University of Florida Press, 1961.

Watson, Alan D. *A History of New Bern and Craven County.* New Bern N.C.: Tryon Palace Commission, 1987.

Williams, Clanton W. "Conservatism in Old Montgomery, 1817–1861." *Alabama Review* 10 (April 1957): 96–110.

———. "Early Ante-Bellum Montgomery: A Black-Belt Constituency." *Journal of Southern History* 7 (November 1941): 495–525.

Williams, Edwin L., Jr. "Negro Slavery In Florida." Pt. 2. *Florida Historical Quarterly* 28 (January 1950): 182–204.

Willoughby, Lynn. *Fair to Middlin': The Antebellum Cotton Trade of the Apalachicola/Chattahoochee River Valley.* Tuscaloosa: University of Alabama Press, 1993.

Womack, Miles Kenan, Jr. *Gadsden: A Florida County in Word and Picture.* Quincy, Fla.: Gadsden County Bicentennial Committee, 1976.

Index

Whitfield, Bryan Croom (son of
Richard Allen and Mary Whit-
field), 158
Whitfield, Edmund, 6
Whitfield, Elizabeth Hatch, 6
Whitfield, George, 44, 46, 51, 60–61,
94, 105, 107, 133, 160, 174, 187,
191, 200
Whitfield, James Bryan, 157
Whitfield, James George, 157–59,
218–19
Whitfield, Mary Croom, 88, 99, 155–
59, 173, 218, 221
Whitfield, Nancy Bryan, 5
Whitfield, Nathan Bryan, 12
Whitfield, Needham, 6
Whitfield, Richard Allen, 157–59,
218, 221
Whitfield, Sally Wooten, 157
Whitfield, Susan Matilda Croom,
5–6, 83, 88, 154–59, 197, 218–19,
221
Whitfield, Winifred, 88
Whitfield, Winifred Bryan, 88
Whiting, Caroline Lee, 85
Whitner, Benjamin F., Jr., 149–50
Whitner, Benjamin F., Sr., 149
Whitner, Eliza, 149
Whitner, Sarah Church, 149

Wilkinson (planter), 13–14
Williams, Joseph John, 158, 195
Williams, Robert W., 37, 39, 45, 118
Williams, William W., 199
Wilson, George, 17, 107
Wilson, Gen. James H., 208
Wilson, Dr. John T. J., 39, 174
Wilmington, N.C., 25, 70
Wilmington Advertiser, 70
Winthrop, Guy, 206
Winthrop, John (colonial governor),
163
Winthrop, John Still, Jr., 163–64,
188–94, 196
Winthrop, John Still, III, 164, 203–
4, 206
Winthrop, Susan Evelyn, 163–64,
168–69, 174, 203, 205–6, 222
Wray, Dr., 55
Wright, John, 223
Wright, William, 44, 73
Wyatt, (William?), 105

Yancey, William L., 207
Yazoo River, 13, 135, 145
Yucatan Peninsula, 66

Zeigler, Nathaniel D., 92